Indiana
Off the Beaten Path®

"Very handy for anyone 'wandering Indiana.' An excellent guide."
—Tim Walter, News Director,
WOAV/WRTB Radio, Vincennes, Ind.

"Thomas is a resident of Indiana and knows the back roads of the Hoosier State, which lead to many special and unusual places. The guide also includes places to eat and stay and is divided into the five geographical areas."
—*The Star,* Chicago, Ill.

"Traveling by car doesn't mean you have to stick to the interstate highways. *Indiana: Off the Beaten Path* points out sights that most books miss."
—*News-Democrat,* Belleville, Ind.

"Well-organized, packed with information, and written with informal clarity. Whether you're just passing through a corner of the state or have lived in Indiana all your life, the book will tell you what's where in Indiana."
—*Palladium Item,* Richmond, Ind.

Help Us Keep This Guide Up to Date

Every effort has been made by the author and editors to make this guide as accurate and useful as possible. However, many things can change after a guide is published—establishments close, phone numbers change, hiking trails are rerouted, facilities come under new management, etc.

We would love to hear from you concerning your experiences with this guide and how you feel it could be improved and be kept up to date. While we may not be able to respond to all comments and suggestions, we'll take them to heart and we'll also make certain to share them with the author. Please send your comments and suggestions to the following address:

The Globe Pequot Press
Reader Response/Editorial Department
P.O. Box 480
Guilford, CT 06437

Or you may e-mail us at:

editorial@globe-pequot.com

Thanks for your input, and happy travels!

OFF THE BEATEN PATH® SERIES

Indiana

SIXTH EDITION

Off the Beaten Path®

by Phyllis Thomas

The Globe Pequot Press

Guilford, Connecticut

Cover and text design by Laura Augustine
Cover photo © Index Stock
Drawing on page 35 rendered from photograph by Helen K. Link
Maps created by Equator Graphics © The Globe Pequot Press
Illustrations by Carole Drong

Off the Beaten Path is a registered trademark of The Globe Pequot Press.

Library of Congress Cataloging-in-Publication Data
Thomas, Phyllis, 1935–
      Indiana : off the beaten path / by Phyllis Thomas.—6th ed.
      p. cm. —(Off the beaten path series)
  Includes index.
  ISBN 0-7627-0711-9
    1. Indiana—Guidebooks. I. Title. II. Series.
  F524.3.T47   2001
  917.7204´44—dc21   00-068173

Manufactured in the United States of America
Sixth Edition/Third Printing

For Bill and Allan —
I was twice blessed

Contents

Hall of Fame Museum, Indianapolis Motor Speedway

Introduction

Ask almost anyone what images Indiana brings to mind, and—after a long pause—he or she is likely to mention the Indy 500, cornfields, and perhaps the steel mills of Gary. This book has been written to advise you that Indiana offers a lot more than auto racing, corn, and steel.

State highways and byways lead to some of the finest travel gems in the nation. There are natural wonders and man-made splendors, irreplaceable slices of Americana and futuristic marvels, places stately and sublime, others weird and wacky—a cornucopia of attractions, restaurants, and inns that for the most part lie off the well-trodden paths and are overlooked by major travel guides.

The most difficult part of writing this book was deciding not what to include but what, because of space limitations, to leave out. Therefore, what you will find within these pages is merely a sampling of all that Indiana has to offer. It is my sincere hope that this book will help awaken your sense of adventure and encourage you to seek out other such places on your own.

Indiana's geography is sometimes a bit puzzling to strangers. They are often surprised to learn that South Bend is one of the northernmost cities in the state, while North Vernon is not far from the Ohio River, which forms Indiana's southern boundary. Along the Ohio-Indiana border on the east lies West College Corner, while way down in the southwest corner, just across the Wabash River from Illinois, there's East Mt. Carmel. And the towns of Center, Center Square, and Centerville are about as off-center as you can get.

To further confuse the traveler, a look at the official state road map (available free from the Indiana Department of Transportation, Room N755, 100 North Senate Avenue, Indianapolis 46204; 317–232–5533) reveals four Buena Vistas, three Fairviews, three Georgetowns, three Jamestowns, two Klondykes and one Klondike, three Mechanicsburgs, four Millersburgs, five Mt. Pleasants, three Needmores, and four Salems. Pairs of towns with the same name are too numerous to mention, but would you believe two Pumpkin Centers? No wonder the U.S. Postal Service insists on zip codes!

But never mind—this book will at least put you in the right county. And if you do get lost, you're likely to meet such warm, friendly people along the way that you won't mind it a bit.

INTRODUCTION

If all else fails, you can call the Indiana tourism hot line for help. Dial (800) 289–6646 to request free printed materials that will help you plan your itinerary. The toll-free number is answered twenty-four hours a day and is accessible from anywhere in the contiguous United States. You can also write to the Indiana Department of Commerce, Tourism Division, One North Capitol Street, Suite 700, Indianapolis 46204–2288; (317) 232–8860.

One final word—understanding Indiana's time zones is not for the faint of heart. As a traveler, however, you should be aware of them. Five counties in northwest Indiana (Jasper, Lake, LaPorte, Newton, and Porter) and five counties in southwest Indiana (Gibson, Posey, Spencer, Vanderburgh, and Warrick) observe Central Time; i.e., they are on Central Standard Time during winter months and Central Daylight Saving Time in summer. Three counties in south central Indiana (Clark, Floyd, and Harrison) and two counties in southeast Indiana (Dearborn and Ohio) officially observe Eastern Standard Time in winter and unofficially observe Eastern Daylight Savings Time in summer. This allows the many residents of these counties who work in Louisville, Kentucky, or Cincinnati, Ohio, to synchronize their personal timepieces with those of their workplaces. The rest of Indiana's ninety-two counties remain on Eastern Standard Time all year long.

Happy wandering!

The prices, rates, and hours listed in this guidebook were confirmed at press time. We recommend, however, that you call establishments before traveling to obtain current information.

Central Indiana

Indianapolis, at the hub of central Indiana, is crisscrossed by more interstate highways than any other metropolitan area in the country. I–65, I–69, I–70, and I–74 run through the heart of the city, and I–465 encircles it. More than 800,000 people live in Indianapolis (affectionately known to Hoosiers as Indy), making this the twelfth largest city in the country.

Leave Indy behind and head in any direction, and in minutes you will find yourself in the heart of rural Indiana—open fields that seem to stretch forever, patches of scenic woodland, and charming small towns rich with local color.

Central Indiana offers a mix of the best Indiana has to offer—big city excitement, pastoral serenity, and the friendly folks for which the Hoosier State is justly famous.

Boone County

The entire community has pitched in to help restore the glory of yesteryear to Zionsville's 125-year-old downtown business district, and its citizens have succeeded admirably. Now known as the *Zionsville Colonial Village*, it's filled with interesting shops to explore. At *Lilly's Boutique Gallery,* the selection of unusual apparel and accessories includes many items by some 200 artists. Three vine-covered buildings filled with a variety of unusual items and nestled in a garden setting are known collectively as *Brown's Antiques.*

The Cedar Street Shoppes, a cluster of thirty-five individual shops under one roof, are located at the corner of Cedar and Main Streets; they feature a wide variety of arts and crafts. At 10 North Main Street, *My Mother's Doll Shop* provides a test market for the newest Turner dolls before they are marketed nationally (the exquisite collectibles, which range in price from $130 to $1,000, are designed by Virginia Turner, a southern Indiana resident whose daughter owns this aptly-named shop).

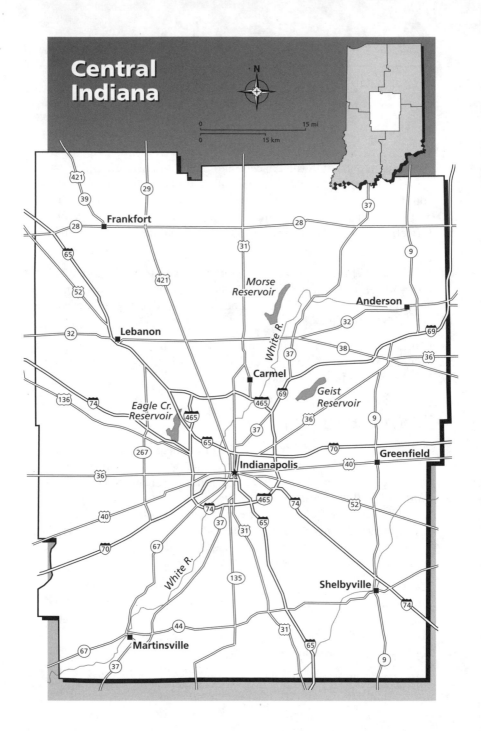

Central Indiana

N

0   15 mi

0   15 km

421

39

29

37

Frankfort

28

28

9

65

31

52

421

Morse
Reservoir

Anderson

32

Lebanon

32

White R.

37

38

69

36

Carmel

69

Geist
Reservoir

136

74

Eagle Cr.
Reservoir

465

465

36

9

37

267

65

70

40

Greenfield

Indianapolis

36

40

465

74

74

52

40

74

37

31

65

67

White R.

70

135

Shelbyville

74

44

31

Martinsville

67

65

37

9

Brick-paved Main Street, which runs through the heart of the village, is decorated with gas lamps and planters. It's here you'll find **Adam's Rib,** often selected as one of the Indianapolis area's ten best restaurants. The adventurous come here to sample the appetizers—such exotic treats as buffalo, llama, giraffe, camel, alligator, zebra, antelope, gnu, lion, kangaroo, and rattlesnake. Not all of this unusual fare is available at all times, so it's best to call ahead if you're yearning for something special. You can, however, enjoy excellent American and Continental cuisine any day except Sunday. The prime rib and fresh seafood have been luring customers back for years. Prices are moderate to expensive, and reservations are advisable for dinner. Located at 40 South Main Street, it's open 11:30 A.M. to 2:00 P.M. Tuesday through Saturday; 5:30 to 9:00 P.M. Tuesday through Thursday; 5:30 to 9:30 P.M. Friday and Saturday; (317) 873–3301.

For additional information contact the Greater Zionsville Chamber of Commerce, 135 South Elm Street, P.O. Box 148, Zionsville 46077; (317) 873–3836.

Zionsville is also home to the **Patrick Henry Sullivan Museum,** a small gem dedicated to assembling and preserving local history. The museum is named for Boone County's first white settler, great-grandfather to the late Iva Etta Sullivan, a former librarian who set up a trust fund to establish a historical foundation in Zionsville in memory of her illustrious ancestor. Ms. Sullivan had the financial wherewithal to set up the trust in part because she accepted the investment advice of her one-time employer, Cecil B. DeMille.

The museum, patterned after early-nineteenth-century architecture, rotates exhibits that feature period furnishings, antique clothing, farm tools, artwork and quilts. A genealogical library houses a growing collection of family histories, diaries,

AUTHOR'S FAVORITE ATTRACTIONS/
EVENTS IN CENTRAL INDIANA

Camp Chesterfield,
Chesterfield; (765) 378–0235

Conner Prairie Pioneer
Settlement, Fishers;
(317) 776–6000 or
(800) 966–1836

Eiteljorg Museum of
American Indian and
Western Art,
Indianapolis; (317) 636–9378

The Giant,
Pendleton; (765) 778–2757
or (800) 253–7931

Indiana Transportation
Museum,
Noblesville; (317) 773–6000

Indianapolis Children's
Museum,
Indianapolis; (317) 921–4000,
(317) 924–5431, or
(800) 208–KIDS

Indianapolis Medical
History Museum,
Indianapolis; (317) 635–7329

Eiteljorg Museum Indian
Market,
Indianapolis; June
(317) 636–9378

Eiteljorg Museum Western
Festival/Chili & BBQ State
Championships,
Indianapolis; September
(317) 636–9378

Heartland Film Festival,
Indianapolis; November
(317) 464–9405

Indy 500 Festival Parade,
Indianapolis; May
(317) 636–4556

Octoberfest,
Indianapolis; September
(317) 888–6940

Trivia

Hank Aaron, baseball's great home run hitter, made his professional debut with the Indianapolis Clowns as a teenage shortstop in 1951 and 1952. Aaron never played a game in Indianapolis, however. The Negro American League Clowns played all their games on the road.

letters, family Bibles, property deeds, maps, photos, and newspapers. Ms. Sullivan and her great-grandfather would be pleased. Admission is free; hours are 10:00 A.M. to 4:00 P.M. Tuesday through Saturday. Visitors will find the museum at 225 West Hawthorne Street; call (317) 873–4900.

The **Boone County Courthouse** in Lebanon, built in the early 1900s, once drew sightseers from around the world. They came to marvel at the eight limestone columns that adorn the north and south entrances. Each gigantic pillar—38 feet high, 4½ feet in diameter, and weighing about 40 tons—is shaped from a single block of limestone.

Lebanon is also the home of Indiana's answer to Willie Wonka's chocolate factory. Any dyed-in-the-wool chocoholic will love a tour of **Donaldson's Country Home Candy Shoppe.** Watch through glass doors as chocolates are cooked in copper kettles and fudge is kneaded on a marble slab.

A Woman to Look Up To

*W*hen Sandy Allen of Shelbyville was born on June 18, 1955, she weighed six and one-half pounds and gave no indication of the extraordinary life that awaited her. Today she stands 7 feet, 7¼ inches tall and is the tallest living woman in the world. She is also the exact height of the world's tallest living man, who resides in Pakistan.

The excessive growth hormone at work in Sandy's body was triggered by a tumor on her pituitary gland. If she had not had surgery to help control her growth when she was a teen, she might have grown even taller.

Sandy sews most of her own clothes, wears size 22 hand-me-down sneakers provided by players in the National Basketball Association, and sleeps in an eight-foot-long custom-made bed.

She has also held a few jobs along the way, including one as a secretary in the office of a former mayor of Indianapolis and another as part of the staff at the Guinness Museum in Niagara Falls, New York.

Now, in spite of many health problems including difficulty walking, Sandy often makes personal appearances at such places as schools and libraries. Her message that "It's Okay to Be Different" is delivered with great wit and humor. She has even made a video by that name, available at many video stores and by calling (888) BIG–SANDY. Upon meeting Sandy, it is impossible, of course, not to notice her physical stature, but after leaving her presence it is the enormity of her heart that one remembers.

Trivia

Paul Butler, a school bus driver in Anderson, delights his young passengers by going to work in an Elvis Presley costume. Paul also performs as Elvis at charity events around the state. In summer 1999, he went to Memphis, competed against hundreds of Elvis impersonators from thirty different countries, and was crowned the best Elvis impersonator in the world.

Guides are on hand to explain the history of this favorite confection. Donaldson's produces and sells seventy-five varieties of chocolates, includ-ing almond bark, chocolate-covered caramels, hand-dipped creams, and assorted nut clusters. Just when you think you can't stand it another minute, you're given a free sample. The tours won't cost you a cent, and you're certainly under no obligation to buy, but if you don't, you have more willpower than most of us. You'll find Donaldson's at 600 South State Road 39, just south of State Road 39's intersection with I–65 on the south side of Lebanon. Stop by anytime between 9:00 A.M. and 6:00 P.M. Monday through Saturday, but try to avoid November and December; they're understandably very busy months. The management would appreciate it if you could give them at least one day's notice for a guided tour; (765) 482–3334.

Approximately 5 miles north of Thorntown, along U.S. Highway 52, motorists can pause at a pretty roadside stop to eat a picnic lunch and enjoy the pleasant rural panorama. There all similarity to other roadside stops ends, for this is the home of the *Garden of Memories,* a spiritual refuge that is a true labor of love. Reverend Alan Moody, pastor of the nearby Walnut Grove Chapel of Praise, first saw the garden in a vision, and now the vision is well on its way to becoming reality. At present the garden is surrounded by a stone wall that forms the outline of a king's crown. Each of the crown's six points is topped by a glass globe that's lighted all night during summer months and until late in the evening during winter. When you walk through the stone archway in the wall, you're confronted by a rock pile that supports three wooden crosses. There are also winding walkways, a baptismal well, a statue of Christ, and a tiny stone chapel. Eventually Reverend Moody and his interdenomina-tional congregation hope to build a church adjacent to the garden. At the entrance to the roadside rest area a sign reads GARDEN OF MEMORIES— WELCOME! It is altogether a serene and lovely place to be. For additional information call Reverend Moody at (765) 436–7166 or 436–7029.

Hamilton County

onner Prairie Pioneer Settlement, ranked as one of the nation's top five "living museums," remains suspended in 1836 forever. This restored pioneer village breathes life into history, permitting visitors to

Conner Prairie Pioneer Settlement

wander at their leisure through the homes, shops, school, and other buildings that might have made up a pioneer community. "Residents" keep busy at tasks that must be performed to keep the settlement going; they also answer questions about the typical 1836 lifestyle.

Ongoing meticulous research helps ensure the authenticity of the settlement. The orchard, for instance, was first planted in neat rows, but when it was learned that this was a twentieth-century method, fruit trees were scattered about at random. It was also discovered, much to everyone's surprise, that men did not wear beards in 1836, and all whiskers except muttonchops had to go. All lace trim had to be removed from the women's dresses—that was a no-no, too.

Also located on the 250-acre tract is a Federal-style mansion built in 1823 by Indiana statesman William Conner. Visitors can tour the main house and grounds, which feature a springhouse, a still, and a loom house where Conner Prairie staff members duplicate textiles used during the 1830s.

At the Prairie Adventure Center, trained craftspeople are on hand to assist visitors who want to learn pioneer skills firsthand. You can try your hand at such pastimes as weaving on an authentic loom, making candles, and whittling with period tools.

The Museum Center, newly renovated in 1999, includes a shop that sells items handcrafted by Conner Prairie artisans, a restaurant that features a mix of modern and historic foods, and a bakery that offers nineteenth-century breads, pastries, and cookies.

Special events are also in keeping with the times. Once a month the

Trivia

In 1923 Carmel, Indiana installed what is believed to be the first electric traffic light in the United States. Because it had only red and green lights, motorists were unable to judge when the signal would change and were constantly running the red light.

Methodist circuit rider arrives to preach his sermon. A presidential election is held in the fall, just as it was in 1836. Weddings, too, are authentic, and visitors are often surprised to learn that even in the mid-1800s women did not promise to "obey" their spouses. Brides agreed to "love, honor, and assist" their husbands, who in turn promised to "love, honor, and maintain" their wives.

In 1989 staff members from *U.S. News & World Report* magazine visited the seven most popular living-history sites in the country, Conner Prairie included, and rated them for authenticity and entertainment. Conner Prairie was the only one of the seven to receive the top rating of four stars in both categories.

A program of Earlham College in Richmond, Conner Prairie is located 4 miles south of Noblesville. Open 9:30 A.M. to 5:00 P.M. Tuesday through Saturday and 11:00 A.M. to 5:00 P.M. Sunday, April through October; 9:30 A.M. to 5:00 P.M. Wednesday through Saturday and 11:00 A.M. to 5:00 P.M. Sunday in November; also open at other times for special events; historic areas are closed Easter and Thanksgiving. Admission is charged. Contact Conner Prairie Pioneer Settlement, 13400 Allisonville Road, Fishers 46038-4499; (317) 776–6000 or (800) 966–1836.

At the *Indiana Transportation Museum* in Noblesville, you can follow the development of transportation in America, beginning with covered wagons. There are buggies, automobiles, trucks, fire engines, trains to sit in and climb onto, and a clanging trolley to ride along a 1-mile track. Each weekend a different special event takes place. The museum is in Forest Park, just north of Noblesville at 325 Cicero Road. It's open 10:00 A.M. to 5:00 P.M. Tuesday through Sunday, Memorial Day through the last weekend in September; Saturday and Sunday, April to Memorial Day and October through November. There's a nominal admission fee; call (317) 773–6000.

Trivia

The population of Hamilton County grew at a rate of 35 percent in the 1990s—the highest county growth rate in Indiana and the second highest in the country.

The *Canterbury Arabian Horse Farm,* also north of Noblesville, welcomes visitors free of charge. You can pet a horse's nose, see a horse "take a shower" in a wash rack, look on as the animals are exercised, stroll through a state-of-the-art barn that rivals horsedom's finest, and, if your timing is right, watch a foal being born. Owners Flois and Debbie Burrow, who acquired their first Arabian in 1980, currently own or board more than fifty horses. Among them is "Real Mac," the mascot of the Indianapolis Colts professional football team. To substantiate the Burrows' claim that they have some of the best Arabians in the country, they point to two bulletin boards covered with show ribbons. The Burrows' farm is located at 12131 East 196th Street; call (317) 776–0779 before visiting and to obtain directions.

Bundy Decoy in Noblesville produces duck decoys that are shipped to countries all over the world, including Japan, Italy, England, and Norway. Each decoy is a work of art—hand-carved from solid white cedar, hand-finished, and stained. Visitors can watch the entire process during a tour of the factory and showroom at 16506 Strawtown Avenue. Open 9:00 A.M. to 4:00 P.M. Monday through Friday and by appointment on weekends; admission is free. Call (765) 734–1148 or (800) 387–3831.

If you appreciate cleanliness in the restaurant of your choice, try the *Classic Kitchen* in Noblesville. You can eat off the floor. Not only is the restaurant impeccably clean, but also it serves some of the best food in central Indiana. Its herb bread draws raves from customers, who sometimes opt for additional portions of bread instead of dessert. Not to put down the desserts—discerning diners, who come from miles around, heap accolades on the white chocolate mousse and the homemade Key lime ice cream. Prices are moderate to expensive. Open 11:00 A.M. to

Annual Events in Central Indiana

Hoosier Horse Fair and Expo,
Indianapolis; March (317) 927–7500

A.J. Foyt's Hulman Hundred,
Indianapolis; May (317) 927–7500 or
(602) 252–3833

Annual Indian Market,
Indianapolis; June (317) 636–9378

Indiana Black Expo,
Indianapolis; July (317) 925–2702

Heartnut Heritage
Festival and Rendezvous,
Franklin; September (812) 526–6809

Penrod Arts Fair,
Indianapolis; September (317) 923–1331

Blue River Valley Pioneer Craft Fair,
Shelbyville; October (317) 398–6647 or
(800) 223–2210

Heartland Apple Festival,
Danville; October (765) 745–4876

Indian Trails Festival,
Anderson; October (765) 642–7600

Morgan County Fall Foliage Festival,
Martinsville; October (765) 342–0332

Small Town U.S.A. Festival,
Alexandria; October (765) 724–7528

Village Tour of Homes,
Zionsville; October (317) 873–3836

2:00 P.M. for lunch and 2:00 to 4:00 P.M. for tea, Tuesday through Saturday; candlelight dinner 6:00 to 9:00 P.M., Friday and Saturday. Located at 610 Hannibal Street; (317) 773–7385.

One restaurant in Carmel takes great pride in fooling its customers. In fact, the hungry folks who flock to **Illusions** would be disappointed if they *weren't* fooled. Entering via a magical forest that leads to a sword in a stone, they follow directions to open the wall before them and enter a world where little (except the food) is what it seems. Menus that mysteriously appear, tableside sleight of hand, and a showroom that features top magicians from around the world are among the pleasures that await diners. David Copperfield occasionally drops in to check out the talent. Prices are moderate to expensive; reservations are suggested on weeknights and are a must on weekends. Open 5:00 to 9:00 P.M. Monday through Thursday, 5:00 to 10:00 P.M. Friday, and 4:30 to 10:30 P.M. Saturday. Located at 969 Keystone Way; (317) 575–8312.

Atkins Elegant Desserts in Noblesville makes cheesecakes that are served across the country in fine restaurants and above the country in Air Force One. President George Bush is said to have favored Triple Chocolate, while President Bill Clinton prefers St. Honore—a blend of buttery cookie crust, French cream filling, miniature pastry puffs, chocolate fudge sauce, whipped cream, and chopped pecans.

Carmel is also home to the charming **Museum of Miniature Houses,** filled with Lilliputian works of art. Visitors will see an amazing array of wee things faithfully replicated. Kitchens contain tiny canned goods, eating utensils, cookie cutters, and rolling pins. Elsewhere, a cat lays claim to a chair, a dog snoozes on a hearth, and a minuscule Monopoly board stands at the ready. One room box depicts a museum, wherein suits of armor, dinosaurs, and Oriental works of art await the scrutiny of visitors. An antique dollhouse, documented by its English builder, dates to 1861. Special collections that range from cars and cannons to dolls and teddy bears are exhibited on a rotating basis. The not-for-profit museum also offers traveling exhibits and seasonal displays. Visitors may purchase such items as handcrafted miniatures, books, and periodicals in the museum's gift shop (small in size, of course). There's a nominal admission fee. The museum is located at 111 East Main Street; open 11:00 A.M. to 4:00 P.M. Wednesday through Saturday and 1:00 to 4:00 P.M. Sunday; closed major holidays and the first two school weeks of January. Special hours can be arranged in advance for large groups and out-of-town visitors; call (317) 575–9466.

A popular attraction for visitors and locals alike is the artesian well in **Flowing Well Park.** Discovered by accident in 1902, the free-flowing fountain provides mineral water free of charge to anyone who has an

Dave's Mom

*H*er face and smile are known throughout the world—not bad for a woman the world at large had never seen until she was in her seventies and who has no appellation other than Dave's Mom.

The woman, of course, is the mother of Indianapolis native David Letterman; and he, of course, is the late-night television host who popularized top ten lists and stupid pet tricks. Dave's mother, whose real name is Dorothy, first burst upon the world scene as the Letterman show's official Winter Olympics correspondent.

Neither Dorothy nor her son anticipated the way in which viewers would embrace her freshness and charm, nor could they have anticipated the endurance of her fame. Since her first assignment at the 1994 Olympics, Dorothy has been deluged with offers for appearances around the world. She was asked to fly to Iceland for a fashion show, to officiate at a World Wrestling Federation match, and to promote hams. All offers go through her son's agent, who has started considering only those that pay in excess of $1 million (he claims it weeds out the idiots).

empty jug. You'll find the park on the northeast corner of Gray Road and East 116th Street in Carmel. Don't be surprised if the well is surrounded by a crowd of thirsty enthusiasts.

Hancock County

*H*ancock County is James Whitcomb Riley country. Here he was born, grew up, and found the inspiration for many of his poems, including such classics as "When the Frost Is on the Punkin," "Little Orphan Annie," "The Raggedy Man," and "The Old Swimmin' Hole."

Riley was born on October 7, 1849, in what is now the kitchen of a white frame house built by his father, who was an able carpenter as well as a lawyer noted for his oratory. Located at 250 West Main Street (U.S. Highway 40) in Greenfield, this house was immortalized in Riley's poems. It contains the rafter room where "the gobble-uns'll git you ef you don't watch out," the dining room "where they et on Sundays," and the side porch where Mary Alice Smith, who worked for the Riley family and is believed to have been the real-life "Little Orphan Annie," would "shoo the chickens off the porch." The *James Whitcomb Riley Birthplace and Museum,* complete with a collection of Riley memorabilia, is open to the public from 10:00 A.M. to 4:00 P.M.

Monday through Saturday and 1:00 to 4:00 P.M. Sunday, April through late December. There's a nominal admission fee; call (317) 462–8539.

Although Riley was a lifelong bachelor and never had children of his own, he dearly loved them, and they in turn loved him. The statue of the famous Hoosier poet seen today on the lawn of the Hancock County Courthouse (110 South State Street, Greenfield) was purchased entirely with funds contributed by the schoolchildren of Indiana.

Not far east of the Riley home, at the northwest corner of the intersection of U.S. Highway 40 and Apple Street, you'll find *Riley Memorial Park.* A boulder, into which are carved the words "Riley's Old Swimmin' Hole," stands on the banks of Brandywine Creek within the twenty-acre park and marks the exact spot where Riley and the friends of his youth once whiled away the hours on hot summer days. The youth of today frolic in a modern pool nearby. For additional information contact the Greater Greenfield Chamber of Commerce, 110 South State Street, Greenfield 46140; (317) 462–4188.

Although Riley eventually left Greenfield, he maintained his residence in Indiana until his death in 1916. You'll find his Indianapolis home and burial site described later in this section under Marion County.

Another place of interest in Riley Park is the two-story *Old Log Jail Museum.* Since log jails could hardly be called escape-proof, their builders resorted to various ingenious methods to keep prisoners

By Appointment Only

*I*n the United States there are exactly three Rolls-Royce dealerships—one in Beverly Hills, California; one in New York City; and one in Zionsville, Indiana. Albers Rolls-Royce, which has been in business for about thirty years, is the oldest authorized Rolls-Royce dealership in the country. Herman Albers, the owner, also has a service shop that stocks thousands of Rolls-Royce and Bentley parts, including some for cars that were built seventy years ago. People from all over the country order parts from Albers or make the trip to Zionsville to have their Rolls-Royces serviced on the spot. Anyone thinking of dropping by Albers's dealership at 360 South First Street just to browse and dream, however, should be advised that prospective buyers are admitted only by prior appointment—and only very serious prospective buyers are given an appointment. If you happen to fall into that elite group, call (317) 873–2360 to set up a mutually agreeable time.

incarcerated. This jail features an upstairs cell room and logs filled with nails to prevent prisoners from "sawing out." There's a nominal admission fee; call (317) 462–7780.

If on some warm day you are driving along County Road 300 East just north of its intersection with County Road 400 North, you may see a kangaroo bounding across the field next to you. Not to worry—you're not entering a time warp, another dimension, or the twilight zone. You're merely passing the *C. C. Irving Wild Game Farm,* where, in addition to kangaroos, you're just as likely to see camels, peacocks, llamas, zebras, and other exotic wildlife roaming a fenced-in range during warm-weather months. The farm is not open to the public, but the wire fence permits excellent viewing from the road. Call (317) 326–2676 for more information.

A Remarkable Life

*I*ndiana lost one of its most remarkable citizens on January 28, 1998, when John Morton-Finney of Indianapolis died at the age of 108.

The son of two slaves, Dr. Morton-Finney was born on June 25, 1889. During World War I he served in the Army unit of black soldiers known as the Buffalo Soldiers. He loved learning, believing that "when you stop learning, that's about the end of you." During his lifetime he earned fifteen college degrees, including degrees in law, mathematics, history, and French, and became fluent in five languages. He earned his last degree at age seventy-five.

Following World War I, he began a career in education, teaching languages in black colleges. The pay was low, however, so he accepted a position teaching languages in the Indianapolis Public School System. He was the first teacher hired for Crispus Attucks, an Indianapolis high school for black students that opened in 1927.

After retiring from teaching in 1947, he practiced law and actively participated in that profession until his death. He was admitted to practice before the U.S. Supreme Court in 1972 and was inducted into the National Bar Association's Hall of Fame in 1991.

When Dr. Morton-Finney turned 108, the Federal Government invited him to a special ceremony honoring him for his service to his country. He respectfully declined, saying that he was just too busy to attend.

At the time of his death, he was the last remaining survivor of the Buffalo Soldiers and was believed to be the oldest practicing attorney in the United States. He was laid to rest with full military honors in Crown Hill Cemetery.

It was once said of Winston Churchill that he lived a life, not an apology. The same could be said of John Morton-Finney.

At the *Irving Materials* office, located approximately 5 miles northwest of the farm at the intersection of State Roads 9 and 234 near Eden, you can stop by the lobby any business day to see a collection of rare stuffed animals. Contact Irving Materials, Inc., 8032 North State Road 9, Greenfield 46140; (317) 634–5802.

Hendricks County

Rising from the cornfields of Hendricks County near Plainfield, the 124-acre *Islamic Center of North America* has served Muslims throughout the continent as a religious and educational center since 1982. The site, which is the national headquarters for several Islamic organizations, was selected for both its central location and its receptive environment. During the 1991 war with Iraq, the center's staff members were asked by the Pentagon to advise U.S. military leaders of the religious needs of the several thousand Muslims who serve in the military. The center also answers questions from non-Muslims who are interested in learning more about Islam. When former heavyweight boxing champion Mike Tyson was released from a nearby state correctional facility in 1995, after serving nearly four years on a rape conviction, this was the first place he came to. Tyson converted to Islam while in prison. The public is welcome to tour the mosque, library, and teaching center; contact the center's public relations department at (317) 839–8157 to arrange a visit. You'll find the center, distinguished by its modern Middle Eastern design, approximately 3 miles south of Plainfield via Old State Road 267 (Center Street), on the east side of the highway.

Johnson County

The *Johnson County Museum* is well worth the attention of area history buffs. Housed in a former Masonic Temple, the museum displays more than 20,000 items, including antiques, Indian artifacts, guns, tools, and an interesting collection of nineteenth-century dresses. Four of its rooms have been furnished to depict the period between the Civil War and the early 1900s. But perhaps the most interesting (albeit a bit grisly) exhibit is the blood-spattered fan held by a woman who sat in Abraham Lincoln's box at Ford's Theatre in Washington, D.C., the night he was assassinated.

On the lawn outside the museum is an authentic log cabin built in 1835. It was discovered when an old house elsewhere in the county was being demolished—the house had been built around the cabin.

The museum, located at 135 North Main Street in Franklin, is open 9:00 A.M. to 4:00 P.M. Monday through Friday and 10:00 A.M. to 3:00 P.M. the second Saturday of each month. Admission is free; (317) 736–4655.

When one happens upon **Morningside Gardens** in full bloom, it brings to mind a line from a poem by Edna St. Vincent Millay: "Lord, I do fear Thou'st made the world too beautiful this year." The daylilies of Debra and Walt Henricks are that stunning. Sprawling over eight acres at the Henricks' home south of Bargersville, daylilies of nearly 1,000 varieties bloom in multicolored splendor. Although the plants are for sale, visitors are also welcome to stop by just for the view. July is usually a good time to come for daylilies. The Henrickses sell other plants, too—daisies, gladioli, purple cornflowers, coralbells, and roses, to name a few.

The gardens are located on State Road 44 approximately four and one-half miles west of State Road 135. There is a large sign in front of the gardens, which are open 10:00 A.M. to 6:00 P.M. Tuesday through Sunday. For additional information, write the Henrickses at 7201 West State Road 44, Morgantown 46160; call (317) 422–9969, fax (317) 422–5593.

The **grave of Nancy Kerlin Barnett** is a top contender for Indiana's most unusual burial site. Nancy, who died in 1831, often expressed her wish to be buried at a favorite spot overlooking Sugar Creek. Through the years Nancy's grave was joined by others. A footpath through the small cemetery eventually became a road. Increased traffic made it necessary to widen the road, and the graves had to be relocated—all, that is, but Nancy's. It's reported that one of Nancy's relatives greeted the road-wideners with a shotgun and threatened to shoot anyone who disturbed her resting place. That same relative persuaded county officials to give Nancy a special dispensation, and her grave can still be seen today, skirted on both sides by County Road 400 South (Camp Hill Road), near Amity. There's even a historical marker to honor Nancy's memory and, perhaps, to forestall questions from curious passers-by. To see Nancy's grave, go to the intersection of U.S. Highway 31 and County Road 400 South at the south end of Amity; then turn east onto County Road 400 south and drive approximately 1.3 miles to the grave in the middle of the road.

You'll find numerous restaurants in Greenwood, but one of the finest is the **Johnson County Line,** situated at 1265 North Madison Avenue. Readers of *Indianapolis* magazine rated this establishment the "best-kept secret" in central Indiana. They loved its prime rib, smoked salmon, steaks, large variety of appetizers, chocolate fondue, homemade cheesecake, and atmosphere. Although the magazine is now defunct, the restaurant isn't. If you'd like to find out for yourself what all the fuss is about, the Johnson County Line restaurant is open 5:00 to 9:00 P.M. Monday through Thursday, 5:00 to 11:00 P.M. Friday and Saturday, and 5:00 to 8:00 P.M. Sunday; (317) 887–0404.

Madison County

On the north side of the little country town of Chesterfield, two massive stone gateposts mark the entrance to the beautiful parklike grounds of *Camp Chesterfield.* They also mark the entrance to another world, for Camp Chesterfield is one of two major headquarters in this country for spiritualists. (For you curious types, the other is at Lily Dale, New York.)

Spiritualists, in case you don't have a dictionary handy, believe that mortals can communicate with the spirits of the dead through a medium. Using a variety of methods, the mediums at Camp Chesterfield attempt to do just that. They conduct séances, go into trances, evoke ectoplasms, cause spirits to materialize, and predict the future. The mediums are carefully screened before being selected to join the camp's staff, and each has his or her own specialty and sees clients by appointment in one of the cottages scattered about the forty-eight-acre grounds.

Visitors are welcome from 9:00 A.M. to 5:00 P.M. daily and at other times for special events. Fees, quite reasonable, are charged for private consultations with the staff member of your choice, but there is no charge to enter the camp, attend services at the Cathedral in the Woods, view various public demonstrations of psychic phenomena, or tour the fascinating art gallery and museum. The museum houses the memorabilia of the Fox Sisters, who are credited with initiating the modern spiritualism movement.

If you'd like to read up on such subjects as reincarnation, astrology, and faith healing, you'll find books on these and more in the camp's bookstore. A gourmet chef presides over a cafeteria that serves three meals a day, and several hotels offer overnight accommodations. There are even a few campsites for self-contained recreational vehicles. Occasionally you can take courses in such subjects as the technique of spiritual healing, handwriting analysis, and trance development. All rates are reasonable.

Lest you scoff, remember that such notables as Sir Arthur Conan Doyle, creator of Sherlock Holmes, and Thomas Edison dabbled in spiritualism. Even Sigmund Freud expressed an interest in the movement and said, shortly before his death, that if he had his life to live over again he "would concern himself more with these matters." No matter what your beliefs, you will leave here with much food for thought. For a schedule of events and other information, write Camp Chesterfield, P.O. Box 132, Chesterfield 46017; (765) 378–0235. To make hotel reservations write the hotel manager at the same address or call (765) 378–0237. The camp is located at the north end of Washington Street in the town of Chesterfield.

Not far southwest of Chesterfield, atop limestone bluffs overlooking the White River, you can study the curious architecture of mound-building Indians. Of the eleven prehistoric earthworks preserved at **Mounds State Park,** the most exceptional is the circular Great Mound (circa 160 B.C.), nearly 1,200 feet in circumference and 9 feet high. Two other mounds are guitar-shaped, yet another is conical, and one is U-shaped. Excavations can be seen, and a naturalist is available to explain the cultures of the Adena and Hopewell Indians, who are believed to have built these mounds. The park, steeped in Indian legend, is reportedly home to the Puk-wud-ies, a peaceful tribe of little people that continue to inhabit the forest as they have for time immemorial. Some visitors have reported encountering the blue-gowned dwarves on park trails. In addition to historical tours, the park offers a swimming pool, hiking and cross-country ski trails, modern campsites, and canoeing on the White River. Canoes and ski equipment can be rented in the park. You can reach the park by taking Mounds Road (State Road 232) southwest from Chesterfield for about 2 miles. There's a nominal vehicle admission fee. Write Mounds State Park, 4306 Mounds Road, Anderson 46017; (765) 642–6627.

Gospel singer Sandi Patti, who was chosen Female Vocalist of the Year for eleven consecutive years by the Gospel Music Association, makes her home in Madison County. Her pure, clear voice is captured on albums and tapes at **Gaither Studios,** located on State Road 9 South in Alexandria. The state-of-the-art facility also produces the recordings of the Gaither Family and musical scores for television shows and feature-length movies. To make an appointment for a free tour, contact Gaither Family Resource at (765) 724–8244 or (765) 724–8405.

The Church of God, with world headquarters at Anderson, has established **Anderson University** near the north edge of town. On campus is the ultramodern **Warner Auditorium,** noted for its architecture. Five days were required to lift into place its rounded roof, one of the largest thin-shelled concrete domes in the world.

Elsewhere on campus, you can visit the **Charles E. Wilson Library,** which contains the archives and personal papers of the man who served as Secretary of Defense under President Eisenhower. The **Wilson Art Gallery** houses a $250,000 porcelain bird collection donated by Wilson's daughter and a collection of 1,500 napkin rings that range in variety from a solid gold, jewel-encrusted ring once used by Louis XIV of France to rings made from toilet paper spools in a Japanese prison camp during World War II. More than 10,000 artifacts from the Holy Land are displayed in the **Bible Museum,** and **Reardon Auditorium** contains an unusual chandelier that holds some 10,000 light bulbs. For additional information contact the Anderson/Madison County Visitors and Convention Bureau (see address and phone numbers at the end of this chapter). The college is located at the corner of East Fifth Street and College Drive; (765) 641–4145.

At **Alpine Acres** visitors can watch the fascinating process of handcrafting Bavarian wax from beginning to end. Roberta and Jim Rady, considered masters of this centuries-old art form, started their operation in the garage of their Anderson home in 1982. Since then they've moved their growing business to its present three-acre setting just west of town. The first such operation in Indiana and the second in the country, Alpine Acres remains to this day one of only three places in the United States where molds are made to cast a special wax formula in the same way it is done in the woodcarving areas of Germany and Austria, where the art form was born. Wax art was originally developed because it simulated the appearance of woodcarvings but was more affordable. Today the Radys produce more than 250 varieties of unique collectibles. Free tours are offered by appointment between 10:00 A.M. and 7:00 P.M. Monday through Saturday, April through September, and during the first two weeks in December. Alpine Acres is located about 1 mile west of Anderson at 5080 West State Road 32; call (765) 649–4342.

One of the most extraordinary homes in the country belongs to Hoosier musician Vic Cook. Called **The Giant,** the 7,000-square-foot house overlooks Fall Creek near Pendleton. Its rustic design blends well with the patch of woodland that surrounds it, despite the fact that the house is 254 feet long and soars 38 feet high at its tallest point. Vic Cook is rightfully proud of the ingenious home he designed and built himself from fallen trees on his land, and he is happy to show visitors through it.

The Giant (a name excerpted from "one giant leap for mankind") reflects Cook's philosophy that it's time for people to return to a lifestyle that's in balance with nature. Unlike many others who have espoused a similar philosophy, however, Cook believes we can do so without giving up creature comforts.

Visitors will be amazed to learn that, although his fuel bill is $1.00 a day at the most, Cook's home contains a high-tech recording studio with a fantastic sound system, a big-screen television, two computers, and a washing machine. Perhaps the most unique object in the house is the refrigerator Cook fashioned from a hollow beech tree. Lined with a special insulation, it is cooled by underground air and has a separate freezer section (further cooled by a microchip) that keeps even ice cream solid. Air-conditioning also is provided naturally by underground sources. Cook uses a few kerosene heaters in the winter, but he needs minimum fuel because his house is superinsulated. The house is powered by six storage batteries that are charged by solar panels, with a gasoline-powered generator on hand for alternative power when the weather stays cloudy for days. And yes, he does have an indoor toilet—a composting unit.

There's another bonus, too. Because Cook has no utility hookups, his real estate taxes are much lower.

Although The Giant took eight years to build, Cook believes it would be possible for a couple of reasonably fit people to build a similar structure in one summer for about $3,500.

To learn more about the man and The Giant, often described as being at the pinnacle of environmental science, make an appointment for a tour. An admission fee is charged, with proceeds going to a not-for-profit environmental organization. Tours, which include a 1/4-mile hike through the woods, are available by reservation. Contact The Giant, c/o EarthShip Corporation, 2928 West Larry Street, Anderson 46013; (765) 778–2757 or (800) 253–7931.

Marion County

The *Indiana World War Memorial,* built as the centerpiece of five-block plaza in downtown Indianapolis, pays homage to Hoosiers killed during U.S. wars fought in the twentieth century. Patterned after the Tomb of King Mausolus at Halicarnassus, one of the seven wonders of the ancient world, the building is an architectural marvel. It is the Shrine Room, however, that is the glory of the memorial. Massiave dark red marble columns surround a marble altar that commemorates fallen war heroes. A 17-by-30-foot American flag, supported by invisible wires, is suspended above the altar. Tiny blue lightbulbs that flicker off and on in the ceiling surround a huge Swedish-crystal light fixture in the shape of a star. Daylight filters through twenty-four deep blue glass windows. The memorial also houses a museum that contains such artifacts as a Korean War–era helicopter, a Navy Terrier missile, and some jeeps. Located at 431 North Meridian Street, it's open free of charge Wednesday through Sunday. Hours are 9:00 A.M. to 5:00 P.M. October through April 15 and 11:00 A.M. to 7:00 P.M. April 16 through September; call (317) 232–7615.

Not far away, at 700 North Pennsylvania Street, the *American Legion National Headquarters* houses one of the world's most extensive collections of World Wars I and II posters—more than 800 from World War I and 1,200 from World War II. Approximately forty are on display throughout the American Legion Building, with the rest available for view on a slide collection. A museum on the top floor of the four-story building exhibits memorabilia from the wars our country has fought in the twentieth century. You may tour the building free of charge at any time it's open; call (317) 630–1366 for specific hours and for an appointment to view the slide collection.

> ## Trivia
>
> *Hockey great Wayne Gretzky began his professional career in 1978 with the Indianapolis Racers. The then-sixteen-year-old Gretzky played his first eight games with the Racers, scoring three goals and three assists.*

If anyone ever compiles a list of national treasures, the *Indianapolis Children's Museum* should be on it. It is the largest children's museum in the world, and in this case, bigger *is* better. You can ride an early-twentieth-century carousel; explore the twisting passages of a limestone cave; visit a log cabin, an Indian tepee, an igloo, and an Egyptian tomb inhabited by the 3,000-year-old mummy of a princess; stand beside a fifty-five-ton wood-burning locomotive; see a 30-foot-tall glass water clock, the tallest in the world; marvel at an 820-pound yo-yo that actually works (although it has to be lifted by a crane to do so); watch a spectacular collection of toy trains in motion (1,500 sets in total, but who's counting?); examine replicas of prehistoric creatures; and conduct scientific experiments. If you can coax the adults away from it, your child can sit behind the wheel of a 1940 Maserati that once competed in the Indy 500. Other exhibits, such as the computer center, provide a bridge to the future. Budding scientists can explore ScienceWorks. Outer space comes alive at the museum's planetarium, one of the few in the world equipped

> ## Trivia
>
> *Frank Sinatra debuted his singing career in Indianapolis. He appeared at the Lyric Theater with the Tommy Dorsey Orchestra on February 2, 1940.*

Indianapolis Children's Museum

with a computerized star projector (properly known as Digistar) that simulates three-dimensional flight through space; your children will be even more impressed when they learn that it's the same projector used to create special effects in the *Star Trek* movies. Children are enthralled by the magic of live theater productions at the Lilly Theater. The recently opened CineDome Theater is the first of its kind in the nation. Five stories tall and capped with a domed roof, the theater features a screen that totally surrounds you and a powerful stereo system that lets you experience sounds that range from a thundering herd of elephants to the tiniest of raindrops. In the innovative Center for Exploration, designed by teens for teens, young people can develop projects of their own choosing. Playscape offers learning through play for preschoolers, while Babyscape provides activities designed especially for children under three. Even the museum's restaurant offers behind-the-scenes involvement—you can stand at a window and watch the bakers make such goodies as croissants and cookies. The Children's Museum store includes a cave stocked with glow-in-the-dark toys, a learning tree with built-in seating for reading around its base, and a 3-by-6-foot calculator that youngsters can use to total up the cost of their own merchandise.

The five-level museum nourishes all those qualities we cherish in our children—a sense of wonder, curiosity, imagination, the desire to know and to create, and the ability to dream. And if you don't have a child, come anyway; this is an enchanting place for everyone.

There's a general admission fee; admission is free from 5:00 to 8:00 P.M. the first Thursday of each month, the museum's only evening hours. There are nominal additional fees for the Lilly Theater, the CineDome, the carousel and the planetarium at all times. Museum and restaurant hours are 10:00 A.M. to 5:00 P.M. Monday through Saturday and noon to 5:00 P.M. Sunday; closed major winter holidays and Mondays from the day after Labor Day through February. The carousel operates from 2:00 to 5:00 P.M. on school days and during regular museum hours other days. The museum is located directly north of downtown Indianapolis, at the corner of Thirtieth and Meridian Streets; you can't miss the blue-and-yellow sunrise design of the massive entrance. Call (317) 924–5431, (317) 921–4000 (a prerecorded twenty-four-hour information line), or (800) 208–KIDS.

A Woman of Distinction

The world remembers her today as Madame C. J. Walker, but she was born Sara Breedlove. Sara was born on December 23, 1867, the daughter of ex-slaves living in Louisiana. By the time she died in 1919 at the age of fifty-one, she was a self-made millionaire and believed to be the wealthiest black woman in the country.

Madame Walker's fascinating life story includes being orphaned at age seven, getting married at age fourteen, and becoming a widow with a two-year-old daughter at age twenty. When she and her daughter moved to Denver in 1905, she carried her entire life savings of $1.50. There she met and married a newspaper sales agent named Charles Joseph Walker and created the Walker line of hair care products for black women.

In 1910, to take advantage of the city's eight railway systems as a means of distributing her products nationwide, Madame Walker moved her company to Indianapolis and built a sales force of more than 2,000 women that generated annual revenues of $500,000. There she began the development of the triangular-shaped Walker Building and Theatre, a project that was completed by her daughter after Madame Walker's death. Today, the Walker Theatre Center at 617 Indiana Avenue is a National Historic Landmark and a national model for African-American arts.

Because of her lifetime achievements, Madame Walker was elected to the National Business Hall of Fame in 1992. She was further honored on January 28, 1997, when the U.S. Postal Service issued a 32 cent commemorative stamp bearing her likeness. The stamp was dedicated in a special ceremony at the Walker Theatre.

For additional information about the many special events presented at the Walker Theatre and about tours of the building, call (317) 236–2099.

The *Crispus Attucks Museum* showcases and celebrates the accomplishments of African-Americans in Indianapolis, with a special focus on the graduates of Crispus Attucks High School. Back in the 1950s, when Attucks was a consolidated high school for the city's black youngsters, basketball great Oscar Robertson was a student here. Under his leadership the school's basketball team captured the state championship, the first black team and the first team from any Indianapolis high school ever to do so. Visitors can explore some thirty exhibits, including a basketball hall of fame, in four galleries. The museum is housed in the former high school, currently an integrated middle school, at 1140 North Dr. Martin Luther King Jr. Drive. Named for a black man and former slave who was the first patriot to die in the American Revolution, Crispus Attucks High School was placed on the National Register of Historic Places in 1989. Browse the exhibits on your own any weekday 10:00 A.M. to 2:00 P.M., or schedule an appointment for a guided tour from 9:00 A.M. to 3:00 P.M.; call (317) 226–4613. Admission is free, but donations are welcome.

A bit farther north, an outdoor garden of medicinal plants flourishes year-round on the campus of Butler University. The 40-by-150-foot *Apothecary Garden,* which lines a winding walkway between Robertson Hall and the Pharmacy Building, highlights the ancient medicinal herbs of North America, Europe, and China. Among the herbs that grow here are the narrowleaf coneflower, popular as an immune system booster; St. John's wort, believed to be a natural antidepressant; the weeping forsythia, used in China to treat sore throats and urinary-tract disorders; and elecampane, a Western European herb used to ease respiratory ailments. Each type of plant is labeled with its name and medicinal uses. The garden also includes many unusual landscape plantings that thrive in central Indiana and some native prairie plants and grasses. Butler University is located at 4600 Sunset Avenue in Indianapolis; call (317) 940–9413 or (888) 940–8100.

At *Hook's Historic Drug Store and Pharmacy Museum,* visitors can step into the past, back to a time when the local drug store served as a community's health care center and social hub. Browse through the nation's largest drug store museum, complete with tin signs, apothecary jars, and parent medicines; then stop by the vintage soda fountain for a treat. The chocolate soda is reputed to be the best in Indianapolis. Old time candies, novelties, and souvenirs are also for sale. Open free to the public (donations appreciated) from 11:00 A.M. to 4:00 P.M. Friday through Sunday. The museum is located in the Event Center at the Indiana State Fairgrounds, 1180 East Thirty-eighth Street; call (317) 924–1503. Present plans call for a museum expansion; sometime in 2001 a second museum is expected to open in two historic buildings in downtown Indianapolis, where it will become part of a large educational and family entertainment complex.

The *Indianapolis Museum of Art,* situated on a bluff overlooking the White River, is far more than a museum. It's a 152-acre art park that includes a sculpture garden, botanical and formal gardens, patches of woodland, greenhouses, a wildlife refuge, and a fine restaurant. Among

How to Move a Building

*I*n 1930 the Indiana Bell Telephone Company in downtown Indianapolis badly needed additional space. The decision was made to move its eight-story building to an adjacent lot and erect a larger building on the original location. All this needed to be done, however, without an interruption in the company's around-the-clock service.

The move was begun by emptying the basement and attaching flexible hoses to water, sewage, and gas lines. The wires that carried electricity to the building were given some slack. Cables spliced into the telephone circuits added extra length.

A concrete slab was poured on the existing building's new site to provide the foundation on which it would stand. The entrance to the building was connected to the sidewalk by a movable steel bridge. A system of jacks, I-beams, and rollers was placed next to each of the building's fifty-nine steel support columns.

With everything in place, the move was begun. The jacks raised the columns $1/4$

inch off their foundations, the columns were cut loose, and the weight of the building was transferred to 4,000 steel rollers. The jacks were then simultaneously given six pumps, resulting in a move of about $3/8$ inch. Gradually, moving up to 8 feet a day, the building was turned until its east-facing doors faced north. The building was then inched westward to its new site, and there it stood until 1964, when it was finally torn down and replaced.

Throughout the move, phone company employees continued their work inside the building. They felt no movement but could observe the subtle shift of the view outside the windows. Outside, interested spectators were provided with a 300-seat grandstand built specifically for observation of the monumental occasion.

A new high-rise building was erected on the vacated site while workers continued to provide telephone service in the old building. The history-making move was done in this fashion because at the time it was the most cost-effective way in which to do it.

Trivia

Richard Gatling, an Indianapolis physician, invented the world's first rapid-firing machine gun in 1862. An early model fired 200 shots a minute; by 1898, the Gatling gun could fire 3,000 rounds a minute. Dr. Gatling envisioned his gun as a weapon so terrible that it would end war forever.

its exhibits are the world's largest collection of J. M. W. Turner watercolors and prints outside the United Kingdom, a self-portrait of Rembrandt as a young man, and important collections of Oriental, Chinese, African, and Neo-Impressionist art. The museum site was once the private estate of Mr. and Mrs. J. K. Lilly, Jr. (of Lilly pharmaceutical fame), and there is also much of architectural interest here. The main exhibition buildings are open, free of charge, 10:00 A.M. to 5:00 P.M. Tuesday through Saturday; open Thursday to 8:30 P.M. There's a fee for special exhibitions. A donation is requested at the Lilly Pavilion (the original Lilly mansion), which is open 1:00 to 4:00 P.M. Tuesday through Sunday. Many special events and programs are held here. Visitors can purchase a wide variety of flowering bulbs and plants at the greenhouses (open 9:00 A.M. to 5:00 P.M. daily) and used art objects, clothing, and furniture at the Better-Than-New Shop (open noon to 4:00 P.M. Tuesday through Saturday). The museum is located at 1200 West Thirty-eighth Street; (317) 923–1331.

Indianapolis has gone wild over its state-of-the-art zoo, a model for zoos of the future that opened to the public in June 1988. Stretching along the west bank of the White River, the innovative sixty-four-acre facility is the first zoo ever to be completely designed around the biome concept. Biomes are simulated natural environments in which animals are grouped by habitats rather than by the continents of their origins. Forest animals from around the world, for instance, share the forest biome, while other animals find appropriate homes in the desert, plains, and water biomes. Unlike most of its counterparts, the *Indianapolis Zoo* combines the best elements of a zoo and an aquarium, with particular emphasis on a marine exhibit that has been called the best of its kind outside of Sea World. The totally enclosed Whale and Dolphin Pavilion, the largest in the world, presents animal shows every day of the year, while a vast aquarium offers above- and below-water views of some 200 aquatic species. Only five zoos in the world possess the capabilities to exhibit walruses—this zoo is one of them. Among the things you *won't* find here are cages and bars. Animals and people watch each other across such natural barriers as moats and boulders and, where necessary, through meshwork that disappears as you look at it. One resident giraffe graphically requested a special privilege for his brethren by licking a hole through the wall of the giraffe barn—the barn is now equipped with windows 14 feet above the ground so that the lanky creatures can have a home with a view. Open daily 9:00 A.M. to 5:00 P.M. June 1 through Labor Day; 9:00 A.M. to 4:00 P.M. Monday through Friday; 9:00 A.M. to 5:00 P.M. Saturday and Sunday, April through May and the day after Labor Day through October; 9:00 A.M. to 4:00 P.M. daily the rest of the year. The zoo is located just west of the downtown area at 1200 West Washington Street; (317) 630–2030 or (317) 630–2001.

The *White River Gardens* adjacent to the zoo opened in June 1999 to rave reviews from the public. Included in the gardens' 3.3 acres are a glass-enclosed conservatory, water gardens, outdoor design gardens, and an outdoor wedding garden. Nearly fifty bronze sculptures of small animals are scattered over the grounds. Visitors enter the garden through a cylindrical rotunda that features a 360-degree mural depicting Indiana's changing seasons. Open year-round; 9:00 A.M. to 5:00 P.M. in summer, 9:00 A.M. to 4:00 P.M. the rest of the year, with extended hours from Thanksgiving through December 23. A nominal admission fee is slightly lower from November through February. Call (317) 630–2001 for specific and up-to-date information.

In addition to the reputation it has earned as the amateur sports capital of the world, Indianapolis is also noted for having the country's most impressive collection of American war memorials outside Washington, D.C. The newest—dedicated in May 1999—is the *Congressional Medal of Honor Memorial,* the only memorial in the United States that honors our nation's most highly decorated war heroes. Of the forty million men and women who have served in the military in the twentieth century, just 931 have earned the Medal of Honor; more than half were awarded posthumously. Covering one acre in White River State Park, the memorial comprises twenty-seven curved walls of glass that range from eight to 10 feet in height. The name of each medal recipient is etched into the glass. Although the outdoor memorial is open free of charge at all times, visitors who come at dusk will hear a recording, played over a public address system, of a Medal of Honor winner telling his own story.

> ### Trivia
>
> *The Curtis Management Group (CMG) Worldwide protects the rights of some of the most famous people of the twentieth century, both living and dead, making certain that clients' names and images are not used in exploitative ways. Among the company's clients are such luminaries as Sophia Loren, Michael Jordan, Garfield the Cat, and the estates of James Dean, Marilyn Monroe, Humphrey Bogart, and Babe Ruth. CMG's corporate headquarters is in Indianapolis.*

Not far away, at 500 West Washington Street, the *Eiteljorg Museum of American Indian and Western Art* showcases the arts and crafts of the American West in a $14 million building, reminiscent of an Indian pueblo, that's a work of art in itself. Opened in 1989 primarily to house the collection of the late Indianapolis businessman and philanthropist for whom it's named, the museum is one of only two of its type east of the Mississippi River. Its still-growing collection, currently valued at more than $45 million, includes sculptures by Charles Russell, bronzes by Frederic Remington, and paintings by Georgia O'Keeffe. Special programs, some especially for children, breathe life into the exhibits; visitors may, for instance, see roping demonstrations or attend a lecture series that offers instructions on how to make a cowboy hat or a lariat. The gift shop features authentic arts and crafts from the southwestern United States. There's a nominal admission fee. The museum is open 10:00 A.M. to 5:00 P.M. Tuesday through Saturday and noon to 5:00 P.M. Sunday; also open Monday in July and August; closed major winter holidays; (317) 636–9378.

The zoo, the White River Gardens, the Medal of Honor Memorial, and the Eiteljorg Museum lie within 250-acre **White River State Park,** which borders both sides of the waterway for which it is named. To view drawings and a model of what White River State Park is envisioned to become during the next few years and to obtain up-to-date information about additional planned facilities, stop at the park's visitor center at 801 West Washington Street. The park includes the National Institute for Fitness and Sport, Victory Field (home of the Indianapolis Indians, the city's AAA baseball team), Military Park, the state's only IMAX 3-D theater, and the NCAA Hall of Champions. The visitor center is open 8:30 A.M. to 5:00 P.M. Monday through Friday year-round; also noon to 5:00 P.M. Saturday and Sunday during warm-weather months; (317) 634–4567 or (800) 665–9056.

On August 2, 1995, a group of World War II veterans gathered together in downtown Indianapolis to witness the fruition of a long-cherished dream. They came to dedicate a memorial that would forever honor the memory of their fallen shipmates in one of the nation's greatest wartime tragedies, the sinking of the USS *Indianapolis.* When it was hit by a Japanese torpedo on July 30, 1945, the *Indianapolis* became the last U.S. Navy ship lost in World War II. The heavy cruiser was returning from a top-secret mission—delivering components of the atomic bomb that would be dropped on Hiroshima in early August. Because of the secrecy surrounding the ship's exact whereabouts, crew members spent five days in shark-infested waters 600 miles west of Guam before a Navy seaplane accidentally spotted them. Only 316 of the 1,196 crew members survived. The loss of 880 men remains to this day the single largest loss of life in American naval warfare history.

Visitors can view the **USS Indianapolis *Memorial*** and the plaza it occupies along the east bank of the Central Canal in downtown Indianapolis, just behind the Navy EMPF Building at 714 North Senate Avenue. The south face of the black-and-gray granite monument is engraved with the names of the ship's crew and on the opposite face with a likeness of the USS *Indianapolis.* Engravings on the limestone base tell the story of the ill-fated vessel. Because this is an outdoor site, the memorial, impressive and sobering, can be seen at any time. For additional information call (317) 924–1484 or (800) 482–5242.

One of the largest city parks in the United States, 5,200-acre ***Eagle Creek Park*** is home to bald eagles, coyotes, and deer. An arboretum near the park's nature center boasts a 400-year-old Douglas fir log and a beech tree into which Daniel Boone carved his still-visible but fading initials. (If you wonder why the carving is so high up, naturalists surmise it's because Boone was on horseback when he left his mark there.) Much of the park's summertime appeal centers on 1,300-acre Eagle Creek Reservoir, which features a three-acre swimming beach; pontoon boat cruises; the only internationally sanctioned canoe/kayak regatta course in the country (site of the 1988 U.S. Olympic trials and the 1994 World Rowing Championships); and a marina that rents boats, canoes, and sailboards. Also in the park are hiking, bicycling, and cross-country ski trails; an eighteen-hole golf course; a joggers' outdoor exercise course; a world-class archery field; ice-skating ponds; and sled runs. The park is open dawn to dusk every day of the year; a nominal entrance fee is slightly higher on Saturday and Sunday. Enter the park at 7840 West Fifty-sixth Street; (317) 293–4827.

A marvelous getaway spot, especially in winter, is the serene world within the walls of the ***Garfield Park Conservatory.*** Outside, the world may be white with snow, but inside it is summer eternally. Vividly colored birds live among trees that shade giant ferns and lush vegetation. Tropical fish swim in a series of pools fed by a 15-foot waterfall. Walk beneath the falls and enter the environs of the desert, not barren at all but alive with cacti, succulents, and carnivorous plants. Outside, from May through October, the sunken gardens are brilliant with hundreds of blooms. Garfield Park is located at 2450 South Shelby Street; open daily dawn to dusk; free. The conservatory is open 10:00 A.M. to 5:00 P.M. Tuesday through Saturday and noon to 5:00 P.M. Sunday, with special hours for seasonal shows; free admission except during special shows; (317) 784–3044.

Holliday Park would certainly be a top contender for honors as Indianapolis's most unusual park. Located on the west bank of White River at 6349 Spring Mill Road, the eighty-acre park was initially developed in 1936 as a botanical garden, and the grounds still contain more than 800 species of plants. Children love its innovative new playground, especially a rope-climbing contraption that resembles a giant spider web and some twisty tube slides.

The park is most noted, however, for its "ruins." Three stone statues that formerly resided on the now-vanished St. Paul Building in New York City now perch on a ledge atop three Doric columns, dominating a setting that is the focal point of Holliday Park. Three times life-size, the kneeling figures represent white, black, and Asian males who have labored in unity. Just behind the statues is a grotto with a fountain and reflecting pool. Twenty-five 10-foot-tall columns obtained from a local convent when it was razed a few years back surround the grotto and contribute to the ruins effect. Nearby, four statues that once stood atop Marion County's old courthouse adorn the lawn. The collection of statuary is not only eye-catching but also an imaginative contribution to the recycling effort. Open daily dawn to dusk; free; (317) 327–7180.

In the midst of **Lockerbie Square,** a 6-block area of late-nineteenth-century homes near downtown Indianapolis, stands an old brick house once occupied by poet James Whitcomb Riley (for information about Riley's birthplace, see Hancock County earlier in this chapter). Riley spent the last twenty-three years of his life here, and his memorabilia are everywhere. The structure, built in 1872, is recognized as one of the two best Victorian preservations in the country. Nothing here has been restored to the way someone thought it should look—this is history untouched. Riley's pen is on his desk, his suits are in the closet, and his hat is on the bed. The carpets are slightly faded, and the upholstery shows signs of wear, just as it did when Riley lived here. A humble, unpretentious man, Riley would have been astounded to learn that his home is now a major tourist attraction. Located at 528 Lockerbie Street, the **James Whitcomb Riley House** is open 10:00 A.M. to 4:00 P.M. Tuesday through Saturday and noon to 4:00 P.M. Sunday; closed major holidays. There's a nominal admission fee. For additional information write the James Whitcomb Riley Memorial Association, 50 South Meridian Street, Indianapolis 46204; (317) 631–5885 or 634–4474.

When Riley died in 1916, he was interred in *Crown Hill Cemetery.* His grave, sheltered by an elegant but simple Greek temple, is at the crest of Strawberry Hill, the highest point in Indianapolis.

Among the other notables buried here are Benjamin Harrison, twenty-third president of the United States; three vice presidents; and the infamous John Dillinger. Ironically, it is Dillinger's grave that commands the most attention. His funeral in 1934 was the only occasion in Crown Hill's history that the cemetery had to close its gates and restrict attendance. Since then it has been necessary to replace his grave marker several times. Souvenir hunters chip away at them relentlessly, and one collector actually carried away an entire tombstone.

Also located here is *Crown Hill National Cemetery*—a cemetery-within-a-cemetery and the final resting place for nearly 2,000 soldiers, mostly Civil War veterans. The cemetery's main gate at 3402 Boulevard Place is open daily during daylight hours. Before entering, however, you should stop by the office at 700 West Thirty-eighth Street and ask for a map and/or directions to the various grave sites; the cemetery covers more than 500 acres and is crisscrossed by 50 miles of roads. Office open daily 8:00 A.M. to 6:00 P.M. April through September; 8:00 A.M. to 5:00 P.M. the rest of the year; (317) 925–8231.

Well-traveled deli connoisseurs will tell you that *Shapiro's Delicatessen* in southside Indianapolis is the equal of any in New York or Chicago. Believe them! Shapiro's has been a much-loved local fixture since 1905, growing through the years and several generations of Shapiros from a small grocery store with a few tables into a deli/restaurant that serves approximately 2,500 devotees each day. You'll find all the usual deli fare here and then some, generously served, moderately priced, and deliciously prepared. The corned beef, made from a family recipe that won a blue ribbon at the 1939 World's Fair in New York City, sells by the ton—about three tons a week, to be exact. *USA Today* called it "the best corned beef in America," and *Gourmet* magazine reported that "the corned beef sandwich is superb." Other highly rated treats include matzo ball and vegetable soups, pastrami sandwiches, potato pancakes, liver pâté, pickled herring, and, on Sundays only, *real* mashed potatoes. Don't forget the desserts—food critics and just plain eaters rank them with the best Indianapolis has to offer. The strawberry-topped and

James Whitcomb Riley House in Lockerbie Square

chocolate cheesecakes are without peer. Breakfast, lunch, and dinner are served every day of the week (eat in or carry out); open 6:30 A.M. to 9:00 P.M. Located at 808 South Meridian Street; (317) 631–4041. A smaller northside Shapiro's, established at 2370 West Eighty-sixth Street, is open during the same hours; (317) 872–7255.

It began as one man's dream. That dream became a reality in March 1994 when the *Indiana State Police Historical Museum* opened its doors to the public. One of only about half a dozen police museums in the country, it was funded entirely by private donations and is filled with exhibits that will fascinate visitors of all ages.

Vintage police cars and motorcycles, an aluminum boat used by state police scuba divers, a copper moonshine still, some John Dillinger memorabilia, handcuffs, firearms, and bulletproof vests are among the artifacts. The Harger Drunkometer displayed here was developed in the 1920s; Indiana state troopers were the first in the nation to use it. Many of the exhibits are designed for hands-on inspection, and children especially love the two-headed police car (which is actually the front halves from two police cars welded together and facing in opposite directions). Kids can climb inside, turn on the lights and siren, and talk on the radio. There's also a tornado room where visitors can learn what to do when a tornado is approaching—no dry facts here but an actual simulated tornado complete with sound and fury.

The museum is the brainchild of now-retired Ernie Alder, the former director of youth services for the Indiana State Police. Located at 8500 East Twenty-first Street, the museum is open 8:00 to 11:00 A.M. and 1:00 to 4:00 P.M. Monday through Friday; also open noon to 4:45 P.M. on the first and third Saturdays of each month from January through July and September through November. Admission is free, but donations are appreciated. Group tours and educational programs can be arranged by appointment. Call (317) 899–8293.

Just west of Indianapolis is the ***Indianapolis Motor Speedway,*** where each May the world-famous Indy 500 auto race is held. When the course is not being used for competition or test purposes, you can see the track as professional racers see it by taking a bus tour around the 2½-mile asphalt oval. Your pace, of course, will be much more leisurely, and you'll learn many interesting facts along the way.

In addition to hosting the Indy 500, the track also hosts the Brickyard 400 each August and the U.S. Grand Prix in September. The latter event, inaugurated in 2000, returned Formula One racing to this country for the first time since 1991.

A ***Hall of Fame Museum*** inside the track houses a vast collection of racing, classic, and antique passenger cars—including more than thirty past winners of the Indy 500—and some valuable, jewel-encrusted trophies. Perhaps the best-known artifact is the unusual Borg-Warner Trophy, which displays the sculptured, three-dimensional faces of every 500 winner since 1936. You'll also see film clips of old races.

The museum and track, located at 4790 West Sixteenth Street in the suburb of Speedway, are open 9:00 A.M. to 5:00 P.M. daily, year-round, except Christmas. A nominal fee is charged for both the museum and the track tour. Tour information and tickets are available at the museum; call (317) 248–6747.

Ever wonder what happens to Indianapolis 500 race cars after the race? They sometimes end up for sale at ***Chip Gnassi Racing Teams, Inc.,*** where recent offerings included a 1990 Lola that once belonged to Eddie Cheever. Estimated to go from 0 to 60 miles per hour in 1½ to 2½ seconds, driven only 4,000 miles, and undamaged except for one minor fender-bender, it carried an asking price of $150,000 (sorry, engine and tires not included, but you do get to keep the decals). A winning race car, such as the one driven by Emerson Fittipaldi in 1989, is a bit pricier, but Gnassi Racing, located at 3821 Industrial Boulevard in Indianapolis, will be happy to work out a deal for you. Call (317) 297–4772.

Ever dreamed of jumping into a race car and speeding around that oval?

Well, now you can! The **Track Attack Racing School,** based at Indianapolis Raceway Park in Indianapolis, will put you in the driver's seat of a real race car on a real race track. Professional instructors show you the ropes and allow you to increase speed as your confidence level builds. Eventually, if you choose, you'll be allowed to race other students. A variety of programs are offered; contact the school at 8573 Zionsville Road, Indianapolis 46268, or call (317) 870–7223 or (888) 722– 3879 for rates and details.

Trivia

The summer of 1816 was the coldest Indiana summer on record. It began with ice, sleet, and snow in late April, then more snow in May and June. Temperatures dipped to the freezing mark in July, and August brought blizzards. With livestock frozen and food crops destroyed, Hoosiers ate such wilderness fare as raccoons and groundhogs to survive.

Indianapolis, which has a well-deserved reputation for being the amateur sports capital of the country, is the home of the **National Track and Field Hall of Fame.** Among the exhibits are a track shoe worn by the legendary Jesse Owens, a hurdle used in 1884, a photographic tribute to Jim Thorpe, and an unfinished poster publicizing the 1940 Olympics in Tokyo (canceled because of the impending war). Located at 200 South Capitol Avenue in the RCA Dome, home of the National Football League's Indianapolis Colts, the Hall of Fame is open 11:00 A.M. to 5:00 P.M. Monday through Saturday and 1:00 to 5:00 P.M. Sunday daily except during some Dome events and on major holidays; hours may be reduced December through February. There's a nominal admission fee; call (317) 261–0483 or 262–3406.

The **Ropkey Armor Museum,** housed in the (big!) front yard of its owner, is the oldest military museum in the state. Owner Fred Ropkey has amassed an incredible collection of war relics that includes the first Patton tank ever produced—serial number 1—and two World War I, horse-drawn, German cannons that once reposed on Monument Circle in downtown Indianapolis. A more recent acquisition is a Soviet-built amphibious artillery piece used by the Iraqi Army during Operation Desert Storm. Other displays in the combination indoor/outdoor museum include military motorcycles, armored personnel carriers, and firearms.

A natural-born collector, Ropkey also invests in antique automobiles, and his is probably the only home in the country that has a NASA Apollo 5 space capsule floating in the family pond.

Occasionally, Ropkey's equipment appears in films or commercials. James Garner drove one of Ropkey's tanks in the movie *Tank,* and another of Ropkey's armored vehicles was seen briefly during a chase scene in *The*

Blues Brothers. Ropkey and his staff drove some of the museum's tanks themselves in *Mars Attacks.*

The eighty-acre museum, located on the northwest side of Indianapolis, is open free of charge by appointment; you will be given instructions on how to get there when you call. Phone (317) 879–1312.

The state's first medical center is also the nation's oldest surviving pathology laboratory. Housed in the Old Pathology Building on the grounds of the now-closed Central State Hospital, it remains virtually untouched by time. Known as the *Indiana Medical History Museum,* it features a fascinating collection of some 15,000 medical artifacts, including "quack" devices, used in the nineteenth and early twentieth centuries. *Medical Landmarks USA,* a travel guide published by McGraw-Hill in 1990, describes it as a "marvelous museum quite simply without peer in the entire country." Nominal admission fee; open 10:00 A.M. to 4:00 P.M. Wednesday through Saturday, other days and times by appointment. The museum is located at 3045 West Vermont Street in Indianapolis; (317) 635–7329.

Twinkie lovers can watch the spongy treats being made, along with Ding Dongs, doughnuts, and other goodies, at the *Wonder and Hostess Bakery* in Indianapolis. Best of all, the free tours conclude with free samples, coffee or milk, and even some take-home snacks. Located at 2929 North Shadeland Avenue; call (317) 547–9421 for tour hours.

Morgan County

Indiana limestone has been used on a grand scale to build some of the world's most durable and majestic buildings. Since 1970 it has also been used by Martinsville *sculptor Charles Schiefer* to create some much smaller but equally memorable works of art. Schiefer saws, shapes, sands, and polishes his abstract sculptures in a shop adjacent to his country home at 5270 Low Gap Road. Outside, the more than 150 sculptures that populate his ten-acre yard and surround his lake startle passersby and, as the sculptor's fame grows, lure visitors from all over. Most days they find the artist at work in his shop, cutting and shaping his latest creation amid the stone dust that constantly swirls through the air. Schiefer's customers, like his statues, come in all shapes and sizes; they range from municipalities and corporations to homeowners and a group of schoolchildren who raised enough money to purchase a stone rhinoceros they cherished. For additional information call (765) 342–6211.

If you're the type whose curiosity is piqued by life's mysteries, head for

Mooresville and nearby *Gravity Hill.* Legend has it that an Indian witch doctor was buried long ago at the foot of this low hill, and the great energy and power he possessed in life still emanates from the good doctor's grave. Anyone who stops his car at the bottom of the hill and puts it in neutral will find himself coasting backward up the slope for nearly ¼ mile. Don't scoff until you've tried it—witch doctor or no, it really works! Gravity Hill is located on Keller Hill Road, which runs west off State Road 42 on the south side of Mooresville; for exact directions ask local residents or contact the Mooresville Chamber of Commerce, 25 East Main Street (P.O. Box 62), Mooresville 46158; (317) 831–6509.

Amateur astronomers can visit the *Goethe Link Observatory* near Mooresville to keep an eye on happenings in the universe. On Saturday nights when the weather is clear, the general public can view the heavens

Other Attractions Worth Seeing in Central Indiana

ANDERSON

Gruenewald Historic House,
626 Main Street; (765) 646–5771

Historical Military Armor Museum,
2330 Crystal Street;
(765) 649–TANK or (800) 875–8265

Paramount Theatre and Ballroom Tour, *1124 Meridian Plaza;*
(765) 642–1234

ELWOOD

House of Glass,
7900 State Road 28 West; (765) 552–6841

INDIANAPOLIS

Indiana State Museum and Freetown Village,
202 North Alabama Street;
(317) 232–1637

Morris-Butler House Museum,
1204 North Park Avenue;
(317) 636–5409

National Art Museum of Sport,
University Place Conference Center,
850 West Michigan Street;
(317) 274–3627

President Benjamin Harrison Home,
1230 North Delaware Street;
(317) 631–1898

RCA Dome Tour,
100 South Capitol Avenue;
(317) 237–3663 or (800) 323–4639

Scottish Rite Cathedral,
650 North Meridian Street;
(317) 262–3100

NOBLESVILLE

Stoneycreek Farm,
11366 State Road 38 East;
(317) 773–3344

Goethe Link Observatory and Link Daffodil Gardens

free of charge through the observatory's 36-inch reflector and 10-inch refractor telescopes. The observatory is owned by Indiana University, which rarely uses it because these days professional astronomers use computers instead. In 1986 the university granted sole use of the observatory to the Indiana Astronomical Society. For additional information, contact the Astronomy Department, Swain Hall West, Room 319, Indiana University, Bloomington 47405, or call (812) 855–6911.

Sharing the one hundred–acre grounds of the Link estate with the observatory are the fifteen-acre **Link Daffodil Gardens,** resplendent with hundreds of thousands of blooms for about two weeks in April. The gardens are open daily, free of charge, during daylight hours. Mrs. Helen Link, a nationally recognized authority on the daffodil, raises an array of different types here. She has personally bred more than forty named varieties, and several of her creations are on exhibit at the National Arboretum in Washington, D.C. You can call (765) 832–3283 to check blooming times or watch for an announcement in the Indianapolis newspapers. The Link estate, which is at 1660 Observatory Road, lies 1½ miles west of State Road 67, about 5 miles south of Mooresville near the tiny community of Brooklyn; follow observatory signs.

An eye-catching house in Morgantown has for many years been luring architects, geologists, and just plain folks from across the nation. Built between 1894 and 1896 as a private residence, the house is adorned with the turrets, gables, and cones that were popular in the Victorian era, but there any similarity to other houses of its time ends. The walls are constructed of concrete blocks, embedded on the exterior with rocks and geodes of all shapes and sizes, bits of colored glass, seashells, Indian relics, jewelry, marbles, dolls' heads, keys, a boar's skull, and even a picture of two puppies under glass. Since the original owner kept enlarging the house to accommodate a family that eventually included twenty-two children, many of the items on the walls depict segments of family history. Today the fanciful house is a bed-and-breakfast inn that welcomes guests for $50 to $75 a night; rates include a full, all-you-can-eat country breakfast. Many guests schedule a stay on one of the several weekends when "mystery nights"—in which guests participate as victim or suspects—are held. Contact the **Rock House Inn,** 380 West Washington Street, Morgantown 46160; (812) 597–5100.

Shelby County

*A*n extraordinary dining experience awaits you in Morristown. Nestled amid lovely gardens, the **Kopper Kettle** is as much a museum as a restaurant. It occupies a picturesque, nineteenth-century manor house accented with stained-glass windows and filled with antiques and art objects from around the world. All this beauty should be re-garded as a bonus, because the meal awaiting you inside would be unforgettable served in any surroundings.

The wide range of entrees changes somewhat from day to day, but you can't go wrong with fried chicken, steak, or seafood. All side dishes are served family style, and you're encouraged to ask for refills. You won't find anything really fancy here—just plain food distinguished by perfect preparation, moderate prices, and an elegant atmosphere.

Located at 135 West Main Street (U.S. Highway 52), the Kopper Kettle is open for lunch from 11:00 A.M. to 3:00 P.M. Tuesday through Friday. The dinner menu is available from 11:00 A.M. to 8:30 P.M. Tuesday through Friday, 11:00 A.M. to 9:00 P.M. Saturday, and noon to 6:30 P.M. Sunday; closed Monday; winter hours vary. Reservations are recommended; (765) 763–6767.

Tiny Boggstown may seem like just another rural Indiana community—a pleasant place to be but in no way distinctive. But since July 1984 when the **Boggstown Inn & Cabaret** opened for business, the "joint has been jumping." At last count, folks from every state and from more than twenty-five countries (including Russia, Thailand, and Australia) have trekked to the Boggstown Inn for a nostalgic dose of ragtime music.

Performers may include piano, banjo, or washboard players; a small band; or singers (a different combination is offered each evening); but the show always features a sing-along. The inn opens for dinner at 5:30 P.M.; the music begins at 7:00 P.M. and continues nonstop until the inn closes at 10:00 P.M. Entertainment charges vary, depending on whether you dine there, what time you arrive, and what night you come. Open Wednesday through Saturday, dinner prices range from $10.00 to $16.00 on Friday and Saturday and from $7.00 to $14.00 on Wednesday and Thursday. Reservations are a must and should be made well ahead of your visit (from four to six weeks for the slightly more popular nights of Friday and Saturday). Since few of the roads leading to Boggstown are marked on any map, you'll be sent directions for getting there when you make your reservation. Write the inn at 6895 West Boggstown Road, Boggstown 46110; call (317) 835-2020 or (800) 672-2656. The inn also offers a Sunday brunch to the accompaniment of live piano music; no reservations required (call for hours).

The excellent *Grover Museum of the Shelby County Historical Society* contains exhibits that depict the history of the local area. In this respect, it is not unlike other county historical museums. One fascinating display, however, is delightfully different. Visitors may view the underwear worn by our nineteenth-century ancestors. Among the many interesting tidbits of knowledge you'll glean from your visit is the fact that women's crotchless underpants did not originate with Victoria's Secret or Frederick's of Hollywood. They were worn for efficiency's sake (all those long skirts and outhouses to contend with, you know) by inventive females in the 1800s. Located at 52 West Broadway Street in downtown Shelbyville, the museum is open from 1:00 to 4:00 P.M. Friday through Sunday. Admission is free; call (317) 392-4634.

PLACES TO STAY IN CENTRAL INDIANA

ALEXANDRIA
Country Gazebo Inn
13867 North 100 West
(765) 754-8783

ANDERSON
Plum Retreat Bed
and Breakfast
926 Historic West
Eighth Street
(765) 649-7586

ATLANTA
The Walton House
Main and Railroad Streets
(765) 292-2422
(888) 674-3705

DANVILLE
Marigold Manor Bed
and Breakfast
368 West Main Street
(317) 745-2347

FISHERS
Frederick-Talbott Inn
13805 Allisonville Road
(317) 578-3600

FRANKLIN
Oak Haven
4975 Hurricane Road
(County Road 400 East)
(317) 535–9491

GREENFIELD
Ahlbrand's Inn
4859 West 150 North Road
(317) 894–8839

GREENWOOD
Candlestick Inn
402 Euclid Avenue
(317) 888–3905

Persimmon Tree Bed
and Breakfast
One North Madison Avenue
(317) 889–0849
(888) 894–1482,
Access Code 01

INDIANAPOLIS
Boone Docks on the River
7159 Edgewater Place
(317) 257–3671

Country Hearth Inn
3851 Shore Drive
(317) 297–1848
(800) 217–9182

Friendliness With a Flair
5214 East 20th Place
(317) 356–3149

Harrison House
Fort Harrison State Park
6002 North Post Road
(317) 543–9592

Hoffman House
545 East Eleventh Street
(317) 635–1701
(800) 737–9323

Holland House
1502 East Tenth Street
(317) 685–9326

Le Chateau Delaware
1456 North Delaware Street
(317) 636–9156

Nuthatch Bed
and Breakfast
7161 Edgewater Place
(317) 257–2660

Old Northside Bed
and Breakfast
1340 North Alabama Street
(317) 635–9123
(800) 635–9127
Fax: (317) 635–9243

Renaissance Tower
Historic Inn
230 East Ninth Street
(317) 261–1652
(800) 676–7786

Speedway Bed
and Breakfast
1829 Cunningham Road
(317) 487–6531
(800) 975–3412

Stone Soup Inn
1304 North Central Avenue
(317) 639–9550

Stonegate B&B
8955 A Stonegate Road
(317) 887–9614

The Tranquil Cherub
2164 North Capitol Avenue
(317) 923–9036
Fax: (317) 923–8676

JAMESTOWN
Oakwood Bed and
Breakfast
9530 West U.S. Highway 136
(765) 676–5114
Fax: (765) 676–5802

LAPEL
Kati-Scarlett B&B
1037 North Main Street
P.O. Box 756
(765) 534–4937

MCCORDSVILLE
Round Barn Inn Bed
and Breakfast
6794 North County Road
600 West
(317) 335–7023
(888) 743–9819

MORGANTOWN
Rock House Inn
380 West Washington Street
(812) 597–5100

Your Country Home
6883 North State Road 135
(800) 782–8693

NORTH SALEM
Walnut Hill Bed
and Breakfast
5932 State Road 236
(765) 676–4196
(800) 433–5664
Fax: (765) 676–4195

ZIONSVILLE
Brick Street Inn
175 South Main Street
(317) 873–9177
Fax: (317) 873–9294

**PLACES TO EAT IN
CENTRAL INDIANA**

ALEXANDRIA
Hi-way Cafe
State Road 9 South
(765) 724–9969

ANDERSON
Homestretch Restaurant
at Hoosier Park
4500 Dan Patch Boulevard
(765) 683–2585

The Lemon Drop
1701 Mounds Road
(765) 644–9055

Lucy's
2460 East County Road 67
(765) 643–3144

Magic Wok
817 South State Road 9
(765) 643 7000

Nile Restaurant
723 East Eighth Street
(765) 640–9028

Tio's Restaurant
2902 Broadway Street
(765) 649–5655

ATLANTA
Fletcher's of Atlanta
185 West Main Street
(765) 292–2777

BEECH GROVE
Chan's Garden Restaurant
718 Main Street
(317) 788–0601

Napoli Villa Restaurant
758 Main Street
(317) 783–4122

BOGGSTOWN
Boggstown Inn
and Cabaret
6895 West Boggstown Road
(317) 835–2020

CARMEL
Cancun Mexican
Restaurant and Cantina
511 South Rangeline Road
(317) 580–0333

Ice Creams Coffee
Beans Cafe
1404 South Rangeline Road
(317) 844–8643

Illusions
969 Keystone Way
(317) 575–8312

DANVILLE
J. J.'s Bar and Restaurant
28 West Main Street
(317) 745–7444

Mayberry Cafe
78 West Main Street
(317) 745–4067

Schaffers Old Towne Inn
and Museum
107 East Main Cross Street
(812) 526–0275

ELWOOD
Wolff's Tavern
1447 South A Street
(765) 552–9022

FISHERS
Governor Noble's
Eating Place
13400 Allisonville Road
(317) 776–6008

Nickel Plate Bar and Grill
8654 East 116th Street
(317) 841–2888

FRANKLIN
Heiskell's Restaurant
and Lounge
398 South Main Street
(317) 736–4900

GREENFIELD
Dragon Palace
413 North State Street
(317) 462–4965

GREENWOOD
Haus Anna
67 North Madison Avenue
(317) 887–0439

Johnson County Line
1265 North Madison Avenue
(317) 887–0404

INDIANAPOLIS
Acapulco Joe's
365 North Illinois Street
(317) 637–5160

Barringer's Tavern
2535 South Meridian Street
(317) 783–3663

The Blue Heron
11699 Fall Creek Road
(317) 845–8899

Brickyard Restaurant
Indianapolis Motor
Speedway
4400 West Sixteenth Street
(317) 241–2500

Broad Ripple Steakhouse
929 East Westfield
Boulevard
(317) 253–8101

California Pizza Kitchen
8702 Keystone Crossing
(317) 846–2900

Deeter and Gabe's
1462 West
Eighty-sixth Street
(317) 876 1111

Dodd's Town House
5694 North Meridian Street
(317) 257–1872

Durbin's Restaurant
and Lounge
Indianapolis Marriott Hotel
7202 East Twenty-first Street
(317) 352–1231

El Sol de Tala
2444 East Washington
Street
(317) 635–8252

G.T. South's Rib House
5711 East Seventy-first
Street
(317) 849–6997

The Garrison Restaurant
6002 North Post Road
(317) 543–9592

George's Place
2727 East l86th Street
Woodfield Center
(317) 255–7064

Hollyhock Hill
8110 North College Avenue
(317) 251–2294

Iaria's Italian Restaurant
317 South College Avenue
(317) 638–7706

The Iron Skillet
2489 West Thirtieth Street
(317) 923–6353

Johnny B's Sports Bar
373 South Illinois Street
(317) 756–7264

JoJo's Restaurant
2544 South Lynhurst Drive
(317) 247–0237

Kabul Restaurant
8553 Ditch Road
(317) 257–1213

Kona Jack's Fish Market
and Oyster Bar
9413 North Meridian Street
(317) 843–2600

Kory's Restaurant
1850 East Sixty-second
Street
(317) 251–2252

Lauren's Southern Soul
2172 East Fifty-fourth
Street
(317) 255–3554

Mama Carolla's Old
Italian Restaurant
1031 East Fifty-fourth
Street
(317) 259–9412

Montgomery Inn
8580 Allison Pointe
Boulevard
(317) 570–9400

Old Spaghetti Factory
210 South Meridian Street
(317) 635–6325

Patty's Kitchen
5225 East Washington
Street
(317) 353–2908

Plump's Last Shot
6416 Cornell Avenue
(317) 257–5867

Queen of Sheba
936 Indiana Avenue
(317) 638–8426

Rathskeller at the
Athenaeum
401 East Michigan Street
(317) 636–0396

Rick's Cafe Boatyard
4050 Dandy Trail
(317) 290–9300

Shapiro's Delicatessen
808 South Meridian Street
(317) 631–4041

Three Sisters Cafe
and Bakery
6360 North Guilford
Avenue
(317) 257–5556

LEBANON
The Old Trackside Depot
100 South Street
(765) 483–0400

MOORESVILLE
Gray Brothers Cafeteria
555 South Indiana Street
(317) 831–3345

MORRISTOWN
Kopper Kettle
135 West Main Street
(U.S. Highway 52)
(765) 763–6767

NOBLESVILLE
Classic Kitchen
610 Hannibal Street
(317) 773–7385

Lutz's Steak House
3100 Westfield Road
(317) 896–5002

Sinclair's Gourmet
Pizza and Subs
216 South Tenth Street
(317) 770–9099

PENDLETON
Downing's Old Trail
Restaurant
114 North Pendleton
Avenue
(765) 778–7595

Jimmie's Dairy Bar
7065 State Road South
(765) 778–3800

The Pendleton House
118 North Pendleton
Avenue
(765) 778–8061

The Post Restaurant
State Roads 9 and 67
(765) 778–4651

PERKINSVILLE
Bonge's Tavern
9830 West 280 North
(765) 734–1625

PITTSBORO
Frank and Mary's
21–25 East Main Street
(765) 893–3485

SHELBYVILLE
Fiddlers Three
1415 East Michigan Road
(765) 392–4306

SHERIDAN
The Red Onion Restaurant
and Lounge
406 South Main Street
(317) 758–0424

SPEEDWAY
Union Jack Pub
6225 West Twenty-fifth
Street
(317) 243–3300

THORNTOWN
Stookey's Restaurant
125 East Main Street
(765) 436–7202

TIPTON
Jim Dandy Family
Restaurant
203 West Jefferson Street
(765) 675–6199

Sherrill's Restaurant
U.S. Highway 31 and
State Road 28
(765) 675–3550

ZIONSVILLE
Adam's Rib 40 South Main
Street (317) 873–3301

Gisela's Kaffeekranzchen
112 South Main Street
(317) 873–5523

Just Like Home
90 East Pine Street
(317) 733–0050

Panache
60 South Elm Street
(317) 873–1388

Z'Bistro
160 South Main Street
(317) 873–1888

Zorba's Greek and
Middle Eastern Food
30 North Main Street
(317) 733–0633

SOURCES FOR ADDITIONAL
INFORMATION ABOUT
CENTRAL INDIANA

Anderson/Madison County
Visitors and Convention
Bureau
6335 Scatterfield Road
Anderson 46013
(765) 643–5633
(800) 533–6569
Fax: (765) 643–9083
E-mail:
andersonvcb@iquest.net
www.madtourism.com

Boone County Chamber of
Commerce
221 North Lebanon Street
Lebanon 46052
(765) 482–1320

Edinburgh (Johnson
County) Chamber of
Commerce
P.O. Box 306
Edinburgh 46124
(812) 526–5660
Fax: (812) 526–6192

Franklin (Johnson County)
Chamber of Commerce
370 East Jefferson Street
P.O. Box 264
Franklin 46131
(317) 736–6334
Fax: (317) 736–9553

Greater Greenfield
(Hancock County)
Chamber of Commerce
One Courthouse Plaza
Greenfield 46140
(317) 462–4188
Fax: (317) 462–8551

Greater Greenwood
(Johnson County)
Chamber of Commerce
550 South U.S. Highway 31
Greenwood 46142
(317) 888–4856
Fax: (317) 865–2609

Greater Martinsville
(Morgan County) Chamber
of Commerce
210 North Marion Street
P.O. Box 1378
Martinsville 46151
(765) 342–8110
Fax: (765) 342–5713

Greater Zionsville
(Boone County) Chamber
of Commerce
135 South Elm Street
P.O. Box 148
Zionsville 46077
(317) 873–3836

Hamilton County
Convention and Visitors
Bureau
11601 Municipal Drive
Fishers 46038
(317) 598–4444
(800) 776–8687
Fax: (317) 598–4450
www.hccvb.com

Hendricks County Tourism Commission
5201 East U.S. Highway 36, Suite 501
Danville 46122
(800) 321–9666
Fax: (317) 745–0757

Indianapolis City Center
Pan Am Plaza
201 South Capitol Avenue, Suite 200
Indianapolis 46225
(317) 237–5200
(800) 323–4639
Fax: (317) 237–5211
www.indy.org/citycen.htm

Lawrence (Marion County) Chamber of Commerce
5803 North Post Road, Suite 150
Lawrence 46216
(317) 541–9876

Mooresville (Morgan County) Chamber of Commerce
26 South Indiana Street
Mooresville 46158
(317) 831–6509
Fax: (317) 831–9548

Morristown Area (Shelby County) Chamber of Commerce
P.O. Box 476
Morristown 46161
(317) 763–7525
Fax: (317) 763–7414

Shelby County Chamber of Commerce
33 East Washington Street
Shelbyville 46176
(317) 398–6647
(800) 223–2210
Fax: (317) 392–3901

Northeast Indiana

erhaps best known as Amish country, northeast Indiana is home to one of the largest populations of Old Order Amish in the world. For the most part, it is a serene and pastoral world, sculpted long ago by the glaciers of the Ice Age. Beyond the scattering of towns and cities, the gentle hills sometimes seem to march on forever. Natural lakes are small but abundant; Steuben County alone is dotted with 101 of them.

Although travelers can hurry north and south on I–69 or east and west on I–80/90 (Indiana's only toll road), those who want to experience the simple charms of this part of the Hoosier State will set out on backroads and byways. It is there that they will discover the essence of this pocket of peace.

Adams County

ust south of Berne you can drive through a picturesque covered bridge across the Wabash River and leave the twentieth century behind. You are now in the land of the Amish, where windmills replace skyscrapers and horse-drawn buggies move sedately along dusty country roads. This is the home of *Amishville, U.S.A.*, a 120-acre Amish farm open to the public.

While members of the resident family go about their daily business of managing the farm, using the centuries-old methods of their ancestors visitors stroll through the barn, milk house, smokehouse, washhouse, and old-fashioned garden. Modern conveniences have no place here; the Amish live their lives without motors, plumbing, refrigeration, radios, televisions, and automobiles. At Amishville you can learn all about the simple lifestyle these gentle people have chosen to embrace.

Trivia
The Ceylon Covered Bridge, 2 miles northeast of Geneva in Adams County, is the last covered bridge on the fabled Wabash River.

Entrance is free, but nominal fees are charged for a guided tour of the authentic Amish house and outbuildings and for buggy rides and

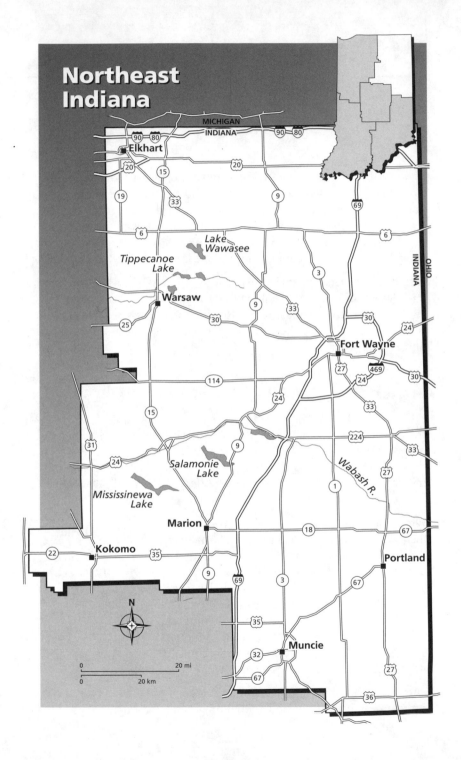

Northeast Indiana

hayrides in the summer and sleigh rides in the winter. In deference to both Amish tradition and the Swiss heritage of surrounding communities, *Der Essen Platz* (The Eating Place) at Amishville serves home-cooked foods that are favorites of both cultures. Two small lakes are available for fishing, swimming, and, in the winter, ice-skating. For those who want to stay a spell and let the peace sink in, there's a large wooded campground.

You can reach Amishville by going south from Berne on U.S. Highway 27 for 3 miles; at County Road 950S, turn east and follow the signs. Open daily from 9:00 A.M. to 5:00 P.M. Monday through Saturday and 1:00 to 5:00 P.M. Sunday; guided tours available daily April through November. Write Amishville, U.S.A., 844 East 900 South, Geneva 46740; (219) 589–3536.

In the Swiss village of Berne, you can visit the **First Mennonite Church.** Located at 566 West Main Street, the classic Gothic structure is one of the two largest Mennonite churches in North America. Some 2,000 people can be seated in the main sanctuary. Of particular note is the Moeller organ, whose 2,281 pipes have resounded with beautiful music for more than seventy-five years. Visitors come from all over the United States, Canada, and Europe to tour the church and listen to the organ. The church is open to visitors daily from 9:00 A.M. to 4:30 P.M.; Sunday services are held at 10:00 A.M.; (219) 589–3108.

For information about Berne's unusual shops and stores, many of which cater to the area's 4,000 Amish residents, contact the Berne Chamber of Commerce, 456 Hendricks Street, P.O. Box 85, Berne 46711; (219) 589–8080.

A turn-of-the-century aura of a different sort is found in Decatur. The **Back 40 Junction Restaurant,** famous for both food and decor, is housed in a country railroad station. Outside, on remnant stretches of train track, you can view such railroad memorabilia as a 1920s-era club car, complete with original lighting fixtures, seats, and berths. The "little

---

AUTHOR'S FAVORITE ATTRACTIONS/ EVENTS IN NORTHEAST INDIANA

Auburn-Cord-Duesenberg Museum, Auburn; (219) 925–1444

International Circus Hall of Fame, Peru; (765) 472–7553

Lincoln Museum, Fort Wayne; (219) 455–3864

Menno-Hof Visitors Center, Shipshewana; (219) 768–4117

Midwest Museum of American Art, Elkhart; (219) 293–6660

Aloha International Hawaiian Steel Guitar Convention, Winchester; July (765) 584–6845, (765) 584–3266, or (800) 905 0514

Auburn-Cord-Duesenberg Festival, Auburn; September (Labor Day weekend) (219) 925–3600

Circus City Festival, Peru; July (765) 472–3918

Easter Pageant, Marion; Easter weekend (765) 664–3947 or (800) 662–9474

Fairmount Museum Days/ Remembering James Dean, Fairmount; September (765) 948–4555

Amishville, U.S.A.

red caboose" is a gift shop. Inside the station is a fine restaurant decorated with hundreds of antiques and bits of Americana. Antique oil lamps that once belonged to actress Carole Lombard, an Indiana native, are here, as are a Tiffany chandelier, an old ox yoke, and a collection of the Burma Shave signs that once lined our nation's highways and provided many a laugh. Although the Back 40 Junction offers a regular lunch and dinner menu, it is the moderately priced smorgasbord that has brought it fame. It's served from 11:00 A.M. to 2:00 P.M. Monday through Saturday, 3:30 to 9:00 P.M. Monday through Thursday, 3:00 to 10:00 P.M. Friday and Saturday, and 11:00 A.M. to 6:00 P.M. Sunday and holidays; closed Christmas. Sing-alongs are a Friday night special. The restaurant is located at 1011 North Thirteenth Street (U.S. Highway 27/33) on the north side of Decatur. Reservations accepted; (219) 724–3355.

Allen County

*J*ohn Chapman, better known as Johnny Appleseed, traveled on foot through much of the Midwest, planting seeds that would one day grow into vast apple orchards. In his own time he was much beloved, and he remains a folk hero to this day. What most folks don't realize is that Johnny didn't wander about in all those raggedy clothes because he had to. Johnny was a miser—kindly, but a miser nevertheless—who found free room and board with families along the routes he followed, planted some apple seeds in their fields, and eventually moved on. It was no surprise to those who knew him, then, that his death on March 18, 1845, was due to exposure. He died near Fort Wayne and was buried there with honors. His gravesite, open at all times, is located in forty-three-acre *Johnny Appleseed Park,* which lies along East Coliseum Boulevard on the east side of the 4000 block of Parnell Avenue and just north of the St. Joseph River; (219) 427–6720.

The forty-two-acre *Fort Wayne Children's Zoo,* with more than 500 domestic and exotic animals, delights visitors of all ages. Although small, it has been internationally recognized for its landscaping and cleverly designed exhibits. *Travel America* says this is "simply the best children's zoo in the nation," while the *New York Times* calls it one of the top five children's zoos in the country. Children love to feed the animals, pet tame deer, and ride the miniature train; the whole family will love the safari through a re-created African veldt where all animals roam free. An exhibit devoted to Australian wildlife—the largest of its kind in North America—includes a 20,000-gallon Great Barrier Reef aquarium. The Indonesian Rain Forest features a Sumatran elephant skeleton, an endangered species carousel, and, since 1996, two Sumatran tigers roaming free in a half-acre re-creation of their outdoor habitat. Open 9:00 A.M. to 5:00 P.M. daily late April through mid-October. Nominal admission fee. Located at 3411 Sherman Boulevard in Fort Wayne's Franke Park; (219) 427–6800.

The world's largest private collection of Abraham Lincoln memorabilia, housed at the *Lincoln Museum,* includes some 18,000 books in twenty-six languages dealing exclusively with Lincoln; paintings, letters, and personal possessions of the family; and such curios as the flag that draped Lincoln's box at Ford's Theatre. The first item in the collection was the photograph of Lincoln that was used on the $5.00 bill; it was contributed by Robert Todd Lincoln, Lincoln's son, in 1928. One of the most recent acquisitions is the inkwell Lincoln used to sign the Emancipation Proclamation. A remarkable collection of some 100 pictures of the sixteenth president and his descendants—the existence of these pictures was known only to family members for many decades—was acquired by the museum after the death in 1985 of the last of the Lincolns (the president's great-grandson, Robert Beckwith). The museum also features computerized exhibits, film clips about Lincoln's life as depicted in the movies and on television, and a gift shop. Open 10:00 A.M. to 5:00 P.M. Tuesday through Saturday and 1:00 to 5:00 P.M. Sunday; nominal admission fee. The 30,000-square-foot state-of-the-art facility is located at 200 East Berry Street; (219) 455–3864.

One of the most breathtaking sights in downtown Fort Wayne is the *Foellinger-Freimann Botanical Conservatory,* a series of three buildings connected by tunnels and one of the largest passive solar structures in the United States. Some 1,300 panels of insulating glass permit the sunshine to enter; moreover, to ensure that all available sunlight could reach 'the buildings unimpeded, the city passed special zoning laws. Visitors will see displays of North American desert plants, rare tropical plants from around the world, and changing seasonal exhibits. Nominal admission fee. Open 10:00 A.M. to 5:00 P.M. Monday through Saturday and noon to 4:00 P.M. Sunday and holidays; closed Christmas. Located at 1100 South Calhoun Street; (219) 427–1267.

Lakeside Rose Garden, which covers more than three acres, is Indiana's only All-American Rose Selection Display Garden. Currently some 220 varieties flourish on nearly 2,500 labeled rosebushes against a backdrop of a lagoon, reflecting pools, and a Grecian-style pergola. The blooms are glorious from June to mid-October, but the scenic grounds are open daily throughout the year during daylight hours. Free admission; located in Lakeside City Park at the corner of East Lake Avenue and Forest Park Boulevard; (219) 427–6000.

Anyone interested in architecture will want to see the *Cathedral of the Immaculate Conception,* a Gothic-style church in the center of Fort

Eight's Company

*B*erne is home to one of Indiana's best-known families. Keith and Becki Dilley were catapulted into the national spotlight when Becki gave birth to sextuplets on May 25, 1993, in an Indianapolis hospital. For a while, the family resided in Indianapolis, with Keith and Becki working different shifts so they could take turns watching over their brood. When Keith accepted a job in Fort Wayne, about forty-five minutes from Berne, the Dilleys left their five-bedroom, four-bathroom home in Indianapolis to take up residence in a three-bedroom, one-bathroom home in Berne. The bathroom isn't free for more than ten minutes at a time on any given day. Needless to say, a second bathroom is high on the family's wish list.

The Dilleys (Keith, Becki, four boys, two girls, and a dog named Bonnie) are enjoying small-town life. One of the children's favorite things to do is to visit nearby Amishville, where they can pet Shetland ponies and long-haired llamas.

People across the country have watched the six children grow through their regular appearances on the ABC-TV show Prime Time. In May 1999 ABC also aired a made-for-TV movie about the sextuplets entitled Half a Dozen Babies.

Trivia

Wayne. Its Bavarian stained-glass windows are recognized as the finest in the Western Hemisphere, and its hand-carved wood altar is considered one of the finest woodcarvings in the country. Maps are available for self-guided tours. Open 10:00 A.M. to 2:00 P.M. Wednesday and Friday and noon to 3:00 P.M. the second and fourth Sundays of each month; other times by appointment. Located on Cathedral Square at 1122 South Calhoun Street; (219) 424–1485.

Other notable architectural sights are the ***Concordia Theological Seminary*** campus buildings designed by Eero Saarinen to resemble an early northern European village. They have won numerous national and worldwide awards for both design and landscaping. For a free tour contact the Seminary Relations Department on the campus at 6600 North Clinton Street in Fort Wayne; (219) 452–2100.

The campus of the ***University of St. Francis*** boasts a college library housed in a mansion that in the early 1900s was a residential showplace. A stairway that spirals to the third floor of the thirty-three-room Romanesque structure is truly magnificent. A map and self-guided cassette tour describe the lavish wall hangings, hand-painted murals, and period rooms. Located at 2701 Spring Street in Fort Wayne; free admission. Open daily except on school holidays during the academic year, but hours vary; (219) 434–3279 or (800) 729–4732.

Residents of Fort Wayne have something new to brag about. According to the fifth edition of Places Rated Almanac, *published in 1997, Indiana's second-largest city is the best-read metropolitan area in North America.*

A city's reading quotient is determined by adding the number of books on local libraries' shelves to the number of times the books are checked out, then dividing the total by the population served.

Fort Wayne's reading quotient of 19.0 is slightly higher than the 18.6 reading quotient of runner-up Jamestown, New York, but is well above the average metro area's score of 6.7.

Indiana's most honored gourmet restaurant—the ***Cafe Johnell*** in Fort Wayne—has won front-page recommendations in the *Wall Street Journal* and the *Chicago Tribune,* the *Travel/Holiday* Magazine Award for Dining Distinction (for more than twenty consecutive years), the Mobil Guide Four Star Award (the lone restaurant in Indiana to be so honored), and the Ordre du Merite Agricole from the Republic of France. In 1984 it was the only Indiana restaurant chosen by *Playboy* magazine as one of the country's one hundred finest. With recommendations like that, almost anything you select should provide a real taste treat. The cuisine, of course, is decidedly French, and the owners say that among their current selections, sole amandine de Dover, caneton à l'orange flambé, and tournedos de boeuf Rossini are customer favorites. The chef guarantees that you can cut all steaks with a fork, and the food is complemented by a notable art collection. Dinners range from $30 to $50—prices that are a bit trendy for Indiana but are a bargain elsewhere. Open 11:30 A.M. to 2:00 P.M. weekdays, 6:00 to 10:00 P.M. Monday through Thursday, and 5:00 to 10:00 P.M. Friday and Saturday; closed Sunday and major holidays. Reservations are advised. Located at 2529 South Calhoun Street; (219) 456–1939.

While touring Fort Wayne you might want to take advantage of a free potato chip–making lesson. *Seyfert Foods, Inc.,* goes through nearly 200,000 pounds of potatoes every eight hours, transforming them into potato chips known to aficionados for their extraordinary taste and texture. The secret to the chips' success, say company executives, is twofold—the thickness of the potato slices and the secret-formula cooking oil, neither of which has changed in some sixty years. Seyfert's makes other goodies, too, including cheese-flavored popcorn, corn chips, butter pretzels, and various nut products. Reservations are required for the tours, which are offered at 9:15 A.M. and 1:15 P.M. each Tuesday and Thursday; participants must be age twelve or older. The plant is located at 1001 Paramount Road; call (219) 483–9521.

For a get-away-from-it-all experience, travel southwest from downtown Fort Wayne to *Fox Island County Park.* There, in a 270-acre state nature preserve, you'll see a 40-foot sand dune and an unusual (for Indiana) quaking bog whose surface ripples when you stamp your feet. A new nature center opened in 1999. Located at 7324 Yohne Road; (219) 449–3180 or (219) 427–6000.

The peaceful little town of Grabill, northeast of Fort Wayne, is a lovely place to explore crafts and antiques shops. Each year in early September, the *Grabill County Fair* lures more than 100,000 people from throughout the Midwest. The fun includes contests for seed spitting, frog jumping, chicken flying, and wife calling. Go north from Fort Wayne onto State Road 1 to Hosler Road in the town of Leo, then turn east onto Hosler Road. For additional information contact the Fort Wayne/Allen County Convention and Visitors Bureau, 1021 South Calhoun Street, Fort Wayne 46802; (219) 424–3700 or (800) 767–7552.

DeKalb County

A rare treat awaits old car buffs in the town of Auburn. Housed in the administration building of the old Auburn Automobile Company is one of the country's finest collections of cars.

The *Auburn-Cord-Duesenberg Museum* and its contents complement each other perfectly. Constructed in 1930, the building is an architectural masterpiece of the art deco style. The automobiles within it are among the most beautiful ever produced—products of a golden age when luxury and power were the gods of the road. Some 140 classic, antique, special-interest, and one-of-a-kind cars dating from 1898 to the present are on permanent display here.

Indiana was once the automobile capital of the world, and Auburn was its heart, the birthplace of twenty-one of America's early motorcars. The Duesenbergs designed and produced here were the costliest domestic automobiles of the 1920s and 1930s—commanding prices of $15,000 to $20,000 even in the midst of the Great Depression. Greta Garbo owned one, as did Gary Cooper, Clark Gable, and many of the crowned heads of Europe. The cars were not only symbols of extravagant wealth but also supremely engineered machines that could hurtle down the highway at speeds up to 130 miles per hour. Today Duesenbergs are worth hundreds of thousands of dollars as collector cars.

Various models of the Cord, more modest than the Duesenberg but still a cut above the rest, and the Auburn are displayed, along with more obscure cars, such as the Locomotive, Rauch-Lang, and McIntyre. A flamboyant 1956 Bentley was owned by John Lennon in the 1960s. Visitors will also see a 1948 Tucker and a 1981 DeLorean.

The museum is open daily year-round, except for major winter holidays, from 9:00 A.M. to 6:00 P.M. Admission fee; contact the Auburn-Cord-Duesenberg Museum, 1600 South Wayne Street, P.O. Box 271, Auburn 46706; (219) 925–1444.

Each year on Labor Day weekend Auburns, Cords, and Duesenbergs from all regions of the United States return to the city of their creation for an annual festival. A highlight of the event is the collector car auction, which has produced many world-record prices. Even for spectators it's an exciting show. In 1997, for instance, some 5,000 collector cars were sold. Among them were the late Scott Brayton's two Indianapolis 500 pole cars, the Taco Bell *Star Wars* Hummer, Roy Orbison's 1985 Porsche 911, and a 1990 BMW 750 IL that once belonged to singer John Mellencamp. Because of a tragic coincidence, an armor-plated Rolls-Royce used by Princess Diana during her visits to the United States fetched $100,000, more than three times the price auctioneers had anticipated. Diana was killed in an automobile accident the day before the auction. The 1998 auction featured Michael Jordan's 1990 Corvette Z R-1, Clark Gable's 1955 Mercedes Benz 300SL Gullwing coupe, and the Batmobile from the 1995 movie *Batman Forever.*

Write the Auburn-Cord-Duesenberg Festival at the museum's address, or call (219) 925–3600.

Complementing the Auburn-Cord-Duesenberg Museum is the *National Automotive and Truck Museum of the United States.* The museum, known locally as NATMUS, houses post–World War II cars and a truck collection that spans the entire motorized industry. A prize of the collection is the Endeavor, a truck built on a modified International Harvester chassis that set the world land speed record for trucks on the Bonneville Salt Flats of Utah. Thousands of toy model cars and trucks are also on display. NATMUS is located at 1000 Gordon M. Buehrig Place and is open 9:00 A.M. to 5:00 P.M. daily May through October; 9:00

Annual Events in Northeast Indiana

James Dean Birthday Celebration,
Fairmount; early February
(317) 948–4555

Wakarusa Maple Syrup Festival,
Wakarusa; February
(219) 862–4344

Cinco de Mayo,
Warsaw; May (219) 372–9554

Festival of the Wild Rose Moon,
Middlebury; June
(219) 262–8161
(800) 377–3579

Cole Porter Festival,
Peru; June (765) 473–9183

Indian Powwow,
Hartford City; June (765) 348–3541

Haynes-Apperson Festival,
Kokomo; July 4th weekend
(765) 459–4191

Quilters Hall of Fame Celebration,
Marion; July (765) 664–9333

Three Rivers Festival,
Fort Wayne; July (219) 745–5556

Popular Rotorcraft Association Convention Fly-In,
Mentone; July (219) 353–7227

Swiss Days,
Berne; July (219) 589–8080

Marshmallow Festival,
Ligonier; July/August (219) 894–4159

National Aeromodeling Championships,
Muncie; July/August
(765) 287–1256, extension 235

Auburn-Cord-Duesenberg Festival,
Auburn; Labor Day weekend
(219) 925–3600

Grabill County Fair,
Grabill; September (219) 627–3202

Forks of the Wabash Pioneer Festival,
Huntington; September
(219) 359–TOUR or (800) 848–4282

Johnny Appleseed Festival,
Fort Wayne; September (219) 427–6000

Apple Festival,
Nappanee; September (219) 773–7812

The International Walkway of Lights,
Marion; late November–early January
(765) 668–5435 or (800) 662–9474

A.M. to 4:00 P.M. Saturday November through April. Nominal admission fee. For additional information contact NATMUS, P.O. Box 686, Auburn 46706-0686; (219) 925–4560; fax (219) 925–4563.

In the tiny town of St. Joe, you can tour **Sechler's Pickle Factory,** where multitudes of midwestern cucumbers have been transformed into pickles since 1921. Along with the traditional types, the factory produces such unique varieties as candied orange strip, lemon strip, apple cinnamon, and raisin crispy pickles. Now a third-generation family operation, Sechler's is believed to be the only pickle manufacturer that makes an aged-in-wood genuine dill pickle (the same pickle made in the same way by the first generation of Sechler pickle producers). Free tours are offered by appointment (drop-in visitors can sometimes be accommodated) from 9:00 to 11:00 A.M. and 12:30 to 2:30 P.M. Monday through Friday, May through October. Located at 5686 State Road 1; (219) 337–5461. A salesroom on the premises displays Sechler's plethora of pickles. Mail orders are also accepted; the late Frank Sinatra ordered his favorites, the candied sweet dill strips, a case at a time.

Delaware County

In Muncie the winter winds can be fierce, the snows deep, and the temperatures subzero, but in a greenhouse on the campus of **Ball State University** a tropical garden of orchids blooms all year long. The **Wheeler Orchid Collection** contains more varieties of this exquisite flower than any other collection in the world. More than 7,000 plants thrive here, and the collection's species bank was the first such bank anywhere.

The greenhouse is situated in seventeen-acre **Christy Woods,** a mix of arboretum, flower gardens, research facilities, and nature center that serves as an outdoor laboratory for both Ball State students and the general public. Recorded messages guide visitors along trails that wind through the arboretum (tape recorders are available at the Orchid House). If you come in April or May, you'll also see a profusion of wildflowers. Free admission; open 8:00 A.M. to 4:00 P.M. Monday through Saturday year-round; 1:00 to 5:00 P.M. Sunday, April through October. Call the Department of Biology at (765) 285–8820.

The university's art gallery, located in the Fine Arts Building, houses the **Ball/Kraft collection of ancient glass.** Free admission; open 9:00 A.M. to 4:30 P.M. Monday through Friday and 1:30 to 4:30 P.M. Saturday and

Sunday; hours may vary during spring and winter breaks and in the summer; (765) 285–5242.

For a unique browsing and/or shopping experience, head for the **House of Fogg** at 418 East Main Street in Muncie. The 3,000-square-foot art gallery and studio features works of art handmade from paper. Sculptor Ann Johnson adopted her legal pseudonym of F. B. Fogg when she invented and patented her unique art form. A former teacher, she left that profession in 1986 to become a full-time artist. She made that decision while she was standing in the White House Rose Garden being presented with the Presidential Scholar of the Arts Outstanding Teacher of the Year Award.

Since then she has achieved international fame and now sells her work in some 1,600 galleries throughout the United States and in several foreign countries. Her art has been purchased by such celebrities as Steven Spielberg, Elizabeth Taylor, Lauren Bacall, Kevin Kline, Whoopi Goldberg, and Mariel Hemingway. Three of her dog clocks will be featured in an upcoming Disney movie.

Visitors can watch Johnson and other Fogg artists she personally trained create her trademark jewelry, clocks, and sculptures. Prices range from $5.00 to $3,000.00. The gallery is open 10:00 A.M. to 4:00 P.M. Monday through Saturday; (765) 289–7464.

Nationally recognized for the hands-on experience it provides, the **Muncie Children's Museum** occupies a 2,000-square-foot exhibit center at 515 South High Street. Children can burrow through a human-size ant farm, learn how to escape from a building "on fire," join a railroad crew laying track across the country, and climb over, under, through, and on ten separate structures. Sunday-afternoon visitors are treated to free "Garfield the Cat" movies (Indiana-born Jim Davis, Garfield's creator, lives near Muncie). Children may also participate as characters in a life-size Garfield cartoon that is videotaped and sent home with the young stars. Nominal admission fee; open 10:00 A.M. to 5:00 P.M. Tuesday through Saturday and 1:00 to 5:00 P.M. Sunday; closed July 4, Thanksgiving, December 25, and January 1; (765) 286–1660.

At a private museum in Muncie, you can see one of the most diverse collections of fruit jars in the country. **Robinson's Jars** features a fascinating display that will especially appeal to collectors and a mind-boggling assortment that will appeal to the merely curious. It is the largest museum of its kind in the world. Located at the corner of Wheeling Avenue and West Cowing Drive. Free admission, but hours vary. Call for information and/or an appointment; (765) 282–9707.

Other Attractions Worth Seeing in Northeast Indiana

BERNE

Swiss Heritage Village;
(219) 589–8007

DUNKIRK

Dunkirk Glass Museum;
(765) 768–6809

ELKHART

National New York Central
Railroad Museum;
(219) 294–3001

Ruthmere Museum;
(219) 264–0330

S. Ray Miller Antique
Auto Museum;
(219) 522–0539

FORT WAYNE

Science Central;
(800) 4–HANDS-ON

GREENTOWN

The Glass Museum;
(765) 628–7818 or 628–3346

HUNTINGTON

Historic Forks of
the Wabash;
(219) 356–1903

KOKOMO

Automotive Heritage Museum;
(765) 454–9999.

Seiberling Mansion (Howard
County Museum);
(765) 452–4314

MUNCIE

Minnetrista Cultural
Center and Oakhurst
Gardens; (317) 282–4848 or
(800) 4–CULTURE

WARSAW

Warsaw Cut Glass Factory;
(219) 267–6581

For five years, the 20-foot-tall wooden statue that stands outside the **Oasis Bar & Grill** on Muncie's southside was merely a curiosity—a ficti-tious basketball player named Barfly Cortez. Barfly wore a red uniform with the word "Oasis" printed across his chest. In 1994, however, the statue underwent a transformation. Barfly's uniform was repainted in green and white. He was given a mustache, and his solid white tennis shoes were changed to black-and-white. No one really knew who Barfly was, but virtually everyone in Indiana knows his replacement on sight. Larry Bird, the former Boston Celtics star forward and current Indiana Pacers head coach, is a much-beloved Hoosier basketball legend. You can see this larger-than-life Larry at 1811 South Burlington Drive; (765) 282–8326.

Muncie became the world headquarters for model aviation in 1994, when the Academy of Model Aeronautics (AMA) moved here from Reston, Virginia. The 1,000-acre complex consists of the **National Model Aviation Museum** and a model airplane flying field. Visitors to the museum will see the largest collection of model aircraft in the country. The craftsmanship and artistry of the master builders are astonishing. Academy members stage flying competitions on an almost continuous basis from mid-May until the end of September. The events include rocket launches, helicopter meets, jet power contests, air combat, soaring competitions, and a vintage radio control reunion. Museum hours are 8:00 A.M. to 4:30 P.M. Monday through Friday; call for weekend hours, which vary. There's a nominal admission fee to the museum for non-AMA members. Former astronaut Neil Armstrong can come for free because he's an AMA member. Admission to the flying site is free at all times for everyone. The complex is located at 5151 East Memorial Drive; (765) 287–1256.

Elkhart County

Some of the best farm cooking you'll ever treat your taste buds to is served up at the **Patchwork Quilt Country Inn** in Middlebury. Located on a 260-acre working farm, the dining room is famous for the family-style, all-you-can-eat dinners it serves five nights a week.

When guests arrive they're served seasonal drinks (no alcohol) in the parlor and encouraged to mingle until the dinner bell sounds. No printed menu—your waitress will give you a choice of foods as each course is served. The entree may be open-hearth-baked ham, herb roast beef, burgundy steak, seafood, or buttermilk pecan chicken (the latter once won a $5,000 first prize for the best chicken recipe in the United States). When the dessert tray arrives, you'll find it almost impossible to choose from the luscious-looking treats displayed thereon—if indeed you have enough room left to make any choice at all. You'll be confronted with such unusual meal toppers as cheddar cheesecake, coffee toffee pie, charlotte russe, walnut torte, fruit parfait, grasshopper pie, and candied violet cake—delectable one and all. At least one dessert will probably feature strawberries—the inn's strawberry recipes, too, have won national fame.

> ### Trivia
>
> *Alka-Seltzer was developed in the 1930s by Miles Laboratories of Elkhart.*

The Patchwork Quilt also offers overnight bed-and-breakfast accommodations Tuesday through Friday. Three guest bedrooms are available, each with its own handmade patchwork quilt. A deluxe continental breakfast is included in the room rate.

Middlebury is in the heart of one of the largest Amish settlements in the country, and the inn offers a guided tour that affords a look at the lifestyle of these people. It also hosts a quilts and crafts tour.

The Beast of 'Busco

*I*n the long-ago spring of 1949, the small Whitley County town of Churubusco was consumed with the tale of the "Beast of 'Busco." Local farmer Gale Harris had reported seeing a turtle as large as a dining room table in a lake on his land, and the hunt was on.

Tales about a 400-pound turtle quickly spread far and wide. Newspaper reporters swarmed along the lake's shoreline, and small planes filled with photographers circled overhead. Divers suited up and plunged into the murky waters. In the course of one day, some 3,000 people tramped through Harris's fields to watch the goings-on. At the height of the search, some 400 cars an hour crept past the lake.

Traps were set but remained empty. Gale Harris tried to drain his lake but was unsuccessful. The huge turtle, dubbed Oscar, was never found, nor was he ever seen again. Experts who heard the story of Oscar speculate that, if the elusive reptile did indeed exist, he was probably a rare, unusually large alligator snapping turtle.

Whatever Oscar might or might not have been, he holds a very special place in the history of Churubusco. Recently, there has even been talk about setting up a museum memorializing him. A documentary film entitled The Hunt for Oscar premiered locally in November 1994. Signs in Churubusco still welcome visitors to "Turtle Town U.S.A.," and each June the community hosts a Turtle Days festival.

You can learn more about the festival that honors Oscar by contacting the Columbia City/Whitley County Chamber of Commerce at 104 South Chauncey Street, P.O. Box 166, Columbia City 46725; (219) 248–8131.

To reach the Patchwork Quilt Inn, go north from Middlebury on State Road 13 for 8 miles to County Road 2, then turn west for about 1 mile to the inn. Lunch is served from 11:00 A.M. to 2:00 P.M., dinner from 4:30 to 8:00 P.M. Tuesday through Saturday. Dinner guests can choose between family-style and plate dinners. Closed all major holidays and three weeks in January/February (exact dates depend on the weather). Prices are moderate; reservations are recommended at all times and are required for tours and overnight accommodations. Smoking is not permitted anywhere on the premises. Write the Patchwork Quilt Inn, 11748 County Road 2, Middlebury 46540; (219) 825–2417.

You can sample authentic Amish cuisine, as well as good country cooking, in Middlebury. The **Village Inn Restaurant** is a small lunchroom whose customers are as apt to ride up in horse-drawn buggies as in automobiles. All the food is hearty and good (not to mention loaded with calories), but the pies are splendid, the prices quite reasonable, and the people—both staff and guests—delightful. The Village Inn, located at 107 South Main Street, is open from 5:00 A.M. to 9:00 P.M. Monday through Saturday; (219) 825–2043.

Three miles east of Middlebury at 11275 County Road 250N, you can tour the **Deutsch Kase Haus** and watch Amish cheesemakers at work. The free samples in the gift shop will help you choose your favorite flavor. Open 8:00 A.M. to 5:00 P.M. Monday through Friday and 8:00 A.M. to 3:00 P.M. Saturday; call (219) 825–9511 for the cheese-making schedule.

The area in which Middlebury lies, known as the Crystal Valley, is chockfull of fascinating places to explore and enjoy—quilt shops, antiques shops, country stores, craft shops, furniture stores, and restaurants. For a map of the area and additional information, write the Crystal Valley Tourist Association, 426 North Main Street, P.O. Box 55, Middlebury 46540; (219) 825–5413.

One of the best ways to gain insight into the lifestyle of the Amish is through a visit to **Amish Acres,** an authentic eighty-acre restoration of a century-old farming community in Nappanee. Amish farmhouses dot the countryside, flat-topped black buggies wander the roads, farmers plow the fields, livestock graze behind split-rail fences, and women quilt, bake in an outdoor oven, and dip candles. You can see demonstrations of soap making, horseshoeing, and meat preserving and visit a bakery, a meat and cheese shop, an antique soda fountain and fudgery, a cider mill, a smokehouse, a mint still, and a sawmill. For the 2,000 Old Order Amish who live in this area, life goes on as it did a hundred years ago.

You may want to take a horse-drawn buggy ride or enjoy the excellent Amish cooking at the **Restaurant Barn.** The soup is always on in big iron kettles, and such typical dishes as noodles, spiced apples, sweet-and-sour cabbage salad, and shoofly pie are on the menu.

Amish Acres is located on U.S. Highway 6, 1 mile west of Nappanee. The restored farm is open 7:00 A.M. to 8:00 P.M. Monday through Saturday and 11:00 A.M. to 6:00 P.M. Sunday, May through October; tours, rides, and some shops close at 5:00 P.M. Closed Sunday from November through April. The restaurant is open 7:00 A.M. to 8:00 P.M. Monday through Saturday and 7:00 A.M. to 6:00 P.M. Sunday, February through December. Admission fee; special package price for a guided tour. Write the Amish Acres Visitor Information Center, 1600 West Market Street, Nappanee 46550; (219) 773–4188. The information center also can assist you in making reservations for an overnight stay in an area farm home.

Like the Crystal Valley to the northeast, the area in and around Nappanee abounds with interesting shops and Amish businesses that can be toured. The Nappanee Chamber of Commerce, at 215 West Market Street, Nappanee 46550, will be happy to provide you with additional information; (219) 773–7812.

Directly north of Nappanee via State Road 19 is the village of Wakarusa, where you can visit the unusual *Bird's-Eye View Museum.* Area build-

ings of distinctive architectural style are reconstructed from toothpicks, popsicle sticks, and other pint-size materials—all built on the same scale (1 inch equals 5 feet). The project began when Devon Rose built a miniature feed mill for his son's electric-train layout and continued until the town of Wakarusa had been replicated in the most minute detail. Now one of the largest collections of miniatures in the world, it has won several awards. Located at 325 South Elkhart Street, the museum is open 8:00 A.M. to 5:00 P.M. Monday through Friday and 8:00 A.M. to noon Saturday. Nominal admission fee; (219) 862–2367.

The *Midwest Museum of American Art* would be a gem anywhere, but in the small municipality of Elkhart (population 43,000) it is a crown jewel. Noted for its extensive collection of Norman Rockwell lithographs (believed to be the largest collection anywhere) and photographs by such distinguished photographers as Ansel Adams, the museum has become one of Indiana's most important art institutions. Nominal admission fee; open 11:00 A.M. to 5:00 P.M. Tuesday through Friday and 1:00 to 4:00 P.M. Saturday and Sunday. Open free of charge 7:00 to 9:00 P.M. Thursday. Located at 429 South Main Street; (219) 293–6660.

Elkhart is also home to a museum that will warm the hearts of owners and want-to-be owners of recreational vehicles. The *RV/MH Heritage Foundation Hall of Fame* showcases the growth, history, and accomplishments of the recreational vehicle and manufactured housing industries. Originally located in Washington, D.C., the Hall of Fame was moved to Elkhart, widely recognized as the RV Capital of the World, in 1991. Nearly forty companies affiliated with the RV industry are headquartered here.

Among the exhibits are the first RV ever made (built in 1915), camping trailers of the 1930s, and the classic art deco Airstream. There's even a tiny pink trailer suitable for small pets and some scale models of trailer high-rises. Believe it or not, someone once envisioned building whole communities of vertical trailer parks with 20 stories of single-wide trailers stacked on top of one another. The more mundane RV Wall of Fame pays tribute to more than 170 people who are famous in the RV industry.

The museum is open 9:00 A.M. to 5:00 P.M. Monday through Friday; admission is free. Located at 810 Benham Avenue; (219) 293–2344; fax (219) 293–3466.

On the northwest corner of Main Street and Lincoln Avenue in **Goshen** stands an intriguing-looking **limestone booth.** The octagonal structure, complete with gun ports and bulletproof green glass, was erected in 1939 by the WPA (Works Progress Administration) to provide a lookout for local police. At that time, two banks stood at the intersection. A slew of recent robberies in surrounding communities had been widely publicized, and the local citizenry decided to take some precautionary measures. Their jitters apparently were not easily dispelled, because police continued to man the enclosure twenty-four hours a day until 1969. Since 1983 it has been owned by the Goshen Historical Society.

Grant County

The death of **James Dean** on September 30, 1955, catapulted the popular young actor to enduring fame as a cult hero. Although he made only three movies—*East of Eden, Rebel Without a Cause,* and *Giant*—Dean gave voice through his roles to the restlessness and discontent of his generation. He died at the age of twenty-four, the victim of an automobile accident on a lonely California highway. Dean was speeding along in his silver Porsche when he collided with a car making a left turn across the highway in front of him. Ironically, Dean had been given a speeding ticket a little over two hours before the accident that claimed his life. His family brought him home to Indiana to bury him. Today rarely a day goes by—no matter what the weather—that someone doesn't show up in **Park Cemetery** at Fairmount, where Dean grew up, to see his grave and mourn his passing.

For ten years after his death, Warner Brothers received as many as 7,000 letters a month addressed to Dean from devoted fans who refused to accept his death. His tombstone in Park Cemetery, defaced by souvenir seekers, was replaced in 1985. Within a few short months it, too, was defaced. A sign that read THIS WAY TO JAMES DEAN'S GRAVE lasted one afternoon, and handfuls of dirt regularly disappear from his burial site. People from as far away as Germany have wanted to purchase a plot here so

Trivia

Weaver Popcorn Company, headquartered in the Grant County town of Van Buren, is the world's largest popcorn processor. The company produces approximately one-quarter of the world's supply.

that they can "be buried near Jimmy." To this day, books are still being written about Dean. When the U.S. Postal Service began issuing its "Legends of Hollywood" series, it was James Dean whose image was chosen for the second stamp in the series. (Marilyn Monroe's stamp, the first, was released in 1995; the Dean stamp was released in 1996.) Between 1986 and 1996, the estate of James Dean amassed more than $100 million from merchandising materials. The phenomenon of James Dean shows no signs of letting up and can never be fully explained—a charisma that reaches out even from the grave. Park Cemetery, open daily dawn to dusk, is on County Road 150E; (765) 948–4040.

At the **James Dean Gallery** in Fairmount, exhibits from more than twenty different countries constitute the world's largest collection of Dean memorabilia. Visitors will see such items as a rare Warner Brothers

True Love

*R*esidents of Marion, Indiana, population 33,000 or thereabouts, suspected something big was afoot on June 27, 1993. They had their first clue when five tour buses and three stretch limousines pulled up near the county courthouse. Turns out singer Lyle Lovett and actress Julia Roberts had come to town to have a quiet wedding, sans media hype. Like all couples about to be married, they had stopped at the courthouse to pick up a marriage license.

Family and friends (actress Susan Sarandon and actor Tim Robbins among them) were on the scene for one of the surprise weddings of the year—in Marion or anywhere. Amazingly, the couple had managed to keep their romance a virtual secret. Only those closest to the couple knew about their whirlwind courtship.

Because the nuptials were planned only seventy-two hours in advance, the wedding attendants showed up in eclectic dress. No matter. All eyes were on the bride, who wore a simple white dress purchased for her by the bridegroom and walked down the aisle barefoot.

The couple chose Marion for their nuptials for two reasons: It was conveniently located between stops on the groom's summer concert tour, and it offered the privacy they desired. People in Indiana are known for giving celebrities their space.

Sadly, the marriage ended, but the town of Marion hasn't forgotten its happy beginning. Do residents consider the marriage the biggest thing that ever happened here? No; the very biggest thing happened in the mid-1970s. That was when the high school basketball team won back-to-back state championships.

life mask, original movie posters, clothing from the actor's films, and yearbooks from Fairmount High School, which counted Dean among its 1949 graduates. It won't surprise basketball-crazy Hoosiers (others, maybe, but not Hoosiers) to learn that some folks hereabouts remember Dean first as the clutch-shooting guard of the local high school basketball team and a distant second as a movie star. Located at 425 North Main Street; nominal admission fee. Open 10:00 A.M. to 5:00 P.M. daily; (765) 948–3326.

The **Fairmount Historical Museum** at 203 East Washington Street tells the story of Dean's life through a series of exhibits and a display of some of Dean's possessions from a family collection. Each September, near the date of Dean's death, the museum hosts the Fairmount Museum Days and the James Dean Film Festival. The museum also honors Fairmount's other favorite son—**Jim Davis,** creator of "Garfield the Cat." No admission fee, but donations are accepted. Open 10:00 A.M. to 5:00 P.M. Monday through Saturday and noon to 5:00 P.M. Sunday, March through November; also open on February 8 (Dean's birth date), September 30 (the anniversary of his death), and by appointment. Write Fairmount Historical Museum, P.O. Box 92, Fairmount 46928; (765) 948–4555 or 948–4776.

Everyone's Favorite Feline

*I*ndiana's most beloved native is arguably Garfield the Cat. Although Garfield is lazy, fat, and selfish, he gets away with it precisely because he is a cat. It also helps that he is adorable.

Jim Davis, Garfield's creator, grew up in Fairmount, Indiana, where he and his family shared the family farm with about twenty-five cats. Today Davis lives and works near the small town of Albany, which lies a few miles northeast of Muncie, Indiana. Davis's company, Paws Inc., is the licensing and merchandising firm for anything created in Garfield's image.

For the curious among you, here are some interesting facts about the cat and his creator:

- Davis now lives in a house without cats—his wife is allergic to them.

- Davis shares his tubby tabby's love for lasagna.

- Garfield is Davis's grandfather's name (the two reportedly share a few traits).

- More than sixty million Garfield books have been published worldwide, and Garfield has been the star of several CBS–TV specials.

- The comic strip that features Garfield is the most widely syndicated strip in the world, read daily by some 200 million people in more than 2,400 newspapers in 26 different languages.

Fairmount Historical Museum

The nearby town of Marion, where James Dean was born, is noted for its extraordinary *Easter pageant,* presented each Easter morning at 6:00 A.M. Lauded as the equal of Oberammergau's famous passion play, the pageant draws spectators from all fifty states and from overseas. Free admission; for tickets and information contact the Marion Indiana Easter Pageant, Inc., 118 North Washington Street, Marion 46952; (765) 664–3947 or (800) 662–9474.

Ice cream lovers will want to journey to Upland, home of Taylor University, and visit *Ivanhoe's.* When they spy the menu here, they'll think they've died and gone to heaven. Sundae and shake flavors are arranged alphabetically—one hundred delicious flavors each, plus a special section for extras. Hoe's, as it's known locally, also serves ice cream sodas, floats, and excellent sandwiches and salads. Located at 914 South Main Street, it's open from 10:00 A.M. to 10:00 P.M. Monday through Thursday, 10:00 A.M. to 11:00 P.M. Friday and Saturday, and 2:00 to 10:00 P.M. Sunday. Call (765) 998–7261.

Howard County

The world has stainless steel because Kokomo inventor Elwood Haynes wanted to please his wife. Well aware of her husband's ingenuity, Mrs. Haynes asked him to perfect some tarnish-free dinnerware for her. And in 1912, he did.

The remarkable Mr. Haynes also invented the first successful commercial automobile. On July 4, 1894, he put his gasoline-powered creation to the test on Pumpkinvine Pike east of Kokomo, speeding along at 7 miles per hour for a distance of about 6 miles. That same car is now on display at the Smithsonian Institution in Washington, D.C.

Another of Haynes's inventions is stellite, an alloy used today in space-craft, jet engines, dental instruments, and nuclear power plants. New uses are still being found for it.

The *Elwood Haynes Museum,* housed in Haynes's former residence, contains a vast collection of Haynes's personal possessions and his many inventions. Visitors particularly enjoy the 1905 Haynes automobile, in which the driver sits in the backseat. Other exhibits reflect Howard County's history during and after the area's great gas boom.

The largest natural gas gusher ever brought into production in this country was struck in 1887 in what is now southeast Kokomo. Almost overnight the town was transformed into a center of industry. Kokomo's many contributions to the industrial growth of America, in addition to Haynes's inventions, have earned it the nickname "City of Firsts." Many of the items first produced here are among those featured in the upstairs rooms of the Elwood Haynes Museum, located at 1915 South Webster Street. Free of charge, it's open 1:00 to 4:00 P.M. Tuesday through Saturday and 1:00 to 5:00 P.M. Sunday; closed Monday and holidays; (765) 452–3471.

Just to the northwest of the Haynes Museum, at 902 West Deffenbaugh

City of Firsts

*K*okomo bills itself as the City of Firsts. Here are a few of the reasons why.

- First commercially built auto (road tested locally on July 4, 1894)

- First pneumatic rubber tire (1894)

- First aluminum casting (1895)

- First carburetor (1902)

- First stellite cobalt-based alloy (1906)

- First stainless steel (1912)

- First American howitzer shell (1918)

- First aerial bomb with fins (1918)

- First mechanical corn picker (early 1920s)

- First dirilyte golden-hued tableware (1926)

- First canned tomato juice (1928)

- First push-button car radio (1938)

- First all-metal lifeboats (1941) and rafts (1943)

- First signal-seeking car radio (1947)

- First all-transistor car radio (1957)

The Kokomo/Howard County Convention and Visitors Bureau will be happy to elaborate (see Sources for Additional Information at the end of the chapter).

Street, enter *Highland Park* and view Kokomo's own *Old Ben.* Ben was a crossbred Hereford steer who at the time of his birth in 1902 was proclaimed to be the largest calf in the world, weighing in at 135 pounds. When you see Ben, you won't find it hard to believe. At four years of age the steer weighed 4,720 pounds, stood 6 feet 4 inches tall, measured 13 feet 6 inches in girth, and was an astonishing 16 feet 2 inches from his nose to the tip of his tail. For many years he was exhibited around the country in circuses and sideshows. He had to be destroyed in 1910 after breaking his leg, and shortly thereafter he was stuffed and mounted. Today he shares a place of honor with another of Kokomo's giant wonders—*the stump of a huge sycamore tree.* The stump—12 feet tall and 57 feet in circumference—is impressive enough, but it only hints at the magnificent tree of which it once was a part. Originally more than 100 feet in height, the tree grew to maturity on a farm west of Kokomo. Its hollow trunk once housed a telephone booth large enough to accommodate more than a dozen people at a time. When the tree was storm-damaged, around 1915, the enormous stump was pulled to the park by a house mover. Old Ben and the stump now occupy a building built specifically to display and protect them; (765) 452–0063.

The *Kokomo Opalescent Glass Company,* in operation since 1888, once supplied glass to Louis C. Tiffany. Today this small factory is known worldwide as a leading producer of fine art glass, and visitors can watch the glassmaking process from beginning to end. Free tours at 10:00 A.M. Wednesday and Friday, except in December. An adjoining retail shop is open 9:00 A.M. to 5:00 P.M. Monday through Friday; Saturday hours vary. Located at 1310 South Market Street; (765) 457–1829.

Motorists cruising along U.S. Highway 31 often do a double take when they chance upon *Tom Smith's 120-acre farm.* Some of Tom's more than one hundred camels are sometimes seen grazing by the roadside. Tom, who is a licensed exotic animal breeder, sells some of his camels to zoos and rents others. The self-proclaimed Avis of camel renters purports to have more camels than anyone else in the Western Hemisphere. At times, his herd of one- and two-humpers has included some rare white camels. Onlookers once backed up traffic so much that the state contemplated putting up warning signs, but to date no action has been taken. (Well, would *you* take seriously a sign reading BEWARE OF CAMEL-WATCHERS beside a major Indiana highway?) It's okay to pull over and watch, but no feeding of camels is allowed. You'll find the farm on the west side of U.S. Highway 31 about 5 miles south of Kokomo. If you're in the market for a rented camel, contact Tom Smith at Route 1, Box 138A, Galveston 46932; (219) 699–6168.

Huntington County

One of Indiana's most famous sons, J. Danforth Quayle (better known as Dan), is the fifth Hoosier to serve as our country's vice president. Quayle was born in Indianapolis in 1947, but his family moved to Huntington about a year later, and it is Huntington that Quayle calls home.

When George Bush and Quayle launched their campaign for the White House in 1988, they came to the Huntington County Courthouse to do it. When Quayle and his wife, Marilyn, received their law degrees from Indiana University in Bloomington, they came to Huntington to open a law office. When Quayle first ran for public office in 1976 (as a U.S. Representative), he ran as a resident of Huntington.

> **Trivia**
>
> *It is against the law to read* The Stepford Wives *in Warsaw, Indiana.*

In June 1993, Huntington demonstrated its affection for Quayle by opening the *Dan Quayle Center and Museum* at 815 Warren Street. Visitors will see exhibits from every phase of Quayle's life, including a newspaper clipping announcing his birth, a baby footprint taken at the hospital in which he was born, and a photo of the newborn Quayle in a diaper. Of particular interest is Quayle's second-grade report card, boasting all As and Bs. A copy of Quayle's college diploma is missing a few pieces, thanks to a family dog (a photo of the offender, much loved nevertheless, is framed with the diploma). No museum honoring Dan Quayle would be complete without some golf memorabilia; an old golf bag and photos of a teenage Quayle holding trophies won in a junior tournament are among them.

You'll know when you get to Huntington. It would be hard to miss the sign at the city limits that proclaims this to be HUNTINGTON: HOME OF THE 44TH VICE PRESIDENT DAN QUAYLE.

The museum is open 10:00 A.M. to 4:00 P.M. Tuesday through Saturday and 1:00 to 4:00 P.M. Sunday. Free admission, but donations are welcome. Contact the museum at P.O. Box 856, Huntington 46750; (219) 356–6356.

After you've toured Dan Quayle's museum, stop by and see *Hy Goldenberg's Outhouses.* You won't see any signs honoring Hy's outhouses, but the town is fond of them just the same.

Hy purchased his first two outhouses some thirty years ago for strictly utilitarian reasons. He and his wife were building a home in a then-isolated spot on the banks of the Wabash River, and they needed a toilet the carpenters could use while working on the house. Since then, Hy has come to regard outhouses as an important segment of Americana, and his collection now numbers thirteen.

Although most of the outhouses are variations of the typical square wooden ones, Hy also has an octagon-shaped concrete one. A three-seater model boasts a child-size seat in the middle for the family that enjoys togetherness. One of Hy's rarest outhouses is a round privy that sports a copper weather vane atop its roof. Hy paid a whopping $17 for this one. Although most of his outhouses cost $2.00 to $3.00 each, Hy had to bid against someone at an auction before he could call this cherished round privy his own.

Hy points out the fact that building outhouses was a source of employment for many men during the Great Depression. Although comfort and safety were certainly important considerations, beauty was not ignored either. Many were covered with roses and trellises to please the lady of the house.

Visitors are welcome to tour the unusual collection free of charge, but because the outhouses are on private property, please phone Nan Rosenberg before visiting. You will be given exact directions when you call; (219) 356–4467. You may also contact the Huntington County Convention and Visitors Bureau for additional information. Write P.O. Box 212, Huntington 46750-0212; (219) 359–TOUR or (800) 848–4282; fax (219) 356–5434.

Kosciusko County

Some towns will do almost anything to get attention. *Mentone* grabbed its share of publicity by erecting a monument unique in the world. There it stands, right next to Main Street—a 12-foot-high, 3,000-pound *concrete egg.* If, when in Mentone, anyone should ask the perennial puzzler "Which came first, the chicken or the egg?" the answer would almost certainly have to be "the egg." Pity the poor chicken that would have to handle this one!

In 1946, when the monument was first "laid," every farmer in the area had a chicken house, and eggs were shipped all over the Midwest. That enterprise declined in the 1950s, but the lives of the town's 950 residents continue to be intertwined with eggs and chickens. Local businesses hatch eggs, provide chicken meat for soup companies, and separate egg whites from the yolks for bakeries. And each June the community celebrates industry, heritage, and monument with an Egg

Festival. Contact the Mentone Chamber of Commerce, P.O. Box 365, Mentone 46539; (219) 353–7551.

Next to the city park on Oak Street, just south of State Road 25 West in Mentone, you'll find the **Lawrence D. Bell Aircraft Museum.** It contains the memorabilia of Larry Bell, the Mentone native who forsook eggs and instead founded the Bell Aircraft Corporation. Bell produced twenty aviation firsts, including the world's first commercial helicopter, the nation's first jet-propelled airplane, and the first aircraft to shatter the sound barrier. Scale models of many Bell aircraft are on display. Guided tours are offered from 1:00 to 5:00 P.M. Sunday from Memorial Day weekend through Labor Day; other times by appointment. Nominal admission fee; contact the museum at P.O. Box 411, Mentone 46539; (219) 353–7551.

Trivia

South Whitley is home to the Fox Products Corporation, the nation's largest producer of high-quality bassoons. The family-run operation, founded in 1949, ships its musical instruments to countries around the world.

In honor of Kosciusko County's agricultural heritage, the Greater Warsaw Area Chamber of Commerce has put together two **drive-yourself farm tours.** Scenic country roads lead visitors past farms that produce chickens, buffalo, pigs, sheep, and cattle, as well as spearmint and various fruits and vegetables. Maple Leaf Farms is the largest producer of ducklings in the country and maybe the world. Ault Stables trains harness horses. Many facilities, including the country's largest llama farm, offer guided tours by prearrangement. Free maps are available at the Kosciusko County Convention and Visitors Bureau, 313 South Buffalo Street, Warsaw 46580; (800) 800–6090 or (219) 269–6090.

The largest of only five such gardens in the United States, the **Warsaw Biblical Gardens** cover three-quarters of an acre in Warsaw's Center Lake Park. All plants mentioned in the Bible have been meticulously researched for this project, and thus far about sixty of the eighty-five identified varieties have been acquired.

An oasis of tranquility, the gardens are enclosed by a low fieldstone wall. Visitors can meander along stone paths that lead through six distinct plant environs: meadow, crop, orchard, forest, brook, and desert. A plaque for each of the species identifies the plant and its biblical reference.

Water lilies, yellow iris, and sweet flag adorn a water garden that's shaded by an umbrella palm. A unique wooden arbor was designed by famous craftsman David Robinson, who served as the first coordinator

Trivia

for the restoration of New York City's Central Park before going into business for himself. Grapevines planted when the gardens were dedicated in June 1991 now nearly obscure the arbor, creating a cool, shaded retreat on hot summer days.

The gardens, located at the intersection of State Road 15 North and Canal Street, are open free of charge from dawn to dusk, April through October. For additional information contact the Warsaw Community Development Corporation, P.O. Box 1223, Warsaw 46580; (219) 267– 6419.

Charles Ramsey of Dunkirk invented a sixty-four-pound car that got an astonishing 3,803 miles per gallon. The aerodynamic three-wheeler, deemed impractical for regular use, was displayed at a 1985 show of engineering exotica in Chicago.

Stop by The Party Shop in Warsaw and visit the **Hallmark Ornament Museum.** The first Hallmark ornament was created in 1973. That ornament and every Hallmark ornament created since then—at this writing, more than 3,000 ornaments—are on display here. The Party Shop is the first and only place in the country to have a complete collection on public display. Admission is free; open 9:30 A.M. to 9:00 P.M. Monday through Saturday, noon to 5:00 P.M. Sunday. Located at 3418 Lake City Highway; phone (219) 267–8787; fax (219) 267–5740; www. thepartyshop.com.

LaGrange County

No place in this country has done better by its junk than the tiny hamlet of Shipshewana. Each Tuesday and Wednesday from May through October, it puts on what may be the biggest small-town sale in the country. Anything you've ever wanted has almost certainly, at one time or another, been available at the **Shipshewana** (Shipshe for short) **Auction and Flea Market.** The items available at one recent sale included old beer cans, garden tools, round oak tables, new hats and clothing at discount prices, doorknobs, bubble-gum machines, rare books, antique china, long-legged underwear, fenceposts, Aladdin lamps, fishing rods, parts for old wagons, extra pieces for a Lionel train set, hand and power tools, quilts, a worn-out butter churn, a half-full can of green house paint, baseball cards, homemade toy alligators, and—perhaps the most unusual item ever offered here—a used tombstone.

Wednesday is the biggest business day. In addition to the flea market, held over from Tuesday, a livestock sale and a miscellaneous auction take place. The vast array of sale items keeps about a dozen auctioneers busy from 7:00 A.M. on throughout the afternoon, while in the livestock barn farmers do some hot-and-heavy bidding on 2,500 head of cattle, sheep, and pigs.

Outside in the flea market yard, nearly 1,000 vendors display their wares. On an average Wednesday, $200,000 worth of livestock and goods changes hands, not including the several thousand dollars spent at the flea market. Although it would be a compliment to describe some of the merchandise as junk, there are also many valuable antiques and hard-to-find items.

The Shipshe Auction hosts as many as 30,000 visitors a day. License plates reveal they come from every state and Canada. When winter comes the flea market closes down, but the Wednesday auction simply moves under cover and continues throughout the year.

Each Friday the auction yard is the scene of a horse auction that draws buyers and sellers from all over North America to deal in Amish draft horses, reputed to be some of the finest in the land. (Shipshewana is in the heart of one of the largest Amish settlements in the United States.)

Trivia

The Winchester Speedway, located in the town of the same name, is the fastest half-mile speedway in the world. Built in the early 1900s, it's the second oldest speedway still in use in the Hoosier State (after the Indianapolis Motor Speedway). ESPN, the sports cable network, comes to Winchester each year to broadcast sprint, midget, and stock car racing from the nationally known track.

You'll have a grand time at the Shipshe Auction even if you don't buy a thing. It's one of the world's great spectator events. The auction yards are located on State Road 5 at the south edge of Shipshewana. For more details contact the Shipshewana Auction and Flea Market, P.O. Box 185, Shipshewana 46565; (219) 768–4129.

Since all the people who attend Shipshe's various auctions have to eat, a special *Auction Restaurant,* operated from one of the sale barns, is open three days a week in the summer. It dishes up delicious Amish food nonstop from 5:00 A.M. to 7:00 P.M. Tuesday and Wednesday and from 5:00 A.M. until the horse sales close for the day on Friday (open Wednesday and Friday only during winter months); (219) 768–4129.

Another fine Amish meal can be had at the *Buggy Wheel Restaurant* on Morton Street in downtown Shipshewana. Some of the more unusual breakfast fare includes mush, headcheese, and, on Thursday only, tomato gravy, but there are plenty of eggs, bacon, and potatoes on hand, too. All lunches are served cafeteria style, while a soup, salad, and dessert buffet is a specialty on Friday and Saturday evenings. Not all meals are offered every day. Open 5:00 A.M. to 7:00 P.M. Monday through Thursday and 5:00 A.M. to 8:00 P.M. Friday and Saturday, May through October; winter hours vary; (219) 768–4444.

To learn more about the Mennonite/Amish lifestyle and heritage, explore the fascinating exhibits at the *Menno-Hof Visitors Center* on State Road 5 South opposite the Shipshewana Auction grounds. Of particular interest is a booth where visitors actually "feel, see, and hear" a simulated tornado. Admission by donation. Generally open 10:00 A.M. to 5:00 P.M. Monday through Saturday; hours may be seasonally adjusted. Call (219) 768–4117.

Stretching along Pigeon River in northeastern LaGrange County and reaching eastward into Steuben County is the 11,500-acre *Pigeon River State Fish and Wildlife Area.* The hauntingly beautiful stream, edged by lush vegetation choked with hyacinths, flows through an outstanding variety of habitats—marshes, meadows, woods, swamps, and bogs. Bird-watchers love this area; some 216 species of birds, many of them rare, have been sighted here. In the spring and early summer, wildflowers run rampant. It's all reminiscent of the Southland's fabled Suwannee River—a fine and private place in which to study nature; canoe; hunt mushrooms, nuts, and berries; hike; fish; pitch a tent; or ski cross-country.

The *Tamarack Bog State Nature Preserve* near the center of the wildlife area contains the largest tamarack swamp in Indiana and harbors such unique plants as the insectivorous pitcher plant and sundew. Contact the Pigeon River State Fish and Wildlife Area, P.O. Box 71, Mongo 46771; (219) 367–2164.

Miami County

The circus first came to Peru, Indiana, in the late 1800s, and it remains there to this day, the single most dominant force in the community.

It all began with native son *Ben Wallace,* who owned a livery stable in Peru. One winter a broken down animal show limped into town and found shelter in Ben's stable. When spring came, Ben was left with all the animals in lieu of a fee. Using his Hoosier ingenuity, Ben spiffed things up a bit, started his own circus, and built it into one of the world's finest— the *Hagenbeck-Wallace Circus.* Winter quarters were set up on the vast farm fields just outside town, and other major circuses of the day, lured by the excellent facilities, also came to Peru in the off-season.

Among the show business greats who spent at least part of the year here were *Clyde Beatty,* the noted animal trainer (like Ben Wallace, a native son); *Emmett Kelly,* the renowned clown; *Willi Wilno,* "the

Trivia

Winchester native Robert Wise achieved fame as a movie director. Two of the movies he directed, West Side Story *(1961) and* The Sound of Music *(1965), received Academy Awards for Best Picture of the Year. He also worked as an assistant editor on* Citizen Kane, *believed by many to be the best film of all time.*

human cannonball"; and **Tom Mix,** who later starred in Hollywood westerns. The late **Red Skelton** left his home in southern Indiana when he was just a boy to join the *Hagenbeck-Wallace Circus* and to launch one of the most famous and enduring careers in the entertainment business.

The circus—and Peru with it—flourished for many years before passing into near oblivion, but local folks, many of them direct descendants of stars who brightened the firmament of circus history, decided that their town's unique heritage should be preserved forever. And so each year in the third week of July, the circus once again comes to Peru.

The performers, who must be residents of Miami County, range in age from six to their twenties, and they are so skillful you'll find it difficult to believe that this is not a professional show. Since the children of Peru are to the circus born—beginning their training in earliest childhood under the tutelage of some of the finest circus pros in the country—a constant supply of new talent is available. All the components of the old-time circus are here—aerialists, clowns, tightrope walkers, human pyramids, gymnasts, animal trainers, and much more. The whole thing is so authentic and entertaining that NBC-TV once filmed an hour-long documentary about it.

There are several performances during the annual festival, as well as a giant parade complete with calliopes, old circus wagons, and the rousing music of the Circus City Band. For additional information contact the Circus City Festival Office, 154 North Broadway, Peru 46970; (765) 472–3918.

One of the finest collections of circus relics in the world is housed in Peru's **International Circus Hall of Fame.** One relic, an elaborately decorated circus wagon built in Peru in 1903, is the only one of its kind in the world. In 1995 the museum acquired the Italian-made tent of the Big Apple Circus, which plays at Lincoln Center in New York. Still under development, the museum currently occupies what used to be the Hagenbeck-Wallace Circus's wagon barn at the ten-acre Old Circus Winter Headquarters, a National Historic Landmark since 1988. The Hall of Fame is located just south of U.S. Highway 24 about 3 miles northeast of Peru; follow signs. Open 10:00 A.M. to 4:00 P.M. Monday through Saturday and 1:00 to 4:00 P.M. Sunday, May through October; open November through April by appointment. Nominal admission fee.

For further information, contact the Circus Hall of Fame, P.O. Box 700, Peru 46970; (765) 472–7553.

Even in death Ben Wallace chose to remain in Peru. He is buried in **Mount Hope Cemetery** on Twelfth Street, along with another well-known native son, **Cole Porter.** One of the few songwriters who wrote both words and music, Porter penned such classics as "Night and Day," "When They Begin the Beguine," "I've Got You Under My Skin," and "What Is This Thing Called Love?" The Miami County Historical Society—(317) 472–3901, extension 40—can direct you to Porter's birthplace, his mother's home, and his grandmother's home. None are open to the public, but they can be seen from the road.

Although Cole Porter is gone, the chocolate fudge he loved lingers on. A trip to Peru always included a visit to **Arnold's Candy Store** at 288 East Main Street, where Porter purchased a goodly supply of his favorite confection to take with him wherever he went. The store has changed ownership since then, but the fudge is still made from the original recipe. Open 9:00 A.M. to 5:00 P.M. Monday through Saturday; (765) 473–5363.

A few miles south of Peru along U.S. Highway 31, you'll come upon the **Grissom Air Museum State Historic Site,** where an outdoor museum displays historic military aircraft. A B-17 flying fortress, a massive B-47 Stratojet and its midair refueler, the KC-97; a tank-killing A-10 Warthog, and the celebrated EC-135 air command post of Desert Storm fame can all be seen here. The lone B-58 Hustler, a supersonic bomber, is one of only six remaining in the world. It's okay to climb and sit on several of the planes, and visitors are welcome to climb into the cockpit of an F4 Phantom fighter. An indoor museum houses various types of military memorabilia, including bombs, missiles, and survival gear. The museum is located at the entrance to the Grissom Air Reserve Base, home to the 434th Air Refueling Wing. Each June, the air base stages a weekend-long air show. Admission to all attractions is free. The museum is open from 10:00 A.M. to 4:00 P.M. Tuesday through Saturday, except holidays; the outdoor exhibits are open daily from 7:00 A.M. to dusk. For additional information, contact the Grissom Air Museum, 6500 Hoosier Boulevard, Grissom ARB 46971; (765) 688–2654.

Trivia

On July 14, 1996, a crop circle was discovered in a farm field near Columbia City. Believed by many to be the result of alien spacecraft landings, these circles are characterized by bent (not broken) plant stalks, mutated plant DNA, odd magnetic readings, and abnormally high radiation levels. About 600 feet in circumference, the Columbia City circle consisted of an outer ring, three spiraled centers, and a radiation reading of two times the normal level.

Near the intersection of U.S. Highway 31 and State Road 18, in the southwest corner of Miami County, is the once-upon-a-time hamlet of Bennetts Switch. The only commercial business in town (unless you count the United Methodist Church) is **Miller's Police and Fire Equipment,** a fun place in which to browse. Browsing may be all you can do. Unless you have some identification proving you're an officer of the law or a firefighter, you'll not be allowed to buy much of anything—with the possible exception of a T-shirt and maybe a bumper sticker. Miller's is in business to sell its stock to police and firefighters. Such things as a T-shirt with DON'T FORGET YOUR RUBBERS imprinted on it and a bumper sticker that states COPS LIKE BIG BUSTS are popular items, but there are also more serious offerings like handcuffs and uniforms. Call (765) 457–7930 for hours and what information non–law officers can manage to obtain.

Noble County

F red Schultz of Ligonier, an aficionado of rare historical radios, recently decided to establish the **Indiana Historic Radio Museum.** The building he chose is an old filling station that is itself historic. Fred thought his dream might be short-lived when a professional gave him an estimate of $100,000 to refurbish the filling station, but in the spirit of community the folks in Ligonier volunteered their labor to fix up the place. As a result, the building renovation cost about $10,000, and in 1995 Fred opened his museum. Thus far, more than 15,000 visitors, including some from six foreign countries, have dropped by to take a look at the more than 400 radios on display.

Among the exhibits, which emphasize radios from the 1920s and 1930s, are the first transistor radio, the Regency TR-1, a 1936 Scott ten-tube set, and a 1938 Emerson Mae West. If you're not too knowledgeable about radios, be aware that each item bears an explanatory tag. One radio, you will learn, was carried on the back of a mule during World War I. There are also novelty radios in the improbable shapes of macaroni and cheese, french fries, and Elvis Presley.

At this time, the Indiana Historic Radio Museum is one of only six known museums of its kind in the country. It's sponsored by the Indiana Historical Radio Society, and many of the radios you'll see are owned by, on loan from, or donated by society members. The museum is open from 10:00 A.M. to 3:00 P.M. Tuesday, Wednesday, Thursday and Saturday from May through October; winter hours are from 10:00 A.M. to 2:00 P.M.

on Saturday only. Admission is free. The museum building, located at 800 Lincolnway South, also houses the Ligonier/Noble County Visitor and Convention Bureau. Call (219) 894–9000 or (888) 417–5362.

A few miles east of Ligonier, in Kendallville, is an even rarer museum. Opened in the summer of 1997, the **Mid-America Windmill Museum** is believed to be the only one of its kind in the country. Currently, about thirty windmills have been restored, and most are on display on a sixteen-acre plot on Kendallville's southeast side.

Kendallville seems a logical place for such a museum because it's in the heart of an area that was once referred to as the windmill store of the nation. In the heyday of wind power, nearly eighty windmill manufacturers were located within a 150-mile radius of Kendallville, and the country's second-largest windmill maker was actually in Kendallville.

Trivia
Farmland claims that it is the only town in the world that bears its name. It was in large part because of the appeal of the town's name that Elle *magazine brought an international staff here in spring 1999 for a fashion photo shoot. The photos, taken primarily at four rural locations, appeared in the September 1999 issue.*

Because the museum is so new, it is still a work in progress. Windmills are still being acquired, brought to the site, and reassembled. A replica of the first windmill in North America, erected in 1610 in what is now Virginia, is also being built.

In the museum building are models and displays that show the advances in windmill technology around the globe and through the years, beginning with a wind-powered gristmill in Persia that dates to about A.D. 200. All windmill restorations are done in this building, and visitors can view the process in various stages.

Currently, the museum is open only in the summer, beginning on Memorial Day weekend. You'll find it on the southwest corner of Allen Chapel and Wallace drives. Admission is free, but donations are appreciated. Hours may vary. For up-to-date information, contact the Kendallville Windmill Museum and Historical Society, Inc., P.O. Box 5048, Kendallville 46755; or phone Russell Baker at (219) 347–0875.

Black Pine Animal Park in Albion is home to rescued, rehabilitated, and retired animals. What started out as a backyard menagerie has evolved into a full-time business, prompted by people who enjoyed seeing and learning about the animals that live here. Today the park houses such exotic animals as lions, tigers, bears, chimpanzees, and camels, and visitors meet them on personally guided tours that last ninety minutes to two hours. The park is open daily except Monday from Memorial Day through Labor Day; six tours are available on the hour Tuesday through Saturday, four tours on the hour on Sunday; open weekends only in May before Memorial Day and in September after Labor Day. Several special events are scheduled throughout the open season. Admission is charged; visitors pay slightly more for feeding tours. Located at 349 West Albion Road; phone (219) 636–7383 for additional information.

Randolph County

At the *Silver Towne Coin Shop* in Winchester, all that glitters *is* gold—or silver—and the beautiful antique-decorated showrooms in which the collections are displayed are as dazzling as the shop's wares. Open 9:00 A.M. to 5:00 P.M. Monday through Friday and 9:00 A.M. to 4:00 P.M. Saturday. Located just west of U.S. Highway 27 on the north side of Union Street; (765) 584–7481.

People from all over the world flock to Winchester each July to attend the *Aloha International Hawaiian Steel Guitar Festival.* For three days the air is filled with music, and on Saturday night everyone's invited to a luau. Townsfolk celebrate the annual event with such decorative touches as fake palm trees in a local cafe. Contact the Randolph County Promotion and Visitors Bureau, 111 South Main Street, Winchester 47394; (765) 584–3266 or (800) 905–0514, or call Jack Fowler at (765) 584–6845.

Steuben County

Majestic *Potawatomi Inn,* the only state park inn in northern Indiana, is one of the finest in the system. Resembling an Old English lodge, it sits in a clearing on the shore of Lake James in 1,200-acre *Pokagon State Park* in Angola.

Winter is king here, and the main treat is a refrigerated,1,700-foot-long toboggan slide, generally open from Thanksgiving Day through February, that whisks you over the hills and through the woods at speeds of up to 50 miles per hour. In this snowy park tucked into the northeastern corner of the Hoosier State, winter visitors will also find an ice-skating pond, a sledding hill, and cross-country ski trails. Toboggans and cross-country ski equipment can be rented in the park.

After frolicking in the chilly outdoors all day, retire to the inn for a sauna and whirlpool bath, do a few laps in the indoor pool, or bask in the warmth of the redbrick fireplace.

The recently renovated inn features more than 140 rooms and serves three meals daily in its highly rated dining room. The atmosphere is so down-homey that guests often come to eat in their stocking feet. Roast beef is a daily feature on a dinner menu that usually includes a choice of seafood, steak, and a chicken or ham dish. Rates range from $47 to $89 a night for a double room and from $5.00 to $12.00 for dinner, with lunch and breakfast rates even cheaper.

Although Pokagon State Park and its inn have gained a reputation as a winter resort, people also come here in other seasons, when the forests and the sweeping lawns of the inn are a lush green, park lakes are ice-free for swimmers and fishermen, and park trails accommodate hikers instead of skiers. Horses can be rented at the saddle barn, and the tennis and basketball courts see heavy use.

The Nature Center is popular year-round, with naturalists always on hand to interpret each of nature's moods. Bison and elk reside in nearby pens. One park trail leads to the marshes, swamps, and forests of the ***Potawatomi State Nature Preserve.*** The largest known tamarack and yellow birch trees in the state, the only northern white cedars known to exist in Indiana, and several species of wild orchids grow within the preserve's 208 acres.

For information about either the park or the inn, write Pokagon State Park, 450 Lane 100 Lake James, Angola 46703. The park's phone number is (219) 833–2012; the inn's is (219) 833–1077. To reach the park go west from Angola on U.S. Highway 20 to I–69. Turn north on I–69 and proceed to State Road 727; State Road 727 leads west from I–69 to the park entrance.

> ### Trivia
>
> *In 1890 a major oil strike was made on a farm in Wells County. By 1904 nearly 20,000 producing oil wells were scattered over a 400-square-mile area in Indiana that included Wells County, and Petroleum came into being as the state's newest boomtown. The oil is long gone, and Petroleum has nearly gone with it. Today the tiny town on State Road 1 is inhabited by approximately 150 people.*

All of Steuben County is noted for its natural beauty. Its combination of 101 lakes and verdant forests have earned it the nickname "Switzerland of Indiana," and no less an impresario than P. T. Barnum once pronounced Lake James "the most beautiful body of water I have ever seen!" What's more, Steuben County contains more dedicated state nature preserves than any other county in the state; you can learn more about them by contacting the Department of Natural Resources, Division of Nature Preserves, 402 West Washington Street, Room W267, Indianapolis 46204; (317) 232–4052.

Wells County

B luffton native Charles C. Deam (1865–1953) was the Hoosier State's first state forester and an internationally recognized authority in the field of botany. Approximately 4 miles northwest of Bluffton, you can see the **Deam Oak,** a rare hybrid tree named in the forester's honor. The tree, discovered in 1904, is the first known of its kind, and its acorns have since been distributed to gardens across the country. A natural cross between white and chinquapin oaks, the tree stands at the center of a small tract of state-owned land at the junction of State Road 116 and County Road 250 North.

You can learn more about Deam and his oak tree at the **Wells County Historical Museum** in Bluffton. Also featured here are the memorabilia of Everett Scott, another Bluffton native, who played for the Boston Red Sox and the New York Yankees in the 1920s. A baseball autographed by Scott and his friend and sometimes roommate, Babe Ruth, is a highlight of the exhibit. Civil War buffs can read pages from the Civil War diary of William Bluffton Miller, the first child born in Bluffton. The museum is located at 420 West Market Street; open 1:00 to 4:00 P.M. Wednesday and Sunday, June through August; open 1:00 TO 4:00 P.M. Sunday, September and October. Donations are welcome.

PLACES TO STAY IN NORTHEAST INDIANA

ANGOLA
Potawatomi Inn
Pokagon State Park
450 Lane 100 Lake James
(219) 833–1077

Tulip Tree Inn Bed
and Breakfast
411 North Wayne Street
(219) 668–7000

AUBURN
Yawn to Dawn Bed and
Breakfast
211 West Fifth Street
(219) 925–2583

BERNE
Black Bear Inn and Suites
1335 U.S. Highway 27 North
(219) 589–8955
(888) BERNE–IN

BRISTOL
Rust Hollar B&B
55238 County Road 31
(219) 825–1111

FORT WAYNE
At the Herb Lady's Garden
8214 Maysville Road
(219) 493–8814

GOSHEN
Checkerberry Inn
62644 County Road 37
(219) 642–4445

Indian Creek Bed
and Breakfast
20300 County Road 18
(219) 875–6606
Fax: (219) 875–3968

Rollin' Acres Holsteins Bed
and Breakfast
22151 County Road 40
(219) 831–4406

Royer's 1836 Log House
Bed and Breakfast
22781 County Road 38
(219) 533–1821

HUNTINGTON
Purviance House Bed
and Breakfast
326 South Jefferson
(219) 356–9215
(219) 356–4218

KENDALLVILLE
McCray Mansion Inn
703 East Mitchell Street
(219) 347–3647

LAGRANGE
The 1886 Inn
212 West Factory Street
(219) 463–4227

Atwater Century Farm
4240 West U.S. Highway 20
(219) 463–2743

LEESBURG
Prairie House B&B
495 East 900 North
(219) 658–9211

LIGONIER
Solomon Mier Manor Bed
and Breakfast
508 South Cavin Street
(219) 894–3668

MARION
Golden Oak Bed
and Breakfast
809 West Fourth Street
(765) 651–9950

MIDDLEBURY
Bee Hive Bed and Breakfast
P.O. Box 1191
(219) 825–5023

1898 Varns-Kimes Guest
House
205 South Main Street
P.O. Box 93
(219) 825–9666
(800) 398–5424

Patchwork Quilt
Country Inn
11748 County Road 2
(219) 825–2417

Yoder's Zimmer mit
Fruhstuck Haus Bed and
Breakfast
504 South Main Street
P.O. Box 1396
(219) 825–2378

MUNCIE
Pittenger Student
Center Hotel
Ball State University
2000 University Avenue
(765) 285–1555

NAPPANEE
The Inn at Amish Acres
1234 West Market Street
(219) 773–2011
(800) 800–4942

Olde Buffalo Inn Bed
and Breakfast
1061 Parkwood Drive
(219) 773–2223

The Victorian Guest House
302 East Market Street
(219) 773–4383

NORTH MANCHESTER
Fruitt Basket Inn
116 West Main Street
(219) 982–2443

PERU
Cole House Bed
and Breakfast
27 East Third Street
(765) 473–7636

Rosewood Mansion
54 North Hood Street
(765) 472–7151
Fax: (765) 472–5575

SHIPSHEWANA
Amish Log Cabin Lodging
5970 North State Road 5 at
State Road 120
(219) 768–7770
Fax: (219) 768–7769

Morton Street Bed
and Breakfast
140 Morton Street
(219) 768–4391
(800) 447–6475

SYRACUSE
Anchor Inn
11007 North State Road 13
(219) 457–4714

WABASH
Around Window Inn
313 West Hill Street
(219) 563–6901

Lamp Post Inn Bed
and Breakfast
261 West Hill
(219) 563–3094

WARREN
Huggy Bear Motel
I-69 and State Road 5
(Exit 78) (219) 375–2503

WARSAW
Candlelight Inn
503 East Fort Wayne Street
(219) 267–2906
(800) 352–0640

PLACES TO EAT IN NORTHEAST INDIANA

ALBANY
Osborn's St. Clair
Restaurant
220 West State Street
(765) 789–8487

ANGOLA
The Hatchery
118 South Elizabeth Street
(219) 665–9957

AUBURN
Joshua's Restaurant
and Lounge
640 North Grandstaff Drive
(219) 925–4407

BERNE
The Palmer House
Main and Fulton Streets
(219) 589–2306

BLUFFTON
Dutch Mill Restaurant
402 North Main Street
(219) 824–4000

DECATUR
Back 40 Junction
Restaurant
1011 North Thirteenth
Street
(219) 724–3355

ELKHART
Lucchese's Italian
Restaurant
205 East Jackson
Boulevard
(219) 522–4137

FARMLAND
The Greene Apple
103 North Main Street
(765) 468–8318

FORT WAYNE
Cafe Johnell
2529 South Calhoun Street
(219) 456–1939
(219) 745–4048

Casa D'Angelo
3402 Fairfield Avenue
(219) 745–7200

Cindy's Diner
830 South Harrison Street
(219) 422–1957

Hartley's
4301 South Fairfield Avenue
(219) 744–3141

Old #3 Firehouse Cafe and
Firefighters Museum
226 West Washington
Boulevard
(219) 426–0051

FREMONT
Clay's Family Restaurant
7815 Old North 27
(219) 833–1332
(219) 833–9956

GARRETT
Railroad Inn
104 North Peters Street
(219) 357–5756

T.G.'s Family Restaurant
1346 South Randolph Street
(219) 357–4489

GENEVA
Essen Platz Restaurant
Amishville, U.S.A.
844 East County Road
900 South
(219) 589–3536

GOSHEN
Olympia Candy Kitchen
136 North Main Street
(219) 533–5040

South Side Soda Shop-Diner
1122 South Main Street
(219) 534–3790

HUNTINGTON
Nick's Kitchen
506 North Jefferson Street
(219) 356–6618

LIGONIER
Fashion Farm Restaurant
1680 Lincolnway West
(219) 894–4498

MARION
Good Time Charlie's
3448 South Adams Street
(765) 674–5984

The Nobby Grill
213 East 4th Street
(765) 651–9600

Yesterday's Diner
3015 South Washington
(765) 664–2233

MIDDLEBURY
Das Dutchman Essenhaus
240 U.S. Highway 20
(800) 455–9471

Village Inn Restaurant
107 South Main Street
(219) 825–2043

MONTPELIER
Frosty's
659 West Huntington Street
(765) 728–2257

Grandma Jo's
State Road 18 West
(765) 728–5444

MUNCIE
Foxfires
3300 North Chadham Lane
(765) 284–5235

SunShine Cafe
3113 North Oakwood
Avenue
(765) 288-5221

NAPPANEE
Restaurant Barn
Amish Acres
1600 West Market Street
(219) 773-4188
(800) 800-4942

NORTH MANCHESTER
Mr. Dave's Restaurant
102 East Main Street
(219) 982-4769

ROANOKE
Ambriola's Restaurante
112 North Main Street
(219) 672-3097

SHIPSHEWANA
Blue Gate Restaurant
State Road 5 and
Middlebury Street
(219) 768-4752

Buggy Wheel Restaurant
160 North Morton Street
(219) 768-4444

SWEETSER
Kuch's Kove
102 South Main Street
(765) 384-7820

SYRACUSE
Oakwood Inn
702 Lake View Road East
(219) 457-5600

TOPEKA
The Country Inn
110 Redman Drive
(219) 593-2515

Emma Store
5990 West 200 South
(219) 593-9025

UPLAND
Ivanhoe's
914 South Main Street
(765) 998-7261

WABASH
Mike's Little Italy
1012 North Cass Street
(219) 563-1982

Wabash Sweet Shop
Est. 1938
35 West Market Street
(219) 563-1312

WAKARUSA
Come & Dine
66402 State Road 19
(219) 862-2714

WARSAW
ViewPoint Restaurant
2519 East Center Street
(219) 269-2323

**SOURCES FOR ADDITIONAL
INFORMATION ABOUT
NORTHEAST INDIANA**

Auburn/DeKalb County
Chamber of Commerce
208 South Jackson Street
P.O. Box 168
Auburn 46706
(219) 925-2100

Berne/Adams County
Chamber of Commerce
175 West Main Street
P.O. Box 85
Berne 46711
(219) 589-8080

Bluffton/Wells County
Chamber of Commerce
202 South Main Street
Bluffton 46714
(219) 824-0510

Elkhart County Convention
and Visitors Bureau
219 Caravan Drive
Elkhart 46514
(219) 262-8161
(800) 860-5949
Fax: (219) 262-3925
E-mail:
ecconv@amishcountry.org
www.amishcountry.org

Fort Wayne/Allen County
Convention and
Visitors Bureau
1021 South Calhoun Street
Fort Wayne 46802
(219) 424-3700
(800) 767-7752
Fax: (219) 424-3914
www.fwcvb.org

Huntington County Visitor
and Convention Bureau
305 Warren Street
P.O. Box 212
Huntington 46750
(219) 359-8687
(800) 848-4282
www.visithuntington.org

Kokomo/Howard County
Convention and Visitors
Bureau
1500 North Reed Road
Kokomo 46901
(765) 457-6802
(800) 837-0971
Fax: (765) 457-1572
E-mail: kokomoin@iquest.
net

Kosciusko County
Convention and Visitors
Bureau
111 Capital Drive
Warsaw 46580
(219) 269-6090
(800) 800-6090
Fax: (219) 269-2405

LaGrange County
Convention and Visitors
Bureau
440½ South Van Buren
Street
(State Road 5)
Shipshewana 46565
(219) 768–4008
(800) 254–8090
Fax: (219) 768–4091
E-mail: info@backroads.org

Ligonier/Noble County
Visitor and Convention
Bureau
800 Lincolnway South
P.O. Box 353
Ligonier 46767
(219) 894–9000
(888) 417–5362

Marion/Grant County
Convention and Visitors
Bureau
215 South Adams Street
Marion 46952
(765) 668–5435
(800) 662–9474
Fax: (765) 668–5443

Muncie/Delaware County
Visitors Bureau
425 North High Street
Muncie 47305
(765) 284–2700
(800) 568–6862
Fax: (765) 284–3002
E-mail: mvb@ecicnet.org

Peru/Miami County
Chamber of Commerce
2 North Broadway, Suite 202
Peru 46970
(765) 472–1923
Fax: (765) 472–7099

Randolph County
Promotion and
Visitors Bureau
111 South Main Street
Winchester 47394
(765) 584–3266
(800) 905–0514
Fax: (765) 935–0440

Steuben County Tourism
Bureau
207 South Wayne Street
Angola 46703
(219) 665–5386
(800) LAKE–101
Fax: (219) 665–5461
E-mail: lakes101@locl.net
www.lakes101.org

Northwest Indiana

Northwest Indiana is a land of contrasts. The most heavily industrialized region of the Hoosier State shares the Lake Michigan shoreline with the hauntingly wild and beautiful Indiana Dunes National Lakeshore. Lake County, which covers 501 square miles in Indiana's northwestern corner, is the state's second most populous county—some 475,000 people live within its borders. Not far south lie the rich farmlands of Benton County, whose 407 square miles are inhabited by about 9,000 people.

Two of Indiana's most fabled rivers wend their way through Northwest Indiana. The Kankakee River, which flows southwest from South Bend to the Illinois border, and its adjacent wetlands evoke memories of the lush 500,000-acre Grand Kankakee Marsh it once nourished. Indiana's longest stream, the Wabash River, cuts a swath through four of this region's counties on its 475-mile journey west across the width of the state and then south to the Ohio River.

Visitors travel to and through northwest Indiana on I–80/90, an east-west highway that is Indiana's only toll road; I–65, a north-south route; and several excellent U.S. highways.

Cass County

The pride of **Logansport** is its turn-of-the-century *carousel*. Now nearly 100 years old, it is one of only two all-wood, hand-carved merry-go-rounds still operating in Indiana. (The other is in the Indianapolis Children's Museum.) Delighted riders compete for a mount on the outer side and the chance to snag the coveted brass ring as the carousel spins round and round. Their brightly colored steeds—a mix of thirty-one horses, three goats, three reindeer, three giraffes, a lion, and a tiger—were produced in 1892 by the talented hands of German craftsman Gustav A. Dentzel, who moved to the United States in 1860 and became this country's chief carousel maker.

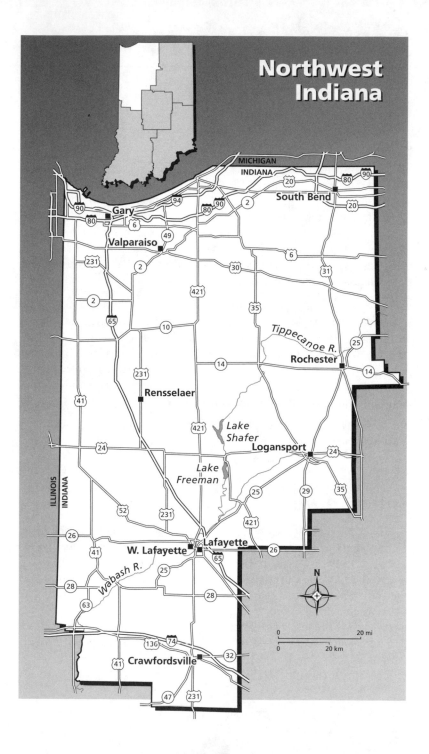

Although the carousel is owned by a nonprofit citizens' group, a small fee is charged for each ride to help offset maintenance costs. You'll find the merry-go-round in *Riverside City Park,* located along the south bank of Eel River at 1300 Riverside Drive—just follow the sound of music. It operates daily 6:30 to 9:30 P.M. Monday through Saturday and 12:30 to 9:30 P.M. Sunday, Memorial Day through Labor Day. Contact the Logansport/Cass County Chamber of Commerce, 300 East Broadway, Suite 103, Logansport 46947; (219) 753–6388.

Four miles west of Logansport off U.S. Highway 24 you'll come upon *France Park* and its picturesque swimming hole. An abandoned limestone quarry, partly hemmed in by precipitous cliffs, is filled with clear, brisk water that's irresistible on a hot summer day. Scuba and cliff divers like it, too.

Patches of woodland and a mossy, 15-foot waterfall on Paw Paw Creek add touches of beauty to the 500-acre county park. Seven miles of hiking/biking trails include a towpath that follows the remains of the old Wabash and Erie Canal. Visitors will also find a water slide, miniature golf course, some 200 campsites, and, near the entrance, a century-old log cabin. Nominal admission fee; beach open Memorial Day through Labor Day; park open daily year-round 9:00 A.M. to 11:00 P.M. Contact France Park, 4505 West U.S. Highway 24, Logansport 46947; (219) 753–2928.

Fountain County

t will never give the folks in Utah anything to worry about, but Indiana does have a stone arch that's so unique it's been declared both a National Natural Landmark and a state nature preserve. Through the years the meanderings of a tiny stream in northwestern Fountain County have carved a 30-by-12-foot opening through a massive sandstone formation and created a natural bridge known as **Portland Arch.** Nearby Bear Creek flows through a deep ravine edged by rugged sandstone cliffs. The rare bush honeysuckle grows here, and this is the only known site in the state where the Canada blueberry is found. At times a cover of mosses and lichens and several species of ferns growing in the crevices of the cliffs create a landscape of green velvet. A quaint pioneer cemetery on the 253-acre preserve contains eleven marked graves.

Portland Arch State Nature Preserve is located on the south side of the town of Fountain. Signs lead the way to the preserve and two parking

Annual Events in Northwest Indiana

Maple Syrup Time,
Merrillville; March
(219) 947–1958 or (800) GRISTMILL

Redbud Trail Rendezvous,
Rochester; April (219) 223–4436

Voyageurs Rendezvous on the Kankakee,
Hebron; May (219) 769–PARK

Rogers Rangers Rendezvous,
Cutler; June (765) 463–7893

Mint Festival,
North Judson; June (219) 896–5481

Marshall County Hot Air Affair Balloon Festival,
Rochester; June (219) 223–4436

Grecian Festival,
South Bend; June (219) 272–6372

Taste of Indiana Wines,
Whiting; June
(219) 659–WINE or (888) TNT–WINE

Round Barn Festival,
Rochester; June (219) 224–2666

Carroll County Wabash and Erie Canal Days,
Delphi; July (219) 965–2262

Ag Day,
Monticello; July
(219) 583–7220

College Football Hall of Fame Enshrinement,
South Bend; August
(219) 235–9999

Renaissance Faire,
Valparaiso; August
(219) 464–9621

Steam and Power Show,
Hesston; September (Labor Day weekend)
(219) 872–7405

International Culture Festival,
Hammond; September (219) 844–8219

Grape Stomp,
Whiting; September
(219) 659–WINE or (888) TNT–WINE

Scarecrow Festival,
Wanatah; September
(219) 733–2183

Wizard of Oz Festival,
Chesterton; September
(219) 926–7048, (219) 926–2255, or
(800) 283–8687

Northwestern Indiana Storytelling Festival,
Chesterton; October
(219) 926–1390

Elvis FANtasy Fest,
Portage; October (219) 926–2255

lots, each adjoined by a self-guiding trail. The loop trail leading from the first and main parking lot follows a hilly route about 1 mile long to Portland Arch. For additional information contact the Department of Natural Resources, Division of Nature Preserves, 402 West Washington Street, Room W267, Indianapolis 46204; (317) 232–4052.

Fulton County

F ulton County is peppered with round barns, the legacy of a turn-of-the-century fad. At last count nine of the original barns, the newest of which was built in 1924, were still standing. They are kept in excellent repair and are both unusual and beautiful to behold. No two are alike. The main idea behind this flurry of round-barn building was to create one centralized feeding station for livestock, thus increasing the efficiency of the farm operation. The barns were billed as being easier, quicker, and less costly to build, but the idea was abandoned.

In 1988 the **Fulton County Museum** near Rochester opened its doors to the public. A round barn, rebuilt on the premises, opened in 1990. Together they offer a glimpse into the county's past and provide information about its unique heritage. Maps are available for a drive-yourself tour of the county's barns. Although officially the barns are not open to the public, many owners, if they're at home when you arrive, are happy to show you through their barns, and several barns are open to the public during the third weekend in June when the county celebrates a Round Barn Festival. Admission to the museum is free; open 9:00 A.M. to 5:00 P.M. Monday through Saturday. Contact the museum at 37 East 375 North, Rochester 46975; (219) 223–4436.

Jasper County

T he world's first Ferris wheel was built by Luther Rice, a native Hoosier from Ladoga, for the 1893 Columbian Exposition in Chicago. It was used again at the World's Fair in Saint Louis in 1904, then was dismantled and sold for scrap. A section of the giant wheel was purchased by Isaac Dunn, another Hoosier, who used it to build a bridge connecting land he owned on both banks of the Kankakee River. Although it's no longer in use, **Dunn's Bridge** can still be seen just west of and parallel to the Tefft Road Bridge, about 3 miles north of the town of Tefft.

Each fall one of Indiana's most magnificent natural spectacles takes place at the 8,000-acre **Jasper-Pulaski State Fish and Wildlife Area.**

Round Barn at
Fulton County Museum

During the last week in October and the first week in November, some 12,000 greater sandhill cranes pause here to rest on their annual journey south for the winter. Jasper-Pulaski is believed to be the only place east of the Mississippi River where this unusual species stops en masse during migration.

These beautiful blue-gray birds, which stand about $3^1/_2$ feet tall and have a wingspan of up to 7 feet, are as impressive to hear as they are to look at. The best times to view them are at dawn, when they rise up from the misty marshes and call to one another in noisy unison, and again at sunset, when they return to the marsh for the night.

You can pick up literature about the cranes and obtain a free observation permit at the area headquarters, then continue on to one of two observation towers.

The cranes also migrate through Jasper-Pulaski between late February and mid-April, but they are usually present in greater concentration in the fall.

Although the sandhills are the main attraction, other wildlife species are here as well. Canada geese, quail, woodcock, and deer live in the wild year-round, and elk and bison roam fenced-in pastures. Part of Jasper-Pulaski serves as a game farm where pheasant are reared as stock for fish and wildlife areas throughout the state. Natural history and wildlife exhibits are maintained in one of the service buildings, and hiking trails wind through the area.

Located in the area's northwest corner is the 480-acre *Tefft Savanna State Nature Preserve,* home to many plants that are extremely rare in the Midwest. The entire fish and wildlife area actually occupies parts of three counties—Jasper, Pulaski, and Starke—but the majority of its 8,000 acres are in Jasper County. It's open daily year-round at all times, and entrance is free. The headquarters office is open 7:00 A.M. to 3:30 P.M. Monday through Friday, but hours may be extended in certain seasons.

To reach the refuge go north from Medaryville (in Pulaski County) on U.S. Highway 421 and turn west onto State Road 143; proceed 1½ miles to the entrance on the right side of the road; follow the signs. Contact Jasper-Pulaski State Fish and Wildlife Area, RR 1, Box 216, Medaryville 47957; (219) 843–4841.

Lake County

When the first white settlers came to Indiana, seven-eighths of the land was covered with a forest so dense that a squirrel could visit every tree in the state without ever once touching the ground. The far northwest corner, including what is now Lake County, was a sea of grass—grass so tall in places that a rider on horseback could not be seen above it. It was a long time before residents realized the value of saving some remnants of that original landscape, and by then most of it was irretrievably gone.

Two of the finest examples still in existence can be seen in Lake County. *German Methodist Cemetery Prairie* covers just one acre at the rear of the cemetery for which it's named, but more than eighty rare and vanishing plant species thrive in its rich black soil. In late summer, when most of them are in bloom, it is a place of incredible beauty.

This tiny preserve is probably the most botanically diverse acre in Indiana. You'll find it in the midst of farm fields on the east side of U.S. Highway 41, 1 mile south of the intersection of U.S. Highway 41 and 141st Street in Cedar Lake. The old cemetery is still there and should be respected. Behind it is the prairie, surrounded by a chain-link fence to protect the fragile plant life. For additional information contact The Nature Conservancy, Indiana Field Office, 1330 West Thirty-eighth Street, Indianapolis 46208; (317) 923–7547; fax (317) 923–7582.

> **Trivia**
>
> It is illegal in Gary to attend the theater within four hours of eating garlic.

Hoosier Prairie, the largest virgin prairie in Indiana, sprawls over 439 acres near Griffith. It contains some 300 species of native plants, including grasses that reach 12 feet in height. A trail about 2 miles long leads through some of the preserve's less sensitive areas and permits a look at the diverse habitats. You may even spot a deer along the way. Hoosier Prairie, a state nature preserve, is located west of Griffith on the south side of Main Street; a small parking lot is near the trailhead. Open daily year-round during daylight hours; admission is free. Contact the Department of Natural Resources, Division of Nature Preserves, 402 West Washington Street, Room W267, Indianapolis 46204; (317) 232–4052.

Pastor Win Worley of the **Hegewisch Baptist Church** in Highland has gained worldwide fame as an exorcist. He began casting out evil spirits in 1970, and within one year, with no publicity other than word of mouth, more than 1,000 first-time visitors were streaming into the small church annually. At an Exorcism Open House sponsored by the church in 1992, for instance, some 500 people from twenty-eight states and three foreign countries showed up. Now several Deliverance Workshops are held each year, and you are welcome to attend. For additional information, contact Pastor Win Worley, Hegewisch Baptist Church, 8711 Cottage Grove Avenue, P.O. Box 9327, Highland 46322; (219) 838–9410. The church also has a Web page at www.hbcdelivers.org.

The **Carmelite Shrines** in Munster offer a haven of serenity. On the grounds are twenty shrines that display Italian sculptures in a grotto studded with crystals and unusual rocks. The overall effect is enhanced by special lighting. You'll also find an arboretum and, in the monastery, a replica of the Vatican's Private Audience Hall. Grounds open free of charge 1:00 to 5:00 P.M. daily, weather permitting; building interiors can usually be seen on request. The shrines are located at 1628 Ridge Road, ¹/₂ mile west of U.S. Highway 41; (219) 838–9657 or (219) 838–7111.

When hunger pangs strike, head for **Teibel's Restaurant** in Schererville. Teibel's first opened its doors in 1929, the year the stock market crashed and launched the Great Depression. That the restaurant operated continuously through those lean years and still thrives today should tell you something. One reason for its longevity is that the old family recipe for fried chicken, which initially earned the restaurant its reputation, is a winner. The chicken (as well as fried perch) is served on an all-you-can-eat basis. Prices are moderate. Open 11:00 A.M. to 10:00 P.M. Sunday through Thursday and 11:00 A.M. to 2:00 A.M. Friday and Saturday. Located at the corner of U.S. Highways 41 and 30; (219) 865–2000; fax (219) 865–2435.

Crown Point is dominated by the "Grand Old Lady of Lake County," the magnificent **Old Lake County Court House,** which many regard as Indiana's most impressive. Built in 1878, it served as the seat of county government until 1974. Today it houses more than twenty crafts and specialty shops, including a fascinating puzzle shop and the Women's Exchange Resale Shop (profits aid courthouse restoration), as well as the Lake County Historical Museum. Don't miss its arched brick ceilings and intriguing hallways. The courthouse is located at the corner of Joliet and Court Streets; its shops are generally open from 10:00 A.M. to 5:00 P.M. Monday through Friday. The museum is open noon to 4:00 P.M. Friday through Sunday, spring through fall; other times by appointment. There's a nominal admission fee for the museum; (219) 663–0660.

Other Attractions Worth Seeing in Northwest Indiana

CEDAR LAKE

Lake of the Red Cedars Museum,
7308 West 138th Place (Constitution Avenue); (219) 374–6157

LAPORTE

Door Prairie Auto Museum,
2405 Indiana Avenue; (219) 326–1337

LINDEN

Linden Junction Depot
Railroad Museum,
514 North Main Street; (765) 339–7245

MICHIGAN CITY

Alyce Bartholomew Children's Museum,
2921 Franklin Street; (219) 874–8222

**Great Lakes Museum of
Military History,**
1710 East U.S. Highway 20;
(219) 872–2702

OGDEN DUNES

Hour Glass Museum and Gallery,
8 Lupine Lane; (219) 762–5184

SOUTH BEND

College Football Hall of Fame,
111 South Joseph Street;
(219) 235–9999 or (800) 440–FAME;
http://collegefootball.org

**Copsaholm Mansion/
Northern Indiana Center
for History,**
808 West Washington Street;
(219) 235–9964

VALPARAISO

Andersons Orchard and Winery,
430 East U.S. Highway 6;
(219) 464–4936

Old Jail Museum,
153 South Franklin Street;
(219) 465–3595

Seven Dolors Shrine,
356 West Seven Mile Road;
(219) 759–2521

WALKERTON

**Stuntz and Hochstetler Pines
Museum of Indian Artifacts,**
20451 North County Line/
Tyler Road;
(219) 586–2663

WEST LAFAYETTE

Fort Ouiatenon,
South River Road;
(765) 742–8411
or 743–3921

In 1896 William Jennings Bryan stood on the courthouse steps and campaigned for the presidency. A then-unknown car designer, Louis Chevrolet, came here to accept the winner's cup for the first major auto race in the United States, a race held in 1909 that was the forerunner of the Indy 500. From 1916 to 1941 the courthouse became famous for its instant marriages; the usual blood test and three-day waiting period were not required here. Among the thousands married at the courthouse during that period were Joe DiMaggio, Red Grange, Colleen Moore, Tom Mix, Muhammad Ali, Ronald Reagan, and, at the height of his career, Rudolph Valentino.

The magnificent **SS Constantine and Helen Greek Orthodox Cathedral** rises from amid thirty-seven acres of grounds at 8000 Madison Street in Merrillville. The only such church in the state, it features twenty-five large stained-glass windows, Byzantine mosaic work, and a rotunda 100 feet in diameter and 50 feet in height. Open 9:00 A.M. to 5:00 P.M. Monday through Friday and 10:00 A.M. to 2:00 P.M. Saturday. Each year on the second weekend of July, a Grecian festival takes place here; (219) 769–2481.

Until recently, the city of Gary was known as Steeltown, U.S.A., but it is perhaps better known now as the **birthplace of Michael Jackson,** the phenomenon of the 1980s. Throughout the city, billboards proclaim that Michael Jackson is ANOTHER GREAT GARY PRODUCT, as well as the WORLD'S NUMBER ONE ENTERTAINER. Michael was born here in August 1958 and grew up in a small, two-bedroom house located at 2300 Jackson Street (named long ago in honor of President Andrew Jackson). Although it's not open to the public, the house can be viewed from the street. Many folks hereabouts still remember the Jackson Five's first public appearance on the stage of Gary's Roosevelt High School in 1965. Shy Michael had to be dragged onto the stage, but what happened from that moment on is show business history.

LTV Steel in East Chicago has been producing steel for more than seventy-five years, contributing to Indiana's ranking as the top steel-producing state in the country. The company's state-of-the-art facilities at **Indiana Harbor Works** are some of the finest in the industry, and visitors may watch the entire process from beginning to end. The raw power and eerie beauty of what you see along the way are fascinating. Free guided tours are offered from March through October, but you must call in advance for an appointment. The plant is located at 3001 Dickey Road; (219) 391–2226. The company also has a drop-in visitor center, where you can watch a video about LTV and learn the history of the industry.

Built in 1917 as a planned worker community for a steel company that has long since vanished, *Marktown* is a historic district that is home to some 650 residents. Marktown's two-story stucco homes, all in Tudor Revival style and painted in pastels for color and variety, line narrow streets that once were given mention in Robert Ripley's *Believe It or Not* column. Ripley, chronicler of the unique, noted that Marktown residents used the streets as walkways and parked their cars on the sidewalks. Although the town never reached completion, ninety-four homes were constructed, and all remain standing today. Marktown is bounded by Pine and 129th Streets and Dickey and Riley Roads in East Chicago. For information about walking and driving tours, contact the Marktown Preservation Society at 405 Prospect Street, Marktown Historic District, East Chicago 46312; (219) 397–2239.

The frogs' legs served at *Phil Smidt's Restaurant* in Hammond have been celebrated for all of the more than seventy-five years the restaurant has been in business. Once the frogs' legs were gathered from the shore of nearby Lake Michigan; today they, like all frogs' legs served in restaurants in the United States, come from Bangladesh. They are still delicious, however, and what's more, they're served in a stunning room. One side is open, two walls are a soft rose hue, and the third bears murals of gigantic roses done in high-gloss paint on a shiny black background. Soft light filters through blocks of aquarium glass. The white tablecloths are bordered in pink, and each place is set with rose-colored napkins and rose-embossed water glasses. Be sure to ask to be seated in the Rose Room; there are five other dining rooms as well.

Another specialty of the house is lake perch, served whole or boned and cooked to perfection. Top off your meal with warm gooseberry pie. Outside, freight trains rumble by, and smokestacks spew smoke—an incredible contrast to the beauty within.

You'll find Phil Smidt's Restaurant at 1205 North Calumet Avenue; it's open for lunch and dinner from 11:15 A.M. to 9:00 P.M. Monday through Thursday and 11:15 A.M. to 10:00 P.M. Friday and Saturday. Call (219) 659–0025; fax (219) 659–6955.

The new building that has housed the *Lake County Convention and Visitors Bureau* since September 1, 1999, is a tourist attraction in itself. Built at a cost of $6 million, the structure is domed with blue glass and stainless steel that symbolize the waves of Lake Michigan crashing against the shore to the north. An undulating south wall represents the Kankakee River, which forms Lake County's southern border. Also along the southern portion of the building is a silo that pays tribute to the county's agricultural heritage. A 2,000-square-foot museum houses the world's largest private collection of John Dillinger memorabilia. Although named after the bank robber who was once designated our county's Public Enemy Number One, the main purpose of the *Dillinger Museum* is to honor our country's law enforcement officers. The museum's entrance is a simulated jail door that includes thirty-nine bricks, each bearing the name of a Lake County officer killed in the line of duty. Located at the intersection of Kennedy Avenue and I–94 in Hammond, the Visitors Bureau is open 8:00 A.M. to 5:00 P.M. daily. Call (800) ALL–LAKE or (219) 980–1617.

LaPorte County

At the tiny town of Hesston, on County Road 1000 North, northeast of LaPorte, you can see the *Hesston Steam Museum*. Spread out over a 155-acre site is an assemblage of steam-powered equipment worth several million dollars—trains, cranes, buzz saws, and a boat among them. You can take a 2-mile ride on a steam train or watch a miniature train, authentic to the tiniest detail, whiz by on a 3$^1/_2$-inch track. Feel free to toot a horn or ring a bell—it's that type of place.

Trivia

Dr. Scholl, friend to sore feet everywhere, was a real person and a real doctor. A native of LaPorte County, Dr. William Scholl graduated from medical school in 1904.

You can walk through the exhibit any day except Monday, but the equipment is in operation noon to 5:00 P.M. on Saturday, Sunday, and holidays, Memorial Day weekend through Labor Day; and Sunday only from Labor Day through October. An especially exuberant celebration takes place during the Annual Labor Day Weekend Steam Show. The outdoor museum is located at 1201 East County Road 1000 North, approximately 2$^1/_2$ miles east of State Road 39. Admission is free except during special events; a nominal fee is charged at all times for train rides. Contact the LaPorte County Historical Steam Society at 2940 Mt. Claire Way, Long Beach, Michigan City 46360; (219) 872–7405.

When *Oprah Winfrey* needs to get away from it all, she retreats to her secluded 160-acre estate near an Indiana town with the lyrical name of Rolling Prairie. Here she can indulge her passions for gardening, antiquing, and horseback riding. Tulips are her favorite flowers, and in 1988, the first year Oprah was here, she planted 50,000 bulbs. Oprah describes her Hoosier home as her favorite place in all the world.

Local residents without exception seem to adore her. Although they don't intrude on her privacy, they certainly notice her when she goes to town. They will tell you with delight that they saw her at a local supermarket or at a nearby Kmart, where she purchased sheets and towels when she was remodeling her mansion. They will also tell you that she is a very nice person and a very good neighbor.

Obviously, you can't visit Oprah's home, but you can drive by and view it from the road. It's located at 9252 North County Road 600 East, and most anyone in the area can tell you how to get there.

In the town of LaPorte you can take a free tour of the *LaPorte County Museum.* The more than 80,000 items on exhibit include the W. A. Jones collection of antique firearms and weapons—recognized as the best collection of its kind in the United States and one of the three best in the world. There's also a folklore display that tells the story of Belle Gunness, LaPorte's Madam Bluebeard, who in the early 1900s lured at least a dozen men to her farm north of town by promising to marry them; once there, the would-be husbands were promptly killed for their money and buried in the farmyard. The museum, located at 809 State Street, is open free of charge 10:00 A.M. to 4:30 P.M. Tuesday through Saturday (closed holidays); (219) 326–6808, extension 276.

At the *Angelo Bernacchi Greenhouses,* you can treat your visual and olfactory senses to the thousands of growing green things that make this the largest grower and retailer of plants in the entire Midwest. There are acres to browse through all year long. The retail shop is open 9:00 A.M. to 5:00 P.M. Monday through Saturday; special tours on May 1 and December 1. Located at 1010 Fox Street, LaPorte; (219) 362–6202 or (800) 759–0978; fax (219) 326–1790.

The *Barker Civic Center* at 631 Washington Street in Michigan City exudes turn-of-the-century elegance. Once the home of millionaire industrialist John H. Barker, it contains thirty-eight rooms; ten bathrooms; several fireplaces with hand-carved teak, walnut, or mahogany woodwork; and a mirrored ballroom. Adjacent to the library terrace is a sunken Italian garden. Tours at 10:00 A.M., 11:30 A.M., and 1:00 P.M. Monday through Friday year-round; also at noon and 2:00 P.M. Saturday and Sunday, June through October; closed major holidays. Nominal admission fee; (219) 873–1520.

A meat market that's a tourist attraction? Yes, say its many visitors. Step through the door and into the past at *Lange's Old-Fashioned Meat Market* in Michigan City. Lange's specializes in homemade mettwurst, bratwurst, and Polish sausage, using recipes handed down from past generations of owners. The real treat, though, is the yesteryear atmosphere of the shop—complete with sawdust-strewn floors—and the character behind the counter. You'll also see a scale model of Michigan City's historic downtown. Located at 218 West Seventh Street; (219) 874–0071. Open 9:00 A.M. to 6:00 P.M. Tuesday through Saturday and 11:00 A.M. to 4:00 P.M. Sunday; closed January and February. Free thirty-minute tours are offered by advance arrangement; visitors are encouraged to ask questions as they learn how old-world sausage is made and how meats are smoked and cured.

Not far away, a fishing pier that extends into Lake Michigan offers a view of Indiana's only operating lighthouse. On a clear day you can also see the Chicago skyline

The area's natural history is explored at the *Old Lighthouse Museum* in *Washington Park,* Michigan City's ninety-acre lakefront park. Situated on Heisman Harbor Road at the park's west entrance, the museum contains a rare fourth-order Fresnel lens, shipbuilding tools, and other maritime artifacts. Open 1:00 to 4:00 P.M. Tuesday through Sunday, year-round; closed Monday and holidays. There's a nominal admission charge; (219) 872–6133.

The Washington Park Zoo features more than 180 species of animals and is a major breeder of Bengal tigers. Within its boundaries an observation tower atop a dune offers spectacular bird's-eye views. The zoo is open daily 10:30 A.M. to 6:00 P.M., March through December; 10:30 A.M. to 3:00 P.M. daily the rest of the year. There's a nominal admission fee. Phone (219) 873–1510; fax (219) 873–1539.

As the folks at the *Guse Tree Farm* can tell you, raising Christmas trees is a year-round business. They're happy to show visitors all about it, including how different trees grow and how Christmas wreaths are made. Among the varieties raised here on more than 125 acres are Scotch pine, white pine, Douglas fir, Frasier fir, and blue spruce. Free tours are offered by advance appointment. Contact the farm at 6177 West 1450 South, Wanatah 46390; phone (219) 733–2213.

Marshall County

I f you visit the small town of Argos, you're likely to see a lot of people looking up. That's because they're scanning the skies for a glimpse of the powered parachutes manufactured at *Buckeye Industries,* the world's

Old Lighthouse Museum

largest manufacturer of these colorful aircraft. The company, which has its national headquarters in Argos, gives demonstration rides to curious spectators, and the skies are almost constantly filled with action.

The powered parachute was originally developed at the University of Notre Dame (in South Bend, Indiana) in the late 1960s and early 1970s and has only been on the market since 1985. The popularity of the lightweight craft has soared since then, in part because it is the most inexpensive way to fly and no previous flight experience is necessary. The pilot sits in an open-air machine that vaguely resembles a motorized go-cart attached to a huge, rectangular parachute. Most people can solo after approximately two hours of instruction.

Although people from all over the world flock in and fly in for Buckeye's annual Fourth of July Five-Day Fly-In, visitors are welcome at any time. The late John F. Kennedy, Jr., came here in 1997 to trade in the single-passenger model he'd purchased in 1996 for a two-seater. His late wife, Carolyn, who accompanied him, said that her husband liked the solitude he experienced when piloting his parachute.

For additional information, contact Buckeye Industries at 16095 Linden Road, Argos 46501; (219) 892–5566.

Since the U.S. Army Cavalry was disbanded in 1950, the **Black Horse Troop** of Culver Military Academy (a college preparatory boarding school in the town of Culver) has been the nation's largest remaining cavalry unit. The 144 young men who compose its ranks hone their skills in the academy's extensive horsemanship programs. Organized in 1897, the troop has taken part in eleven presidential inaugurations,

The Trail of Death Regional Historic Trail

*I*n 1838, the Potawatomi Indians of northern Indiana were rounded up by federal troops and led on foot to the land on which the government had decreed they should henceforth live. The tribe of Chief Alexis Menominee numbered more than 850 when it started its westward walk. During the 900-mile trek to Kansas, some 150 Potawatomis perished from disease, fatigue, and adverse weather conditions. That fateful journey is recorded in history as the Trail of Death.

From the north bank of Twin Lakes in Marshall County, where the long walk began, the trail leads south to Logansport before turning southwest to follow the banks of the Wabash River to the Indiana-Illinois border. Numerous markers and memorials have been established along the trail, but the most impressive of all is the granite statue of Chief Menominee that stands on the site his tribe once called home. Visitors will find it on South Peach Road not far southwest of the town of Plymouth.

Within the next few years, the state's Native American history may be explored at Prophetstown State Park near Battle Ground in Tippecanoe County. Land is currently being purchased for development of the park, which will become the official Native American Cultural Center in Indiana.

escorted kings and queens, and been featured in major horse shows throughout the country, but you can see it free, with all its pomp and pageantry, each Sunday afternoon from May through October. That's when the troopers don their military dress, mount their black steeds, and parade across the academy's well-kept grounds. While you're there, pick up a map at the administration office and tour the 1,500-acre campus, beautifully situated near the shoreline of Lake Maxinkuckee. Contact Culver Military Academy, CEF 129, Culver 46511; (219) 842–7000 or (800) 5–CULVER; fax (219) 842–8267.

For an informative one-hour tour, visit the *Pioneer Seed Company* in Plymouth. You'll learn firsthand how corn gets from the stalk back to seed again. Workers at the plant unload, dry, and shell the corn, then sort it according to the size of the kernel and package it for storing. The tour is free, but call in advance to schedule a time. Located at 7900 North Pine Road; (219) 936–3243.

Montgomery County

*F*or sheer natural beauty it's hard to beat *Shades State Park* near Waveland, but to fully appreciate its magnificent scenery and outstanding geologic features you'll have to do some hiking. Only by taking to the trails can you see the primeval terrain for which the park is noted. Some first-time hikers do a double take when they see what awaits them—a landscape like this just isn't associated with Indiana.

About 470 acres of the 3,000-acre park have been set aside as the **Pine Hills State Nature Preserve.** Within its boundaries are four narrow rock ridges from 75 to 100 feet tall that are recognized as the finest example of incised meanders in the eastern United States. This observation was made by no less an authority than the National Park Service, which designated the preserve a National Natural Landmark.

In 1836 siltstone slabs covered with crinoid (sea lily) fossils were first discovered at the north edge of Crawfordsville. The location is now internationally famous, yielding some of the best crinoid fossils ever found. Crawfordsville crinoids can be seen in museums around the world.

Native white pine and hemlock, not usually found this far south, are relics of a long-ago past when this area was much cooler. The arrival of spring is first announced by the flowering of the rare snow trillium, and the coloring of the land continues through May, when the dogwoods and redbuds show off their blossoms. Through it all flows Sugar Creek, the most beautiful stream in the state.

When early European settlers first cast eyes on the lush forests and deep gorges along Sugar Creek, they referred to this place as "the Shades of Death." The long shadows cast by the heavy growth of trees initially appeared ominous to them, but as they became more familiar with the area the nickname was shortened to "the Shades." It remains appropriate to this day since the land has remained virtually untouched by human hands.

Two other impressive features are Silver Cascade Falls, one of eleven waterfalls in the park, and Devil's Punchbowl, a large, circular grotto cut into the sandstone by two small streams.

Canoeists take to Sugar Creek in droves, and if you're into solitude you'll want to avoid a trip on summer weekends. Weekdays in May or June or any day in August or September when the water level is down promises quieter floats. The most scenic stretch, which lies between Shades State Park and Turkey Run State Park (located to the southwest in adjoining Parke County), can be seen in one day. Put in at Deer's Mill Covered Bridge, which spans Sugar Creek along State Road 234 on the eastern edge of Shades State Park. For an enjoyable two-day trip, put in at Elston Park in Crawfordsville. Both trips end at West Union Covered Bridge in Parke County. Always check water conditions at park headquarters before starting out, however; the creek can be dangerous at flood stage.

Although most of the park is undeveloped, visitors will find more than one hundred primitive campsites, special campgrounds for backpackers and canoeists, and several picnic areas, some with shelters. Bicycles can be rented in the park, and a naturalist is on duty in the summer.

Shades State Park is located along both banks of Sugar Creek in southwestern Montgomery County and spills over into Parke County. The entrance is on County Road 800S, just west of State Road 234; look for signs. It's open daily year-round; there's a nominal vehicle admission fee. Contact the property manager, Shades State Park, Route 1, Box 72, Waveland 47989; (765) 435–2810.

Just north of Shades State Park, County Road 875W leads north off State Road 234 to the Hoosier State's own *Alamo,* which the town's fifty residents hope you'll remember. There, on the outside front of an old school gymnasium, a local artist has created a series of colorful murals that depict both Alamos—the one in Texas and the one in Indiana.

Another small town in the northwestern corner of the county achieved fame without even trying. When Hollywood came to Hoosierland looking for an idyllic rural area in which to film the principal exterior shots for the movie *Hoosiers,* it chose *New Richmond.* (For readers who missed it, *Hoosiers* is loosely based on the true story of a small-town high school basketball team that defied all odds to win the Indiana state championship.) It is also the movie that, in 1998, was voted the best sports movie of all time by readers of *USA Today.* Now tourists, enthralled with what they saw on the screen, travel here to see the real thing—the storefronts, the main street with its single traffic light, the farm fields bathed in sunset gold. The sign that identifies the community as New Richmond is now embellished with the words WELCOME TO HICKORY (the town's movie name), and the Hickory Festival, held in late September, features a basketball game and *Hoosiers* film clips.

For information about Alamo and New Richmond, contact the Montgomery County Visitors and Convention Bureau, 412 East Main Street, Crawfordsville 47933; (765) 362–5200 or (800) 866–3973.

The Old Montgomery County Jail at 225 North Washington Street in Crawfordsville was the first of only seven rotary jails ever built worldwide and is the only one still operational. Completed in 1882, it remained in daily use until 1973. The cell blocks are arranged in a circle in such a way that the sheriff, with the turn of a crank, could rotate the cells around him and check on his prisoners without ever taking a step. Now known as the *Old Jail Museum,* it's open free of charge from 1:00

to 4:30 P.M. Wednesday through Sunday, April, May, September, and October; 10:00 A.M. to 4:30 P.M. Wednesday through Saturday and 1:00 to 4:30 P.M. Tuesday and Sunday, June through August; (765) 362–5222.

The campus of **Wabash College,** at the corner of West Wabash and Grant Avenues in Crawfordsville, is of interest because of the mid-1800s architecture of its buildings and its arboretum of native Indiana trees. Students apparently find the setting conducive to learning. Out of 1,500 colleges and universities in this country, Wabash ranks sixteenth in the percentage of graduates who go on to earn Ph.D.s. Perhaps it's the lack of distraction—Wabash is an all-male college. Call (765) 362–1400.

Also in Crawfordsville, on the corner of Wallace Avenue and East Pike Street, you'll find a four-acre park that contains the **Ben Hur Museum** housed in the study of General Lew Wallace. Famed as a lawyer, statesman, and Civil War general, Wallace is nevertheless probably best remembered as the author of the novel Ben Hur. Published in 1880, it was one of the most popular novels of all time, becoming the first book ever to exceed the Bible in sales (more than one million copies were sold through the Sears catalog alone). A dramatic version was one of the longest-running plays in history. Hollywood twice made Ben Hur into a movie, once as a silent picture in 1926 and again in 1959. The latter won eleven Academy Awards, including one for Best Picture. Wallace's eclectic study, designed by Wallace himself, is a mix of French, Byzantine, Romanesque, and Greek styles. The 20-foot-tall bronze statue of Wallace that stands nearby is a replica of one that was unveiled in Washington, D.C., in 1910. Each year in mid-October, a Circus Maximus is staged on these grounds, complete with a chariot race and Greek food. Open 10:00 A.M. to 4:30 P.M. Wednesday through Saturday in June, July, and August and 1:00 to 4:30 P.M. Tuesday and Sunday, April through October; nominal admission fee; (765) 362–5769 or (765) 364–5173.

At the **Wal-Mart Photo Lab** in Crawfordsville, film is developed in batches of one hundred canisters at a time. Visitors are welcome to view the highly automated process from beginning to end. If you like, you can even do it in the middle of the night. The plant operates around the clock and will give tours at any time except from 3:00 P.M. Saturday until 5:00 P.M. Sunday (the plant shuts down then). Tours are free; the folks at Wal-Mart ask only that you call at least twenty-four hours in advance of your visit so that they'll know when to expect you. The plant is located at 801 Corda Boulevard, Crawfordsville; (765) 364–0190.

Newton County

hat is often described as the most unique natural feature in Indiana is a peculiar layering of rock near Kentland. Elsewhere in the state, layers of rock are almost horizontal, but here many of the layers are vertical. The deformed rocks bear mute testimony to a force of nature so incredible that it folded and fractured layers of rock that lay in a horizontal position 1,800 feet below the surface of the earth and thrust them above the surface in a nearly vertical position.

Currently, two theories exist. One is that a huge meteorite hit here several million years ago and created the huge crater seen today. A second theory is that a sudden, violent explosion of trapped underground gases caused the faulting.

While geologists have been speculating about the cause of the disruption since the 1880s, when the strange formation was first discovered, no geologic evidence yet exists to explain the origin of what is now called the *Kentland Dome.* To this day, it remains a geologic enigma.

The Governor's Bull

In a lonely field in Newton County, a fading stone monument marks the final resting place of Perfection Fair. The occupant of the grave is the grand champion of the 1907 International Livestock Exposition, a prize bull who brought fame and fortune to his owner.

Warren T. McCray brought his prize-winning perfect bull to his stock farm near Kentland, where the bull became the progenitor of many perfect little bulls and made a tidy sum of money for his owner. When Perfection Fair died in 1920, his owner buried him with much pomp and honor.

The fortune to which Perfection Fair had contributed so much helped propel McCray into Indiana's statehouse, where he served as governor from

1921 to 1924. During his tenure in office, McCray sponsored the amendment to the state constitution that gave women the right to vote, created the state gasoline tax to fund much-needed highway construction, and improved teachers' pensions. Unfortunately, he also earned the dubious distinction of being the only Indiana governor (to date) to go directly from the statehouse to the Big House. Tried and convicted of mail fraud and forgery, McCray was sent to the federal prison in Atlanta, where he resided until 1930 when President Herbert Hoover pardoned him. Some believe the governor was set up because he appointed the attorney who in 1925 successfully prosecuted D. C. Stephenson, grand dragon of the state's then-politically powerful Ku Klux Klan.

Although the formation is on private property, visitors may view it by advance appointment. For further information contact the Newton Stone Company, Inc., Route 24 East, P.O. Box 147, Kentland 47951; (219) 474–5125.

Porter County

Indiana does not have a Grand Canyon or a Yosemite, but it does have some of the largest sand dunes this side of the Sahara. Since 1972, most of them have been part of the 13,000-acre **Indiana Dunes National Lakeshore,** a miracle of survival in the midst of one of the most heavily industrialized regions in the country. Its lovely sand beaches along the southern shoreline of Lake Michigan are legendary for miles around, but they are only part of what can be seen and done here.

Mt. Baldy inches away from the lake each year; its name hints at why. Because it has not been stabilized by vegetation, the 135-foot-tall dune is kept in constant motion by wind and water, forcing the dune to take giant steps backward. Climb to the top for a sweeping view of Lake Michigan.

Not all of the landscape is sand and water. There are also grassy hills, patches of prairie, lush wetlands, and cool forests with a canopy so dense that sunlight barely filters through. Miller Woods, Cowles Bog, and Pinhook Bog would be exceptional natural areas anywhere, but their existence in the midst of such pollution, industry, and urban population is incredible.

The Bailly Homestead, dating to 1822, and the Chellberg Farm, built in the late 1880s, contain historical structures that the public can visit. There are hiking, bicycling, and horseback-riding trails to follow; in the winter they're used by cross-country skiers. At least 223 species of birds have been identified here, and many rare plants live among the dunes. Special programs and events are held all year long.

Although the national lakeshore actually lies in parts of three counties—Lake, Porter, and LaPorte—its visitor center is in Porter County, and this is where you should begin your visit. The center is located on Kemil Road, which runs south from U.S. Highway 12 about 3 miles east of the intersection of U.S. Highway 12 and State Road 49 near Porter, and is open daily year-round, 8:00 A.M. to 6:00 P.M. Memorial Day through Labor Day and 8:00 A.M. to 5:00 P.M. the rest of the year; closed major winter holidays. The park is open daily year-round; hours vary from area to area and are subject to change. A nominal parking fee is charged at West Beach from Memorial Day through Labor Day; everything else is free. For additional information contact Indiana Dunes National Lakeshore, 1100 North Mineral Springs Road, Porter 46304; (219) 926–7561.

Completely surrounded by the national lakeshore are 2,182 acres that make up **Indiana Dunes State Park.** It offers a microcosm of the features found in its big brother and boasts the highest sand dune along the lakeshore—192-foot-tall Mt. Tom.

When conditions are just right, the drifting sand emits a low, humming sound, soothing to the ear and soul, that is akin to the sound produced by drawing a bow across the strings of a bass viola. The unique phenomenon is known locally as the music of the "singing sands."

The 1,500-acre **Dunes State Nature Preserve,** which lies within park boundaries, contains more species of trees than any other area of comparable size in the Midwest; from one spot alone you can identify thirty different varieties. In the summer the myriads of rare flowers and ferns found here create a near-tropical appearance. Recreational facilities include a modern campground, a nature center, a swimming beach, and trails for hiking, bicycling, and cross-country skiing. To reach the park proceed north from I–94 on State Road 49 for about 2 miles. The park is open year-round; a nominal vehicle admission fee is charged from spring through fall. Contact the Indiana

Diana of the Dunes

The story of Diana of the Dunes is one of the most enduring in Indiana lore. Born Alice Mable Gray, she was given the name by which she is remembered in legend when she rejected civilization in 1915 to move into an abandoned fisherman's shack nestled in the wilderness of Porter County's dune country.

Diana, a Phi Beta Kappa from Chicago, was believed to have been inspired by the poetry of Byron, who wrote in his poem "Solitude" that "In solitude . . . we are least alone." It is reported that, when weather permitted, she was often seen wandering over and among the dunes sans clothing.

Diana later married and shared her solitude with Paul Wilson, another lover of solitude who sought out Diana after reading about her unique lifestyle. The public, however, would not permit them their privacy, and when a man's charred body was found near their shack, many people fervently believed the two were guilty of murder.

In 1925, Diana died and was buried in an unmarked grave in a nearby cemetery. Her grieving husband packed up and moved away. It is reported even today that her ghost can sometimes be seen at twilight flitting among the dunes she loved.

Dunes State Park, 1600 North 25 East, Chesterton 46304; (219) 926–1952.

When the Chicago World's Fair of 1933 closed, five homes from the *"Houses of the Future" exhibit* were placed on a barge and transported across Lake Michigan to the then-new community of Beverly Shores. Plans to make Beverly Shores the ultimate vacation resort were thwarted by the lingering effects of the Great Depression, but the houses are still there, lined up along Lake Front Drive and still of interest. Especially startling is the House of Tomorrow, a twelve-sided structure built like a wedding cake (the top two floors are each smaller in circumference than the floor below).

You'll also see a reproduction of Boston's Old North Church; it, too, was carted over from the fair. For more information contact the Porter County Convention, Recreation, and Visitors Commission, 800 Indian Boundary Road, Chesterton 46304; (219) 926–2255 or (800) 283–8687.

The magical kingdom of Oz is also a part of Dune Country. L. Frank Baum, author of the Oz books, used to summer here, and later his son established the International Wizard of Oz Club in this area. Today you can view a collection of Oz memorabilia in the *Wizard of Oz Fantasy Museum,* housed in the Yellow Brick Road shop in Chesterton. There's a nominal fee for the museum. The store is open 10:00 A.M. to 5:00 P.M. Monday through Saturday and 11:00 A.M. to 4:00 P.M. Sunday. It's easy to find: Just follow the yellow brick road (honestly!) to 109 East County Road 950 North, near that road's intersection with State Road 49; (219) 926–7048. Each September a *Wizard of Oz* Festival, complete with several real-life Munchkins from the movie's original cast, evokes memories of the Judy Garland screen classic. Contact the Yellow Brick Road or the Porter County Convention, Recreation, and Visitors Commission (see previous entry).

At 411 Bowser Avenue in Chesterton stands a house that is known by the imposing name of the *All-Steel Porcelain-Enameled Streamlined Historic Home.* Its less imposing and easier-to-remember name is the Lustron home, so called because it is one of the fewer than 3,000 such homes produced by the now-defunct Lustron Corporation of Columbus, Ohio.

During the housing boom following World War II, there was a great demand for affordable starter homes for returning veterans. Lustron's answer was the all-steel prefabricated home.

The Bowser Avenue house, erected in 1950, is today believed to be the only Lustron home in the country open for tours on a continuous basis. Jim Morrow, the current owner, originally purchased the house in 1990. The longer he lived there, however, the more he realized the historical heritage it represented, so he moved out and opened it to the public. Jim's steel and chrome furnishings, including some early 1930s steel bedroom sets, lend credence to the historical aura of the home. Tours are free, but donations are welcome. The home is open from 1:00 to 5:00 P.M. Tuesday through Saturday, May through October. To arrange a tour at other times or to ask questions about the house, contact Jim Morrow at P.O. Box 508, Chesterton 46304-0508; (219) 926–3669.

The showpiece of Valparaiso in central Porter County is the striking *Chapel of the Resurrection* on the campus of Valparaiso University. This magnificent contemporary structure, which is the largest collegiate chapel in the nation, has received accolades from around the world. The entire building focuses on the chancel, whose limestone piers rise skyward for 98 feet and culminate in a roof shaped like a nine-point star. Try to visit here on a sunny day; from inside the chancel the view of the awe-inspiring stained-glass windows will take your breath away. The largest Lutheran university in the country, Valparaiso counts the late Lowell Thomas among its alumni. Visitors are

Corn Off the Cob

*T*he words "popcorn" and "Orville Redenbacher" have become virtual synonyms in the minds of snack lovers all over the world. An Indiana native and a graduate of Purdue University in West Lafayette, Orville began his rise to fame when he and a friend purchased a small agricultural company in Valparaiso. The unassuming entrepreneur dreamed of giving the world a fluffier, higher-quality popcorn, and the world is grateful for his efforts.

Originally marketed as Red Bow popcorn (a blending of Redenbacher and the name of his partner, Charles Bowman), it is now known as Orville Redenbacher's Gourmet Popping Corn.

The two changed the name on the advice of a marketing firm, and sales soared. Perhaps in deference to his roots, one of Orville's trademarks was his red bow tie.

In later years, Orville's company was sold to Hunt-Wesson, Inc., and moved to California. However, until his death in 1995 at the age of 88, Orville never forgot his Indiana roots, returning to the state most every year for the annual Valparaiso Popcorn Festival in September.

Today, Orville Redenbacher's Gourmet Popping Corn remains the top-selling microwave popcorn.

welcome at any time; the campus lies at the east end of Union Street; (219) 464–5000.

Housed in a facility that simulates a medieval village, **Marc T. Nielsen Interiors, Inc.,** features crafts shops for upholstery work, cabinet making, and furniture building in a Tudor-style farm structure. There's also a display of Old World furniture and accessories that may be unlike any you've ever seen. Owner Virginia Phillips travels the world to buy antiques for the stunning collection. Store open 9:00 A.M. to 4:30 P.M. Monday through Friday; crafts shops by appointment. Located at 734 North Old Suman Road near Valparaiso. Phone (219) 462–9812; fax (219) 465–1550.

At the **Strongbow Turkey Inn** it's Thanksgiving all year long. You can have almost any part of the gobbler cooked nearly any way imaginable here. Turkey appears in salads, soups, sandwiches, crepes, pies, and pâtés, not to mention sliced up on a plate and accompanied by all the traditional fixings. Everything is made on the premises—breads, rolls, cranberry-orange relish, cakes, pies, and a delicious cup custard. If you're in the mood for something Continental, try the veal Oscar, coquilles St. Jacques, or shrimp Pescatore. You'll find the inn at 2405 U.S. Highway 30 East, Valparaiso. Open 11:00 A.M. to 9:00 P.M. Sunday through Thursday; 11:00 A.M. to 10:00 P.M. Friday and Saturday; closed Christmas week. Reservations advised; (219) 462–5121 or (800) 462–5121. Stop at the Strongbow Bakery on the premises for some delectable take-home treats; (219) 464–8643.

St. Joseph County

█ f you ever wonder where all that spearmint in your Wrigley's
▅▅chewing gum comes from, here's your chance to find out. Call the **Martin Blad Mint Farm** near South Bend and make an appointment to visit the place in July. That's when the bright yellow mint wagons haul a newly harvested crop into the mint-press building. You can watch as the oil is separated, picked up, guided through coils, and pumped into fifty-five-gallon containers. Then it's packed up and sent off to Wrigley's en masse. The 2,500-acre farm is located at 58995 Mayflower Road (State Road 123), $^1/_2$ mile north of its junction with State Road 23, just southwest of South Bend; (219) 234–7271.

From nearly every vantage point in South Bend, you can see the renowned golden dome that tops the administration building of the **University of Notre Dame.** A walking tour of the 1,250-acre campus

Trivia

The original boundary line between Indiana and Michigan in St. Joseph County was established on June 30, 1805. When Indiana became a state in 1816, that line was moved 10 miles north. Hoosiers refused to agree to statehood that did not include waterfront property on Lake Michigan.

will take you to such places as the Grotto of Our Lady of Lourdes, an exact reproduction of the original in France; the Sacred Heart Church, an awe-inspiring Gothic structure that contains one of North America's oldest carillons; the Snite Museum of Art, which houses rare religious artworks and masterpieces by such noted artists as Chagall, Picasso, and Rodin; and the Notre Dame Memorial Library, a huge, fourteen-story building noted for its rare books room and the 132-foot-high granite mural that adorns its outer wall. To reach the university go north from South Bend on U.S. Highway 31/33 to Angela Boulevard and turn east; call (219) 631–5000 for general information, (219) 631–5726 for tour information.

Of all the citizens of South Bend, past or present, Knute Rockne is perhaps the best known. The famous coach, who maintained that football was a game of brains rather than brawn, shaped the Fighting Irish into a legend. When he died in a plane crash in 1931, he was just forty-two years old. His funeral service, attended by an estimated 100,000 people and carried by radio across the nation and to Norway (the land of his birth), was one of the most emotional in American history. You can visit his grave in **Highland Cemetery,** at 2557 Portage Avenue, not far from his beloved university.

The Taking of Oliver

On the evening of December 24, 1889, friends and relatives gathered at the Matthew Larch farmstead near South Bend to celebrate the Christmas holiday. It was pitch black when eleven-year-old Oliver Larch was sent outside to fetch water from the well.

A few minutes later, Oliver's screams of pure terror reached the ears of those in the house. When they rushed outside to investigate, they clearly heard Oliver's voice from somewhere high above their heads proclaiming "Help!

They've got me!" Horrified and helpless, people could only listen as Oliver's cries trailed off into the darkness.

The boy's footprints on the snow-covered ground simply ended. The oak bucket he had carried with him lay on the ground beside his trail. When questioned later by investigators, everyone present, including a local minister and a judge, told identical stories.

Oliver Larch was never seen again.

NORTHWEST INDIANA

Trivia

Another name that's famous around South Bend is Studebaker. Clement Studebaker began his career as a wagon maker, making wagons for the Union Army during the Civil War and later for the thousands who trekked west. As he progressed from wagons to carriages to automobiles, he kept a collection of company vehicles. They are housed today in the **Studebaker National Museum** at 525 South Main Street. Among the exhibits is the Studebaker carriage in which Abraham Lincoln rode to Ford's Theatre the night he was assassinated. The museum is open from 9:00 A.M. to 5:00 P.M. Monday through Saturday and noon to 5:00 P.M. Sunday; closed holidays. Admission fee; (219) 235–9479 (information line), (219) 235–9108 (museum), or (219) 235–9714 (office).

J. Paul Barnett of South Bend has a most unusual sideline—he plays the cannon. The original 1880 score of Tchaikovsky's 1812 Overture calls for sixteen cannon blasts. When symphony orchestras across the country want to perform a historically accurate 1812, they call Barnett. Barnett also owns South Bend Replicas, the company that makes the cannons he plays.

By 1888 Studebaker had become a wealthy man, and he built himself a forty-room mansion worthy of his station, complete with twenty fireplaces and 24,000 square feet of space. Its massive stone walls, turrets, and irregular roofs gave it the appearance of a feudal castle. Today the historic mansion is called **Tippecanoe Place** and houses a fine gourmet restaurant that serves Continental cuisine. Lunch is available from 11:30 A.M. to 2:00 P.M. Monday through Friday; dinner from 5:00 to 10:00 P.M. Monday through Thursday, 5:00 to 11:00 P.M. Friday, 4:30 to 11:00 P.M. Saturday, and 4:00 to 9:00 P.M. Sunday. A Sunday brunch is served buffet style from 9:00 A.M. to 2:00 P.M. Located at 620 West Washington Street; (219) 234–9077. Tours are available outside of dining hours. Reservations are advised for both meals and tours.

Trivia

The only artificial white-water course in North America and one of only three in the world is located in the heart of downtown South Bend. Called the **Dust Race Waterway**, it's a 2,000 foot long channel that bypasses the South Bend Dam across the St. Joseph River. The elite of white-water paddlers from around the globe come here each summer to take part in national and international competitions. Because the flow of water can be controlled, the waterway can generate the churning rapids and 6-foot-tall waves needed for athletic events or can present a surface calm enough for whole families to embark on. It's open to the public for rafting, kayaking, and other water sports, under the watchful eyes of a well-trained rescue team, for approximately thirty hours per week

In South Bend it is illegal for monkeys to smoke cigarettes.

Bendix Woods County Park in New Carlisle contains the world's largest living sign. Back in the 1920s, when the land was owned by the Studebaker Corporation, 8,200 pine trees were planted over an area 250 feet wide and a half-mile long. The trees spell out "Studebaker," but the sign can only be read from the air.

throughout the summer; hours vary. The many adjacent walkways and bridges provide landlubbers with a close-up view of waterway happenings. Located east of the St. Joseph River, along the west side of Niles Avenue and between Jefferson Boulevard on the south and Madison Street on the north. For additional information about competitive events, hours open to the public, and watercraft rental, contact the East Race Waterway and Recreation Corp., 126 North Niles Avenue, South Bend 46617; (219) 233–6121 or the South Bend Parks Department, 301 South St. Louis Boulevard, South Bend 46617; (219) 235–9401.

During spawning season the East Race Waterway also functions as a fish ladder, one of four such ladders on the St. Joseph River. Steelhead trout and Chinook salmon are able to detour around four dams and travel freely along the 63-mile stretch of river between Mishawaka and Lake Michigan. Some 600,000 of those fish are reared annually at the **Richard Clay Bodine State Fish Hatchery** in Mishawaka. Visitors can take a free, self-guided tour of the facilities daily between 8:00 A.M. and 4:00 P.M. Monday through Friday and from 8:00 A.M. to noon Saturday and Sunday. Located at 13200 East Jefferson Boulevard; (219) 255–4199.

In Mishawaka the **100 Center Complex** of shops, restaurants, art galleries, and theaters occupies the original brick buildings of the Kamm & Schellinger Brewery (circa 1853). Located on the south bank of the St. Joseph River at 700 Lincoln Way West; (219) 259–7861.

To the military it's a Humvee; to civilians it's a Hummer. By any name, it's the ultimate sports utility vehicle, and it's made only by A.M. General of South Bend. Aficionado Arnold Schwarzenegger came to South Bend in 1992 to purchase the first one off the assembly line.

Landscape architect Shoji Kanaoka went to Florida and designed the grounds at Epcot Center. He also came to Indiana and designed **Shiojiri Niwa,** a lovely 1.3-acre Japanese strolling garden located in the Merrifield Park Complex at 1000 East Mishawaka Avenue in Mishawaka. Among the garden's many pleasures are Oriental plantings, bridges, a tea garden, and dry waterfalls and streams. Visitors can sample its serenity at any hour of any day. Admission is free. Call the Mishawaka Parks and Recreation Department at (219) 258–1664; fax (219) 258–1736.

On the campus of Bethel College in Mishawaka, you can visit the

Bowen Museum. Dr. Otis Bowen, a physician from Bremen, Indiana, entered politics in 1952. After serving six years as Marshall County Coroner, he was elected to the Indiana House of Representatives, a post he held for fourteen years. Bowen was elected as Indiana's forty-second governor in 1972 and was reelected to a second term by a then-record high margin, the first Indiana governor to serve eight consecutive years. In 1985, at the request of President Ronald Reagan, Bowen became the first physician ever to fill the position of the U.S. Secretary of Health and Human Services. The museum honors the life of one of Indiana's most revered statesmen through displays of personal items, mementos, and official documents. Located in the Bowen Library at 1001 West McKinley Avenue; open from 2:00 to 4:00 P.M. on Wednesday and Saturday or by appointment. Admission is free, but donations are welcome. Call (219) 257–2567 or 257–3347 for additional information.

In 1863 one of the shortest business contracts ever written was signed by the Studebaker brothers for their wagon-making firm at South Bend. It contained two sentences: "I, Henry Studebaker, agree to sell all the wagons my brother Clem can make," and "I, Clem Studebaker, agree to make all the wagons my brother Henry can sell."

Tippecanoe County

The tiny town of Cairo is home to the *Operation Skywatch Memorial,* a limestone statue honoring civilian volunteers in the Korean War. Because there was no national radar system during that conflict, the U.S. Air Force commissioned a nationwide system of observation towers that were manned around the clock by the Civilian Ground Observation Corps. Approximately ninety volunteers from the Cairo area worked in shifts, scanning the skies for enemy planes. The life-size figures of a man, woman, and child, faces turned upward, stand atop the base of the monument, which is inscribed with the words THEY ALSO SERVE WHO STAND AND WATCH. Located in Memorial Park at the junction of County Roads 850 North and 100 West; open during daylight hours.

On November 7, 1811, William Henry Harrison, then governor of the Indiana Territory, led his men in battle against the last all-Indian army to be assembled east of the Mississippi River. The Indians, representing a confederacy of tribes organized by Tecumseh and his brother, the Prophet, went down in defeat, ending any organized Indian resistance to the Europeans' settlement of the Northwest Territory. In later years Harrison's victory was a prominent factor in his successful bid for the presidency of the United States.

In August 1859 the city of Lafayette became the site for the first official airmail flight by the United States Postal Service. Professor John Wise took off in his balloon, the Jupiter, *with a mail pouch that included 123 letters and 23 circulars. Because of a capricious wind, he landed at the wrong destination, but the flight was officially recognized.*

You can see an impressive 85-foot-tall monument and stroll the ninety-six-acre grounds where the battle was actually fought at the *Tippecanoe Battlefield State Memorial* near the town of Battle Ground. A scenic trail leads past several trees that stood during the battle; musket balls are still found in the older trees when they fall. The park is also a peaceful and lovely spot for a picnic— except on those summer weekends when two noisy annual events take place. Players of dulcimers, guitars, mandolins, and more hold all-day, all-night jam sessions during the *Indiana Fiddler's Gathering;* less lyrical sounds fill the air when various types of old machinery rev up their motors at the *Antique Farm Power Show.* The park is open daily, free of charge, year-round during daylight hours. A museum on the grounds presents the history of the battle from both sides' points of view. Open 10:00 A.M. to 5:00 P.M. daily, March through November; 10:00 A.M. through 4:00 P.M. daily, December through February; closed winter holidays. There's a nominal admission fee. Located on Prophet's Rock Road just west of Battle Ground; follow signs; (765) 567–2147.

Construction on nearby *Prophetstown State Park,* under way at press time, can be viewed from the Tippecanoe Battlefield site. The 3,000-acre park will be home to the *Woodland Native American Cultural Center,* the result of more than twenty Great Lakes tribes working together to create a world center for Native American education. Among the planned attractions in Phase I, scheduled for completion in 2001, are a living history village and nearly 200 acres of prairie restoration containing plants native to Indiana. For up-to-date information, contact the Museums at Prophetstown, Inc., 1 Prophetstown Road, General Delivery, Battle Ground 47920; (765) 423–4617.

Movie director Sydney Pollack, born in Lafayette in 1934, won a Best Director Oscar for Out of Africa. *Other movies he's directed include* Tootsie *and* The Way We Were.

On certain nights, full moon or not, you can join a howling at Battle Ground's *Wolf Park.* The eerie but beautiful voices of the resident wolf pack drift through the air and send chills up and down your spine. If you like these misunderstood creatures, it is an experience you will never forget.

This unique wildlife park is a research facility, and you can visit during the day to watch scientists at work. Docents are on hand to tell you each wolf's name and rank order in the pack, and you can see the wolves interact with human beings whom the wolves have accepted as members of their "society." At 1:00 P.M. each Sunday from May through November, predators (wolves) and prey (bison) are placed together to demonstrate that a healthy animal has nothing to fear from wolves.

The park is operated by the nonprofit North American Wildlife Park Foundation, which charges a nominal admission fee to the park to help offset expenses. Advance reservations are required for the howls. The park is open 1:00 to 5:00 P.M. Tuesday through Sunday from the first weekend in May to November 30; howls are held at 7:30 P.M. on Saturday year-round and also at 7:30 P.M. on Friday from May through November (weather permitting). To reach the park go north from Battle Ground on Harrison Road for about 1 mile; Wolf Park signs point the way. Write Wolf Park, c/o North American Wildlife Park Foundation, RFD 1, Battle Ground 47920; (765) 567–2265.

In Lafayette the twenty-acre *Clegg Botanical Gardens* perch on the high bank of Wildcat Creek. Wander along a mile of marked trails that lead past ancient white oaks, sugar maples, and dogwoods. Daffodils bloom in the spring; hybrid daylilies unfold their petals in June and July, followed by resurrection lilies in August and Japanese anemones in September. From Lookout Point you can see the Indiana countryside for miles around. Open 10:00 A.M. to sunset daily; free. Located at 1782 North County Road 400 East; (765) 463–2306 or (800) 872–6648.

The *Red Crown Mini-Museum* in downtown Lafayette can be viewed only from the outside in. Housed in a restored 1928 Standard Oil gas station, one of only seven remaining Standard Oil Products buildings in the nation, the museum exhibits gas station memorabilia and antique cars. Admission is free. Located at 605 South Street, Lafayette; (765) 742–0280.

Trivia
Amelia Earhart joined the staff at Purdue University in West Lafayette in 1935 as a visiting lecturer and counselor for women. In March 1937 she took off from the campus airport in a Lockheed Electra purchased for her by the university. She and her Electra were beginning the now famous around-the-world trip on which she vanished. To this day, her disappearance remains one of the world's great unsolved mysteries.

White County

The small town of Brookston is home to the only professional handmade-paper mill in the country. Located at 100 East Third Street, *Twinrocker Handmade Paper* produces a wide variety of quality papers that range from nonsilver photography paper to archival paper to stationery and everything in between. Owners Kathryn and Howard Clark will design and produce any paper to any specifications a customer wants. Visitors can view the fascinating process on a thirty-minute tour offered at 1:30 P.M. on Tuesday and Thursday. No advance reservations are required. A nominal fee is charged; but after the tour, visitors can purchase paper products for a 25 percent discount. The mill is open from 8:00 A.M. to 5:00 P.M. Monday through Friday.

The Greatest Pacer of Them All

*L*ong before Hoosier basketball fans fell in love with the Indiana Pacers, Hoosiers and the rest of the world fell in love with another pacer. To this day, Dan Patch remains a legend in harness racing.

Born near Oxford in Benton County on April 29, 1896, the mahogany-colored colt was at first a great disappointment to his owner. Dan's sire had been an outstanding pacer, and Dan's owner had hoped the son would inherit his father's greatness. When Dan was born bow-legged and awkward, that hope dimmed, but the ugly duckling grew into a swan.

Dan began racing in 1900 at age four and won every race he entered. By July 1902 there was no one left who wanted to match his horse against Dan, so Dan began racing only against the clock in exhibitions. At the 1906 Minnesota State Fair, Dan paced a mile in one minute, fifty-five seconds, a world record. Although unofficial, the record was generally accepted and remained unbroken for thirty-two years.

During his lifetime the charismatic Dan Patch became one of the most successfully merchandised sports figures in history. His name and likeness were used to endorse thirty products, including china, stopwatches, livestock feed, tobacco, washing machines, toys, and manure spreaders.

There was a Dan Patch automobile that sold for $525. People danced the Dan Patch Two-Step to the song of the same name. Hollywood immortalized him in a 1949 movie called The Great Dan Patch. A Dan Patch thermometer, originally a promotional giveaway, was on sale at an Indiana antiques store in 1998 for $3,000.

Dan is still remembered in his hometown, too. Beginning in 1901, Oxford has honored its famous son with an annual event known as Dan Patch Days. The humble white barn near Oxford in which Dan Patch was born proudly bears the words DAN PATCH 1:55 in large letters on a green-shingled roof.

Dan had more than one owner in his lifetime. His final owner, M. W. Savage of Minneapolis, cherished and provided well for his champion horse. Dan traveled around the country in a private railroad car adorned on each side with his portrait. The huge Minnesota barn in which Dan was stabled was so elaborate it was nicknamed the "Taj Mahal." It was in this barn that Dan died on July 7, 1916, at the age of twenty. His owner died thirty-two hours later.

On September 14, 1999, USA Today featured its choices for the eight great animal athletes of the century. Among them was Dan Patch, described by the newspaper as probably the greatest pacer of all time.

Twinrocker also sells papermaking supplies and offers workshops. For additional information contact Twinrocker Handmade Paper, P.O. Box 413, Brookston 47923; (765) 563–3119.

Before leaving Brookston, stop in at the *Klein Brot Haus,* a German bakery and cafe whose homemade breads are as unique as the papers made by its neighbor. Located at 106 East Third Street; (765) 563–3788.

> **Trivia**
>
> *In the 1800s Yale University owned nearly ten square miles of land in Benton County. The school purchased the rich farmland as an investment.*

PLACES TO STAY IN NORTHWEST INDIANA

ATTICA
Apple Inn Museum B&B
604 South Brady Street
(765) 762–6574

BEVERLY SHORES
Dunes Shore Inn
33 Lakeshore County Road
(219) 879–9029

CHESTERTON
Gray Goose Inn
350 Indiana Boundary Road
(219) 926–5781

COVINGTON
Green Gables Bed and Breakfast
504 Fancy Street
(765) 793–7164

CRAWFORDSVILLE
Yount's Mill Inn
3729 Old State Road 32 West
(765) 362–5864

DARLINGTON
Our Country Home Bed and Breakfast Stable and Carriage Company
Route 1, Box 103 (County Road 550 North)
(765) 794–3139

LADOGA
Vintage Reflections
125 West Main Street
(765) 942–1002

LAFAYETTE
Historic Loeb House Inn
708 Cincinnati Street
(765) 420–7737

LAPORTE
Arbor Hill Inn
263 West Johnson Road
(219) 362–9200

Boathouses on the East Shore
1004 Lakeside Street
(219) 362–5077
(800) 720–3990

MICHIGAN CITY
Brickstone Bed and Breakfast
215 West Sixth Street
(219) 878–1819

Creekwood Inn
U.S. Highways 20/35 at I–94 (Exit 40B)
(219) 872–8357

Duneland Beach Inn
3311 Pottawattamie Trail
(219) 874–7729

The Hutchinson Mansion Inn
220 West Tenth Street
(219) 879–1700

MISHAWAKA
Beiger Mansion Inn
317 Lincoln Way East
(800) 437–0131

MONTICELLO
1887 Black Dog Inn
2390 Untaluti Street
(219) 583–8297

Quiet Water Bed and Breakfast
4794 East Harbor Court
(219) 583–6023

The Victoria Bed and Breakfast
206 South Bluff Street
(219) 583–3440

SOUTH BEND
The Book Inn Bed and Breakfast
508 West Washington Street
(219) 288–1990
http://members.aol.com/bookinn/

The Inn at Saint Mary's
53993 U.S. Highways 31/33 North
(219) 232–4000
(800) 947–8627

The Oliver Inn Bed and Breakfast
630 West Washington Street
(219) 232–4545
Fax: (219) 288–9788
e-mail: oliver@michiana.org
http://michiana.org/users/oliver

Queen Anne Inn
420 West Washington Street
(219) 234–5959

TIPPECANOE
Bessinger's Hillfarm
Wildlife Refuge
4588 State Road 110
(219) 223–3288

VALPARAISO
Inn at Aberdeen
3158 South State Road 2
(219) 465–3753

WALKERTON
Hesters Log B&B
71880 State Road 23
(219) 586–2105

Koontz House Bed and
Breakfast
7514 North State Road 23
(219) 586–2105

WINAMAC
Tortuga Inn
2142 North 125 East
(219) 946–6969

**PLACES TO EAT IN
NORTHWEST INDIANA**

BATTLE GROUND
TC's Restaurant and
Tavern
109 North Railroad Street
(765) 567–2838

BROOKSTON
Klein Brot Haus
106 East Third Street
(765) 563–3788

Top Notch Bar and Grill
113 South Third Street
(765) 563–6508

CEDAR LAKE
The Bread Basket
13951 Huseman Street
(219) 374–4661

COVINGTON
Beef House
I–74 and State Road 63
(765) 793–3947

Maple Corner Restaurant
1126 Liberty Street
(765) 793–2224

CROWN POINT
Bronko's
1244 North Main Street
(219) 662–0145

Chocolate Cafe
192 West Joliet Street
(219) 662–9667

Crown Kitchen
111 North Main Street
(219) 663–7466

Cynthia's Cafe
110 South Main Street
(219) 662–7779
Fax: (219) 662–8390

Truffles Caffe
400 North Main Street
(219) 662–7764

Twelve Islands
114 South Main Street
(219) 663–5070

CULVER
Cafe Max
113 South Main Street
(219) 842–2511

Pinder's
South Main and Ohio Streets
(219) 842–3415

GRIFFITH
Stan's Steak and
Seafood House
216 South Broad Street
(219) 924–4767

HAMMOND
El Taco Real
935 Hoffman Street
(219) 932–8333

Phil Smidt's Restaurant
1205 North Calumet Avenue
(219) 659–0025

HEBRON
Marti's Place at
Ramsey's Landing
17519 North 700 West
(219) 996–3363

HOBART
Country Lounge
3700 Montgomery Street
(219) 942–6699

KNOX
Ernie's Fireside Inn
902 South Heaton Street
(219) 772–3746

The Shore Club Restaurant
3698 South County
Road 210
(219) 772–3363

KOUTS
Birky's Cafe
205 South Main Street
(219) 766–3851

LAFAYETTE
Arni's
2200 Elmwood Avenue
(765) 447–1108

Hacienda Mexican
Restaurant
112 North Main Street
(765) 423–2347

Patout's of New Orleans
3614 State Road 38 East
(765) 447–5400

Romney's Coffee Shop
Intersection of U.S.
Highways 28 and 231
(765) 538–2834

Sarge Oak
721 Main Street
(765) 742–5230

Sergeant Preston's of
the North
6 North Second Street
(765) 742–7378

LAKEVILLE
Jack's Bar and Grill
117 South Michigan Street
(219) 784–9939

LAPORTE
Christo's Family Dining
1462 West State Road 2
(219) 326–1644

Kelsey's Steak House
304 Detroit Street
(219) 325–0000

Roskoe's
1004 Lakeside Street
(219) 325–3880

Tangerine
601 Michigan Avenue
(219) 326–8000

LOWELL
George's Family Restaurant
1910 East Commercial
Avenue
(219) 696–0313

The Hindquarter
1900 Lucas Parkway
(219) 696–8344

MERRILLVILLE
The Odyssey Restaurant
7876 Broadway Street
(219) 738–2242

MICHIGAN CITY
The American Grill
5727 North 600 West
(219) 874–4603

Blue Ribbon Cafe
1407 Franklin Street
(219) 879–5702

Fortune House
312 West U.S. Highway 20
(219) 872–6664

Maxine and Heines
Restaurant and Pub
521 Franklin Square
(219) 872–4500

Rodini Restaurant
4125 Franklin Street
(219) 879–7388

Swingbelly's
103 South Lake Avenue
(219) 874–5718

MILLER BEACH (GARY)
The Beach Cafe
903 North Shelby Street
(219) 938–9890

Miller Bakery Cafe
555 South Lake Street
(219) 938–2229

MONTICELLO
Oakdale Inn
U.S. Highway 421 and
State Road 39
(219) 965–9104

MUNSTER
Giovanni's
603 Ridge Road
(U.S. Highway 6)
(219) 836–6220

NEW CARLISLE
Miller's Home Cafe
110 East Michigan Street
(219) 654–3431

PLYMOUTH
Hayloft
15147 Lincolnway West
(219) 936–6680

PORTAGE
The Savoy Supper Club
2542 Portage Mall
(219) 762–4114

RENSSELAER
City Office and Pub
114 South Van
Rensselaer Street
(219) 866–9916

ROCHESTER
Evergreen Cafe
530 Main Street
(219) 223–1809

ROLLING PRAIRIE
Blacksmith Shoppe
Depot and Mechanic
Streets
(219) 879–7944

ST. JOHN
Apollo Family Restaurant
9141 Wicker Avenue
(219) 365–8733

SCHERERVILLE
Teibel's Restaurant
U.S. Highways 30 and 41
(219) 865–2000

SOUTH BEND
East Bank Emporium
Restaurant
121 South Niles Avenue
(219) 234–9000

Hans Haus
2803 South Michigan Street
(219) 291–5522

Heartland Texas Barbecue
222 South Michigan Street
(219) 234–5200

LaSalle Grill
115 West Colfax Avenue
(219) 288–1155
(800) 382–9323

Tippecanoe Place
620 West Washington
Avenue
(219) 234–9077

VALPARAISO
Billy Jack's Cafe and Grill
2904 Calumet Avenue
(219) 477–3797

China House
120 East Lincolnway
(219) 462–5788

Clayton's
66 West Lincolnway
(219) 531–0612

Restaurante Don Quijote
119 East Lincolnway
(219) 462–7976

Strongbow Turkey Inn
Junction of State Road 49
and U.S. Highway 30
(219) 462–5121
(800) 462–5121

Wagner's Ribs Too
597 West U.S. Highway 30
(219) 759–6334

WHITING
Purple Steer Restaurant
1402 Indianapolis
Boulevard
(219) 659–3950

Vogel's
1250 Indianapolis
Boulevard
(219) 659–1250

SOURCES FOR ADDITIONAL
INFORMATION ABOUT
NORTHWEST INDIANA

Greater Lafayette
Convention and Visitors
Bureau (Tippecanoe
County)
301 Frontage Road
Lafayette 47905
(765) 447–9999
(800) 872–6648
Fax: (765) 447–5062
E-mail: glcvb@pop.nlci.com
www.lafayette-in.com

Greater Monticello/White
County Chamber
of Commerce
116 North Main Street
P.O. Box 657
Monticello 47960
(219) 583–7220
(219) 583–3399

Lake County Convention
and Visitors Bureau
7770 Corinne Drive
Hammond 46323
(219) 980–1617
(800) ALL–LAKE

LaPorte County Convention
and Visitors Bureau
1503 South Meer Road
Michigan City 46360
(219) 872–5055
(800) 634–2650
Fax: (219) 872–3660

Logansport/Cass County
Chamber of Commerce
300 East Broadway Street,
Suite 103
Logansport 46947
(219) 753–6388

Marshall County Conven-
tion and Visitors Bureau
220 North Center Street
P.O. Box 669
Plymouth 46563
(219) 936–9000
(800) 626–5353
Fax: (219) 936–9845

Montgomery County
Convention and Visitors
Bureau
412 East Main Street
Crawfordsville 47933
(765) 362–5200
(800) 866–3973
Fax: (765) 362–5215

Newton County Chamber
of Commerce
c/o Kentland Bank
111 North Fourth Street
P.O. Box 273
Kentland 47951
(219) 474–6665
Fax: (219) 474–5071

Porter County Convention,
Recreation, and Visitor's
Commission
800 Indian Boundary Road
Chesterton 46304
(219) 926–2255
(800) 283–8687
Fax: (219) 929–5395

South Bend/Mishawaka
Convention and
Visitors Bureau (St. Joseph
County)
401 East Colfax Street, #310
P.O. Box 1677
South Bend 46634-1677
(219) 234–0051
(800) 828–7881
Fax: (219) 289–0358

Southeast Indiana

Beauty and history exist side by side in southeast Indiana. Although I–70 on the north, I–65 on the west, and I–74 in between carve the landscape into two pie-shaped wedges, the land between those ribbons of highway is some of the loveliest the state has to offer. This is also the land where history began in Indiana, sweeping in on the waters of the beautiful Ohio River. The first settlers found woodlands so dense, it is said, that a squirrel could make its way across the state without ever once having to touch the ground.

Today a scenic highway winds along the banks of the Ohio, taking those who will spend the time on a voyage of discovery. Antiques lovers may think they've died and gone to heaven. History buffs will find museums galore, with unique treasures tucked away in their corners.

Bartholomew County

According to an article that appeared in the *New York Times Magazine* in recent years, "there is really no equivalent to **Columbus** anywhere." That's just one of many tributes this town of 31,000 people has received from around the world in recognition of its architecture. Sixty-five public and private buildings make up the most concentrated collection of contemporary architecture on Earth, and the names of the architects, artists, designers, and sculptors who created them are right from the pages of *Who's Who*. Where else, for instance, can you walk out of a church designed by Eliel Saarinen, cross the street, pass a Henry Moore sculpture, and enter a library designed by I. M. Pei?

Trivia
The only car to ever complete the Indianapolis 500 without a single stop was a diesel-powered car entered in the 1931 race by Cummins Engine Company of Columbus.

One of the most visually striking buildings is the **North Christian Church,** designed by Eero Saarinen (Eliel's son). A low, hexagon-shaped building, it has a sloping roof centered by a 192-foot-tall needlelike spire

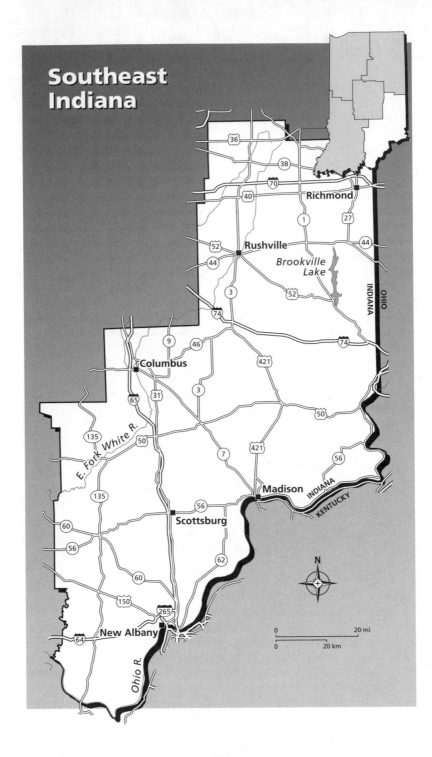

Southeast
Indiana

that's topped by a gold-leaf cross. The multilevels of *Smith Elementary School,* created by John M. Johansen, are connected by several brightly colored, tube-shaped ramps—pure delight for the children who use them. *Clifty Creek Elementary School* was designed by Richard Meier, the architect who also designed the spectacular new J. Paul Getty Fine Arts Center that sprawls atop a Brentwood, California, hilltop. The sanctuary of *St. Peter's Lutheran Church,* topped by an 85-foot-tall, copper-clad steeple, rises in Byzantine-like splendor above its surroundings—beautiful at any time, but especially so when touched by the sun. Just east of town the sprawling *Otter Creek Clubhouse,* designed by Harry Weese, lies adjacent to one of the finest public golf courses in the country; Robert Trent Jones, who laid out the course, says its thirteenth hole is the single best hole he's ever designed.

The beauty of the downtown area is enhanced by a sprawling white structure that serves as the world headquarters of *Cummins Engine Company,* Columbus's oldest and leading firm. Outside, graceful fountains feed shallow ponds and fingers of vines meander up the walls. Inside, within the glassed-in lobby, a diesel engine—the product that first brought fame to the company—is displayed as an abstract sculpture. Since 1957, as part of its commitment to a quality environment for all town residents, the Cummins Foundation has paid the fees of all leading architects chosen by the town leaders, contributing to the overall design of the city itself.

Not all of these buildings will knock the socks off you at first sight. To fully appreciate them, you should learn something about the innovative functions and attention to details that lie behind the facades. Many will amaze you when you learn the years in which they were constructed; the *First Christian Church,* built in 1942, could just as easily have been built yesterday.

Author's Favorite Attractions/ Events in Southeast Indiana

Falls of the Ohio State Park,
Clarksville; (812) 280–9970

Indiana Basketball Hall of Fame,
New Castle; (765) 529–1891

Red Wolf Sanctuary,
Dillsboro; (812) 667–5303

Squire Boone Caverns,
Corydon; (812) 732–4381

Wayne County Historical Museum,
Richmond; (765) 962–5756

Whitewater Canal State Historic Site,
Metamora; (765) 647–2109

Zimmerman Art Glass Factory,
Corydon; (812) 738–2206

Aviation Heritage Air Show, Jeffersonville;
September (Labor Day weekend) (812) 282–6654

Canaan Fall Festival,
Canaan;
September (812) 839–4770

National Muzzle Loading Rifle Association National Championship Shoot,
Friendship; June
(812) 667–5131

Old-Fashioned Christmas Walk, Metamora;
November/December
weekends (765) 647–2109

Railroad Days Festival,
North Vernon; June
(812) 346–7377

Scottish Festival,
Columbus;
July (812) 378–2622
or (800) 468–6564

North Christian Church

Columbus also has its share of renovations and historical buildings, but it is the modern architecture that has brought this small town fame as the "Athens of the Prairie."

Begin your tour at the *Columbus Area Visitors Center,* housed in a nineteenth-century home at 506 Fifth Street; (812) 378–2622. You'll find interactive exhibits that call up images of the area's best-known architecture, including a special child-oriented section, a fifteen-minute video presentation about the city's architectural heritage, and an eye-catching yellow neon chandelier that highlights a two-story bay window.

Measuring 9 feet high by 6 feet across and weighing 1,200 pounds, the chandelier is the creation of world-renowned glass artist Dale Chihuly. The unique work of art contains 900 pieces of hand-blown glass in four shades of yellow and 50 feet of neon tubing. Chihuly, who studied glassblowing in Italy, is the first American glassblower ever

Trivia

Flambeau Products Corporation in Columbus supplies the world with Duncan yo-yos, no easy task since a global craze began in recent years. In 1998 yo-yo sales were estimated at fifty million, breaking the company's previous record of forty-two million sold in 1962.

permitted to work on the island of Murano, a carefully guarded and iso-lated Italian glassmaking center that dates to the thirteenth century. Pres-ident Clinton often gives smaller Chihuly pieces as gifts to world leaders when he travels abroad.

You can also pick up brochures, maps, and descriptive cassette tapes for self-guided tours of the city or make advance reservations for a minibus guided tour, available daily April through October. The center is open 9:00 A.M. to 5:00 P.M. Monday through Saturday and 10:00 A.M. to 2:00 P.M. Sunday, April through October; hours vary the rest of the year. For additional information contact the Columbus Area Visitor Information Commission, P.O. Box 1477, Columbus 47202–1477; (812) 378–2622 or (800) 468–6564.

There's nothing contemporary about *Zaharako's Confectionery* in downtown Columbus—it's pure nostalgia. Located at the same address since October 1900, the store is now a Columbus institution. Its fixtures carry you back to the beginning of the century—Mexican onyx soda fountains purchased from the St. Louis World Exposition in 1905, a full-concert mechanical pipe organ brought here from Germany in 1908 that rings out with tunes of the Gay Nineties, an exquisite Tiffany lamp, and accessories of carved mahogany. Amid these ornate surroundings you can enjoy homemade ice cream, fountain treats, and an assortment of candy and sandwiches. You'll find the store at 329 Washington Street, (812) 379–9329, across the street from Columbus's ultramodern, award-winning shopping mall and special events center, *The Commons,* designed by Cesar Pelli.

Completely enclosed, The Commons houses a unique playground that children will want to take home with them. Also here is **Chaos I,** a seven-ton, 30-foot-tall, in-motion sculpture crafted out of scrap metal by Swiss artist Jean Tinguely; the piece becomes more intrigu-ing the longer you look at it.

In 1895 the Romanesque Revival building at the corner of Fifth and Franklin Streets was the brand new Columbus City Hall. Today it is an elegant bed-and-breakfast inn that ranks as one of the Midwest's finest. Meticulously renovated, the *Columbus Inn* combines the best of past and present. Each of the thirty rooms and five suites contains American Empire–style cherry furnishings—including beds that were custom-made in France—and some beautiful antiques. The efficiency kitchens in the suites boast microwave ovens, linen nap-kins, and French crystal. For breakfast, guests are served such fare as an egg casserole (a unique dish that has contributed greatly to the

Trivia

One of the most successful self-help books in recent years is The 7 Habits of Highly Effective People. *It has sold upwards of six million copies in North America alone and has been translated into twenty-eight languages. Stephen Covey, its author, is a former business professor at Brigham Young University who is based in Provo, Utah.*

A few years back, Covey signed up six "experimental" communities to be the beneficiaries of 7 Habits *training. One of those communities was Columbus, Indiana (population 35,000). Covey's goal is to train every citizen in the 7* Habits, *thereby improving (theoretically) the performance of every organization and the quality of life for every citizen.*

One Columbus Chamber of Commerce executive expressed the purpose of the city's participation: "What we want is to have productive, happy people. . . . I think this can be life-changing."

Only time will tell, of course, but Columbus would seem an ideal choice for such an experiment. It is a community that personifies civic pride.

inn's growing fame), fruit salad, homemade bread, and imported tea. Rates for two range from about $120 to $190 per night. For reservations write the inn at 445 Fifth Street, Columbus 47201, or call (812) 378–4289. Both guests and nonguests are invited to partake of afternoon tea from noon to 4:00 P.M., and high tea from 4:00 to 6:00 P.M.; prices range from $4.95 to $6.95.

On the north side of Columbus is the city's municipal airport, originally built during World War II as the Atterbury Air Base. The *Atterbury-Bakalar Air Base Museum* at the airport pays tribute to military aviators who served their country between 1942 and 1970. Among the memorabilia are uniforms, flight jackets, and scale models of vintage aircraft. Homage is also paid to one of the least-known units of World War II—the pilots who flew the 6,000 gliders known as the "Silent Wings." Towed aloft by C-47s, the engineless planes were cut loose to silently infiltrate enemy territory and deliver their cargoes of infantrymen and munitions. The U.S. Army trained the pilots to fight on the ground as well, but each flight was obviously a one-way mission, and casualties were high.

The museum also honors the famous Tuskegee Airmen, a special unit of black Americans that was composed of graduates of the Tuskegee Institute in Alabama. During World War II, some of those men trained at Atterbury Air Base in B-25 bombers. Their combat record was unblemished—no bomber flown by a Tuskegee Airman was ever lost to the enemy. In addition to an indoor exhibit, the airmen are memorialized in an outdoor monument that stands on Bakalar Green just south of the airport terminal. The museum is located at 4742 Ray Boll Boulevard; admission is free. Open daily, but hours may vary; call (812) 372–4356.

Clark County

Along the banks of the Ohio River in **Clarksville** lies a 400-million-year-old fossil bed that is one of the world's greatest natural wonders. Its rare and unusual formations date back to the Devonian age and have for decades attracted sightseers and scientists from around the world. Once the reef was covered by the Falls of the Ohio, a raging, 2-mile stretch of water below Louisville in which the Ohio River dropped 22 feet over limestone ledges. Now the Ohio has been reduced to a series of pools by a string of dams, and the controlled water levels have left the reef high and dry. Its fossil corals archaeological sites are among the best in the country, and the variety of its migratory bird life is unparalleled at any other inland location.

For years efforts have been under way to preserve this area. The first step in realizing that dream occurred in October 1984, when the U.S. Senate approved funding for the creation of the **Falls of the Ohio**

Indiana Fried Chicken?

Few people know that Colonel Harland Sanders was born in the tiny southern Indiana town of Henryville. As a matter of fact, few people who live in Henryville knew it until recently. Young Harland loved to cook even as a boy, a skill that served him and his family well. Harland was just five years old when his father died in 1895, and his mother had to go to work to support her family. It fell to Harland to take care of many of the household chores, including much of the cooking. One of his specialties was fried chicken.

When he was barely into his teens, the young man went to work as a farmhand and then as a streetcar conductor in New Albany before enlisting in the army as an underage recruit (easy to do in those days). He later sold insurance in Jeffersonville; started a ferry company that ran boats across the Ohio River between Jeffersonville and Louisville, Kentucky; and worked as a secretary for the Columbus, Indiana, Chamber of Commerce. There he also launched a manufacturing company that went belly-up when his firm's product became obsolete. Off Harland went to Kentucky, where he progressed from tire salesman to gas station manager to restaurant owner. Finally, it seemed, Harland had found his niche. Kentucky Fried Chicken became one of the most successful food franchises in history.

Harland also knew talent when he saw it. During a visit to a Fort Wayne franchise, he was impressed with the work ethic of a young man who worked there and predicted that the industrious employee would someday amount to something. Indeed, the young man did. Dave Thomas moved on to found Wendy's.

Trivia

In October 1803 Meriwether Lewis and William Clark began their epic journey to explore the Louisiana Purchase and the Pacific Northwest near the present-day site of Clarksville. The two explorers and their Corps of Discovery assembled here at the homesite of General George Rogers Clark, a military hero who was William's older brother.

National Wildlife Conservation Area. In 1990 sixty-eight acres of land were dedicated as Indiana's newest state park. Although relatively small itself, the *Falls of the Ohio State Park* lies within the 1,404 acres of the federally protected conservation area, providing lots of wide-open space to explore.

A 16,000-square-foot interpretive center, perched atop a bluff overlooking the fossil beds, opened to the public in January 1994. The building's exterior features horizontal bands of Indiana limestone alternating with bands of earth-toned bricks, creating a layered look reminiscent of the geological treasure that sprawls below it.

Inside, exhibits lead visitors back through the millennia to a time when ancient Indiana lay about twenty degrees south of the equator beneath the warm waters of a tropical sea. An orientation video employs the latest laser technology to portray the history of the falls. The use of underwater oceanic photography to re-create a 400-million-year-old tropical sea is a first in the film industry. In a wildlife observation room, human visitors can view some of the area's 265 species of avian visitors in a small garden area. Elsewhere, the center offers panoramic views of the Ohio River, a historic railroad bridge, the McAlpine Dam and Locks, and the fossil bed itself (best seen from August through October, when the river is at its lowest level).

Low-water periods also provide the best opportunity to explore the fossil bed. More than 600 fossil species have been identified, and two-thirds of those were discovered here for the first time anywhere in the world. Visitors may walk among the eroded rock slabs and search for fossils freed from the bedrock by the powerful waters of the river. Handling of the fossils is encouraged, but they must be returned to their original locations. Collecting is strictly forbidden.

Other activities include fishing, picnicking, and hiking along park trails.

The park is located on the south side of Riverside Drive, about a mile west of U.S. 31. A nominal admission fee is charged for both the park and the interpretive center, which are open 9:00 A.M. to 5:00 P.M. daily year-round. For additional information contact Falls of the Ohio State Park, 201 West Riverside Drive, P.O. Box 1327, Clarksville 47131-1327; (812) 280–9970.

Presiding over Clarksville is the town's own version of London's Big Ben. The main building of the Colgate-Palmolive plant at State and Woerner streets is topped by the *second-largest clock in the world,* which is a monstrous 40 feet in diameter and has a 16-foot-long hour hand that weighs 500 pounds. (The largest clock in the world, 50 feet in diameter, sits on the former site of a Colgate plant in Jersey City, New Jersey.) No one in Clarksville gets away with saying he doesn't know the time—the electric-powered clock is reputed to be accurate to within fifteen seconds a month, the clock's face can be read from a distance of $2^1/_2$ miles, and the clock is illuminated at night.

You can take a free tour of Colgate's facilities at 9:00 A.M. each Tuesday if you make an advance appointment; call Employee Relations at (812) 283–6611. The plant, which produces an array of household and personal care products, is housed in a building that once served as Indiana's first state prison.

Jeffersonville, which adjoins Clarksville to the east, is home to the biggest inland boatbuilders in North America. You can see them at work along the waterfront building cruise ships, ferries, towboats, barges, and—with the recent arrival of riverboat gambling in Indiana—gaming boats. The company, known as *Jeffboat, Inc.,* has its offices at 1030 East Market Street; call (812) 288–0200 or (812) 288–0400.

Annual Events in Southeast Indiana

Madison Regatta,
Madison; July (812) 265–5000
or (800) 559–2956

Swiss Wine Festival,
Vevay; August (800) 435–5688

**Jennings County Historical
Society Labor Day Antique and
Collectibles Market,**
Town of Vernon; Labor Day weekend
(812) 346–4865 or (800) 928–3667

Blue Jeans Festival,
Rising Sun; September
(812) 438–4933 or (888) RSNG–SUN

Madison Chautauqua,
Madison; September
(812) 265–2956 or (800) 559–2956

Steamboat Days Festival,
Jeffersonville; September
(812) 284–BOAT

Autumn on the River Festival,
Bethlehem; October
(812) 282–6654

Ethnic Expo,
Columbus; October (812) 376–2502

Stumler Applefest,
Starlight; October (812) 923–3832
or 923–5819

Tree City Fall Festival,
Greensburg; October (812) 663–2832

Southern Indiana is the only place in the world where Deam's foxglove, a vascular plant, occurs naturally.

Each summer one of Jeffersonville's own comes home to visit. The **Mississippi Queen** passenger steamboat, built locally by Jeffboat, pauses here during its annual treks up and down the Ohio and Mississippi rivers. Her older sister, the **Delta Queen,** also stops here; both can be toured when they're tied up at the pier. Call (800) 543–1949 for schedules and information.

Until 1931 the Howard Shipyards were in Jeffersonville. During their 107 years in business, the yards produced some 3,000 steamboats, reported to be the finest ever to ply the waters of North and Central America. The *J. M. White,* the most luxurious steamboat in history, was built here, as were the *Glendy Burke,* which inspired the Stephen Foster song of the same name; the *City of Louisville,* the fastest steamboat ever built; and the *Cape Girardeau,* captured on film for all time in *Gone with the Wind.*

The steamboat era was flourishing in the 1890s when construction began on the elaborate twenty-two-room Howard mansion at 1101 East Market Street that today houses the **Howard Steamboat Museum.** A striking late-Victorian structure, the house features stained- and leaded-glass windows, a Moorish-style music room that contains its original Louis XV furniture, and intricate embellishments that were hand carved from fifteen types of wood.

You can see all this today, plus a priceless collection of relics that played a role in the golden era of steamboating, miniature models of Howard-built steamboats, and whole rooms furnished like staterooms on the finest turn-of-the-century boats. Open 10:00 A.M. to 3:00 P.M. Tuesday through Saturday and 1:00 to 3:00 P.M. Sunday; closed Monday and major holidays. There's a nominal admission fee. Write the Clark County Historical Society at P.O. Box 606, Jeffersonville 47130, or call (812) 283–3728 for further details.

In 1991 **Schimpff's Confectionery** at 347 Spring Street celebrated its hundredth birthday. An old-fashioned candy store complete with soda fountain and tin ceiling, Schimpff's is one of the oldest continuously family-owned candy businesses in the country. Its cinnamon red-hot squares are a particular favorite, ordered through the mail by people from around the world. The folks in Bakersfield, California, for example, order sixty to eighty pounds of red hots annually. All candies are handmade, just as they were a century ago. They're all scrumptious, and the ice cream's good, too! Open 10:00 A.M. to 5:00 P.M. Monday through Friday and 10:00 A.M. to 3:00 P.M. Saturday; (812) 283–8367.

Something's always going on at the 550-acre Huber Farm near Borden. Officially billed as the *Huber Orchard, Winery, and U-Pick Farm,* it's open to the public year-round. Strawberries are ripe for the picking from mid-May through mid-June. Twelve varieties of apples are in season from late summer through December. You can select your own pumpkin right from the patch in the fall and cut your own Christmas tree in December. Cider made on the farm each fall is available for purchase at any time.

Brothers Gerald and Carl Huber, along with their families, have turned their talents to commercial wine making in recent years, and thus far they've garnered more than one hundred awards for their efforts, including "Best of Show" at several Indiana State Fairs and a silver medal at the prestigious Eastern International Wine Competition in 1991. Visitors can sample their eighteen varieties and tour the winery. The Hubers also make cheese on their farm, and visitors can watch this process as well. You can buy the makings of a picnic lunch, as well as ready-made sandwiches and cheese trays, right on the farm. The winery, the cheese factory, and a gift shop are open Tuesday through Sunday year-round, but hours vary. Call (812) 923–WINE or (800) 345–WINE for hours and exact directions, or write the Hubers at 19816 Huber Road, Starlight 47106. You may also fax the Hubers at (812) 923–3013.

Trivia
The chief engineer on the Hoover Dam project on the Colorado River at the Arizona-Nevada state line was Dr. Elwood Mead of Patriot. Upon completion of the project in 1936, the huge reservoir created by the dam was named Lake Mead in honor of the Hoosier native.

Just down the road, on a 360-acre farm, cousin Joe runs the *Joe Huber Family Farm and Restaurant.* The down-home country cooking, which features fried chicken, fried biscuits, and fresh fruit and vegetables, is served family style. Open 11:00 A.M. to 8:00 P.M. Monday through Thursday, 11:00 A.M. to 10:00 P.M. Friday and Saturday, and 11:00 A.M. to 6:00 P.M. Sunday, March through December. Located at 2421 Scottsville Road; (812) 923–5255; fax (812) 923–0583.

After visiting the *Forest Discovery Center* in Starlight, you may never look at a tree in the same way again. Step into the massive building and enter an indoor forest, complete with trees, a stream, the natural music of the woodlands (recorded), and re-creations of the creatures that live there. A television set imbedded in a tree trunk plays a video describing the many uses of a tree. Elsewhere you'll find a giant, walk-through oak tree, a 1,000-square-foot mural created from small pieces of wood, a children's play area with interactive games, and a gift shop. Artisans and craftspeople display their creations and discuss woodworking techniques.

The center was built by the Koetter family, which owns and operates Koetter Woodworking, a state-of-the-art lumber mill that's adjacent to the center. Visitors can access the plant via a glass-enclosed sidewalk and watch the manufacturing process from a series of elevated catwalks. You'll see logs enter one end of the building and exit the other as a finished product. Along the way, the logs are sawed, planed, dried, ripped for width, and chopped for length—all done by high-tech computerized equipment. What's more, not one bit of a log goes to waste. The sawdust generated along the way is burned to provide the electricity that powers the plant, and the steam created by the burning provides the heat used in the kilns to dry the lumber.

The center is open 9:00 A.M. to 5:00 P.M. Tuesday through Saturday and 1:00 to 5:00 P.M. on Sunday. The mill can be toured during the same

Other Attractions Worth Seeing in Southeast Indiana

CAMBRIDGE CITY

Huddleston Farmhouse Inn Museum,
U.S. Highway 40 East; (765) 478–3172

CENTERVILLE

Scott Shafer Stoneware,
610 North Morton Avenue; (765) 855–2409

COLUMBUS

Irwin Home and Sunken Gardens,
608 Fifth Street; (812) 372–1954

CORYDON

Corydon Capitol State Historic Site,
202 East Walnut Street; (812) 738–4890

KNIGHTSTOWN

Carthage, Knightstown & Shirley Railroad Round-Trip Excursion,
CKS Depot, 112 West Carey Street; (765) 345–5561

Trump's Texaco Museum
39 North Washington Street; (765) 345–7135

MADISON

Madison Railroad Station and Historical Society Museum,
615 West First Street; (812) 265–2335

NEW ALBANY

Culbertson Mansion State Historic Site, 914 East Main Street; (812) 944–9600

RICHMOND

Gaar Mansion,
2593 Pleasant View Road; (765) 935–8687

RISING SUN

Ohio County Historical Society Museum,
212 South Walnut Street; (812) 438–2056 or 438–3751

SALEM

Stevens Memorial Museum,
307 East Market Street; (812) 883–6495

VEVAY

Switzerland County Historical Society Museum,
Main and Market Streets; (812) 427–3560

hours but can be seen in operation only on weekdays. Both are included for a nominal admission fee. For additional information contact the Forest Discovery Center, 533 Louis Smith Road, Starlight 47106; (812) 923–1590; fax (812) 923–1595.

Dearborn County

*A*top a wooded hillside overlooking the village of *Aurora* stands a splendid yellow frame house filled with the memories of a bygone era. It was built in the 1850s by Thomas Gaff, a wealthy industrialist and shipping magnate whose steamboats regularly plied the waters of the Ohio River far below.

Gaff's love for the river ran deep, and that love is reflected in his home, *Hillforest Mansion,* whose architectural style is often referred to as "steamboat Gothic." And indeed it does resemble a steamboat in part, with its rounded front porticoes and cupola, coupled columns, and suspended interior staircase—all features that were typical of the "floating palaces" that graced the nation's rivers in the heyday of river transportation.

Trivia
The ministry of Henry Ward Beecher, a noted nineteenth-century clergyman, began in 1837 at a Presbyterian church in Lawrenceburg. He spoke eloquently against slavery, a cause that was further espoused by his sister, Harriet Beecher Stowe, in her novel Uncle Tom's Cabin.

Now restored and filled with antique furniture, the entire mansion can be toured, from its wine cellar up to the observatory at the top of the house. The view of the Ohio River is just as beautiful as it was when Thomas Gaff himself stood here. Around the one-of-a-kind home are ten acres of grounds laid out in the grand manner of an Italian villa. Open 1:00 to 5:00 P.M. Tuesday through Sunday, April through December 23; admission fee; situated at 213 Fifth Street; (812) 926–0087.

About $2^1/_2$ miles west of Aurora on U.S. Highway 50, you'll find an attractive restaurant built around a living tree; it's called appropriately enough, *The Tree House.* Hanging plants, brick archways, and a glass roof contribute to the garden atmosphere. Specialties of the house include barbecued ribs, veal parmesan, seafood, filet mignon, and prime rib, which, at dinnertime, will cost you from about $11 to $20. Buffets are offered Friday night and Sunday. Children's menus are available; reservations are recommended. Open 11:00 A.M. to 9:00 P.M. Tuesday through Thursday; 11:00 A.M. to 10:00 P.M. Friday and Saturday; 11:00 A.M. to 8:00 P.M. Sunday; closed Monday, January 1–17, and December 25; (812) 926–3737.

Named for an animal now extinct in the wild, the **Red Wolf Sanctuary** near Dillsboro is home to several red and gray wolves, coyotes, foxes, a mountain lion, and an assortment of raptors. The red wolves seen here are hybrids (part coyote)—the few remaining pure red wolves in the United States live on lands managed by the U.S. Fish and Wildlife Service.

Established more than ten years ago by Paul Strasser, a former zookeeper, the twenty-three-acre refuge also serves as a rehabilitation center for sick and injured wildlife from all over the country. Paul and his wife, Jane, nurse their wild charges back to health, returning those who fully recuperate to their natural habitats and adding the others to their growing "family."

The Strassers welcome visitors to their sanctuary free of charge from Thursday through Sunday year-round, but they request that you call in advance and make an appointment. If you want to see the newborn young, come in the spring. Located approximately 5 miles southwest of Dillsboro via State Road 62. Contact the sanctuary at P.O. Box 23, Dillsboro 47018; (812) 667–5303.

Decatur County

It's easy to tell the visitors from the hometown folks in *Greensburg*—the visitors are all looking up. Up, that is, at a tree that's growing where we've all been led to believe trees can't grow—on a roof. Eye-catching, to be sure.

The tree adorns the tower that tops the *Decatur County Courthouse.* When the first tree appeared here in 1870, local authorities, who knew a tree's proper place, grubbed it out. Five years later a second tree appeared. The amazed citizenry, admiring its tenacity, merely stood by and watched this time. That tree thrived until 1929, when it failed to leaf and was removed to the local *Decatur County Museum* for preservation.

At the time of its removal another tree had already started growing on the opposite side of the tower. It was later joined by a second tree, so that today there are actually two trees, both

Trivia

Carl Fisher, born poor and half-blind in Greensburg in 1874, had to quit school and go to work at age twelve. Nevertheless, he founded the town of Speedway, helped create the Indianapolis Motor Speedway (home of the Indianapolis 500), was instrumental in marking the route for the first transcontinental road for automobiles, and created the resort town of Miami Beach, Florida, from a mangrove swamp.

growing without any apparent nourishment (although local comedians conjecture that they are fed by the springs in the tower's clock). The townsfolk have long since made their peace with this peculiar situation, and they even celebrate each September with a *Tree City Fall Festival.*

What type of tree had implanted itself on the courthouse roof? For years no one could agree on the answer, and finally scientists at the Smithsonian Institution in Washington, D.C., were consulted. They declared the trees to be large-toothed aspens. For additional information contact the Greensburg Area Chamber of Commerce, 125 West Main Street, Greensburg 47240; (812) 663–2832.

Fayette County

The *Whitewater Valley Railroad,* the longest steam railroad in Indiana, travels 32 scenic miles between Connersville and Metamora each Saturday, Sunday, and holiday from May through November. All the sights and sounds of old-time steam travel have been re-created to transport you back in time, and places of interest, including some of the original canal locks, are pointed out along the way. Two rare Baldwin locomotives, vintage 1907 and 1919, pull New York Central and Erie Stillwell passenger cars over tracks laid along the towpath of the old Whitewater Canal. At Metamora (see Franklin County) there's time to disembark and explore a restored canal town.

Whitewater Valley Railroad

Both round-trips and one-way trips, as well as caboose rides and special Christmas runs, are available. Round-trips, which are approximately five hours long, originate at the Connersville station, located 1 mile south of town on State Road 121. Write the Whitewater Valley Railroad, Inc., P.O. Box 406, Connersville 47331; call (765) 825–2054 in Connersville or (765) 647–3162 in Metamora.

Seven miles southwest of Connersville on County Road 350 South is the *Mary Gray Bird Sanctuary,* a 684-acre wildlife preserve owned and operated by the Indiana Audubon Society. These peaceful surroundings are crisscrossed by several miles of hiking trails, and a full-time naturalist is on hand to answer your questions. A small museum depicts local flora and fauna. The preserve is open daily, free of charge, from dawn to dusk. Contact the sanctuary at RR 6, Box 165, Connersville 47331; (765) 827–0908.

Floyd County

hen the late W. Fred Conway was tiny tyke about three years old, he heard the clanging of a bell outside his Uniontown, Pennsylvania, home and saw a wondrous red machine go racing by. That was the beginning of a lifelong love affair with firefighting equipment. Through the years, he authored several books on the history of fire fighting and amassed a private collection so large he had to build a museum to contain it.

A Labor of Love

If you happen to travel through northeastern Floyd County during the Easter or Christmas holidays, you may see one of southern Indiana's most cherished landmarks.

Atop a rise that overlooks the tiny town of St. Joseph, a 50-foot-tall lighted cross dominates the landscape. It was erected in the early 1950s by the Clark County REMC (Rural Electric Management Company) and became an instant holiday tradition. Equipped with three 350-watt lamps and 105 100-watt lamps, it could be seen by pilots from more than 100 miles away.

The cross was a constant on the holiday scene until the mid-1960s, when repeated damage by some incorrigible vandals forced REMC to discontinue the tradition. In 1972, however, the congregations of three local churches asked REMC to resume operation of the cross, and the company responded by repairing it. The cross has illuminated the skies ever since, a lovely and enduring symbol of the holidays.

The *Vintage Fire Engines Museum,* housed in a replica of a fire-house, opened to the public in mid-June 1999. Of the approximately three dozen significant fire-fighting museums in the country, Conway's is ranked in the top five by the nation's foremost appraiser of vintage fire equipment.

The oldest piece in the museum is a hand pumper that was built in London in 1756. An elegant 1870 Parade Hose carriage is the beauty of the collection, built solely for use in parades to show off a fire company's equipment. Also on display is the very first chemical fire engine in the United States, shipped to this country from Paris in 1870 to serve as the prototype for U.S. manufacturers; more than 10,000 were produced by the time this type of engine became obsolete in the 1920s.

There are small treasures here, too—fire department lanterns, leather helmets and buckets, models of fire stations in a variety of architectural styles, a wooden water main (circa 1832), and a brass fire pole. Perhaps the most unique of all is a bed key used in Colonial times; the key enabled fire companies to quickly disassemble metal bed frames and carry the pieces from a burning home.

Other intriguing exhibits include a fire-related video game, an interactive fire alarm display, and a library of films where visitors can select the films they'd like to watch. One is a documentary that was aired several years ago on *NOVA,* the award-winning PBS television show; Conway was a consultant for the program. A knowledgeable staff imparts fascinating tidbits of lore, such as the fact that George Washington, Benjamin Franklin, and Paul Revere all served as volunteer firefighters.

The museum is located at 402 Mount Tabor Road in New Albany; it's open Monday through Friday from 11:00 A.M. to 4:00 P.M. and at other times by special appointment. A nominal admission fee is charged. Call (812) 941–9901 or (800) 995–9901 for additional information.

In the mood for something exotic to eat in a setting that's unique? Then head for the *Creekside Outpost Cafe* in New Albany and indulge in one of the more than three dozen types of game served there. How about some ground camel? Or an elk steak? Maybe a bison burger or some buffalo jerky? Then, of course, there's always ground beaver.

Owners Phil and Donna "Ladyhawk" Young once operated a more conventional restaurant in New Albany. That was before Ladyhawk came down with a mysterious illness that even the famed Mayo Clinic could not treat. In desperation, they turned to an alternative treatment that involved a special macrobiotic diet. Ladyhawk recovered and, to supply the special foods that she needed, the Youngs opened up a health food store in a converted stable behind their home. Before long, they were back in the restaurant mode and serving meals, too.

In addition to their exotic meat, the Youngs serve a wide range of vegetarian foods and, each week, a different macrobiotic special. Some of the fare can be a bit pricey (it isn't cheap to import camel to southern Indiana), but that doesn't seem to deter the clientele. Thus far, the Youngs have expanded three times—and still the customers come.

The Creekside Outpost Cafe is located at 614 Hausfeldt Lane in New Albany. Call for hours; (812) 948–9118.

Franklin County

Not too long ago, Metamora was a dying town, its days numbered by the end of the canal era. That was before the state of Indiana decided to restore a 14-mile section of the old *Whitewater Canal,* originally a 76-mile waterway constructed in the mid-1800s, and now the small village hums with activity.

An 80-foot-long covered wooden aqueduct in Metamora was built in 1848 to carry the canal 16 feet above Duck Creek. Believed to be the only such structure in existence, it was once featured in *Ripley's Believe It or Not.*

A horse-drawn canal boat takes visitors for a leisurely thirty-minute cruise through the aqueduct and a restored lock. Occasionally the Whitewater Valley Railroad's steam train chugs by carrying passengers between its Connersville station (see Fayette County) and Metamora.

Many of the town's fine arts, crafts, and specialty shops are housed in pre–Civil War buildings that cling to the banks of the canal; others occupy reconstructed and reproduced buildings elsewhere in a section known as Old Metamora. An aged brick gristmill still grinds and sells flour, cornmeal, and grits. The total effect is that of a country village suspended in the 1830s.

Of the many special events scheduled throughout the year, the loveliest is the Christmas Walk that's held evenings on the first three Fridays and Saturdays after Thanksgiving. Some 3,000 luminaries line the banks of the canal, roads, and walkways. Carolers stroll through the streets; horses clippity-clop along, pulling carriages behind them. The aroma of hot spiced cider perfumes the air. Quite a show for a town that has a population of about sixty permanent residents!

If while in Metamora you experience a bit of déjà vu, it may be because you've seen the movie *Rain Man*. Dustin Hoffman and Tom Cruise came here to shoot part of the film.

Most shops are open 10:00 A.M. to 5:00 P.M. Tuesday through Friday and 9:00 A.M. to 6:00 P.M. Saturday, Sunday, and holidays, from mid-April to mid-December, while some are open only on weekends. Head for the shops flying bright yellow flags; that's Metamoraese for "Come on in! We're open!" For additional information contact the Metamora Visitor Center, P.O. Box 117, Metamora 47030; (765) 647–2109.

The canal boat operates on the hour from noon to 3:00 P.M. Wednesday through Friday and 11:00 A.M. to 4:00 P.M. Saturday and Sunday, May through October (by reservation only on May weekdays); a nominal fee is charged. Contact the Whitewater Canal State Memorial, P.O. Box 88, Metamora 47030; (765) 647–6512.

Oldenburg is another architectural and historical gem that has dwelt in the past since it was founded in 1837. Known as the *"Village of Spires"* because of its many soaring steeples, Oldenburg is the home of the *convent and academy of the Sisters of St. Francis,* an order that originally came here from Austria. The peaceful grounds, which invite leisurely strolls, include a cemetery reserved for the sisters. In warm-weather months the cemetery is a stunning mosaic in green and white—paths edged by low-cut green hedges, emerald lawns shaded by the sprawling branches of ancient shade trees, and row on row of small, white, identical stone crosses. The convent itself, renowned for its ceiling frescoes, basilica-like chapel, iron stairways, and solid oak woodwork, can be toured by appointment. Call (812) 934–2475.

Elsewhere in the picturesque community are houses and storefronts adorned with the ornate tinwork of master craftsman Gasper Gaupel. The lovely tree-lined streets bear German names, ranging from the mundane Haupstrasse (Main Street) to the lyrical Schweincochwantz Gasse (Pigtail Alley). Every so often the aroma of brats and sauerkraut escapes from a local eatery. If you'd like to sample some German cuisine, just follow your nose.

Harrison County

few miles south of Corydon is a peaceful valley laced with subterranean caverns and edged by forested hills. Squire Boone first saw this area in the late 1700s while hunting with his older brother, Daniel, and eventually returned here to settle down, building

Gone Too Soon

*L*ova Cline, born in 1902, was the only child of George and Mary Cline of Arlington, Indiana. Unfortunately, Lova suffered from a serious illness and had to spend much of her short life in bed. Her father, hoping to bring some joy to his daughter's life, built her a dollhouse. He and Lova's mother filled it with toys, dolls, and love.

When Lova died at the age of six, her parents placed her beloved dollhouse above her grave. That dollhouse still marks the spot in the Rush County cemetery where little Lova lies.

Lova's parents have long since joined her in death, but they bequeathed the upkeep of the dollhouse to Lova Wooten, the daughter of some friends of the Clines who was named after the first Lova. The second Lova has faithfully tended the unusual monument and still fills it with handmade items of sentimental value.

Now fitted with aluminum siding and anchored by a cement foundation, the dollhouse draws visitors from across the state and beyond. Visitors may see it in the Rush County cemetery along U.S. Highway 52, just east of Arlington—a poignant monument to a little girl who died much too soon.

a home for his family and a gristmill that provided their means of support. When he died in 1815 he was buried at his own request in the cave that today bears his name, and the walnut coffin that contains his remains can be seen on a guided tour.

Squire Boone Caverns offer a wondrous mix of colorful stalactites and stalagmites, underground streams, waterfalls, twisted helictites, massive pillars of stone, and the world's largest travertine dam formation. Cave crickets, blind crayfish, isopods, amphipods, and a few bats live in the cave's deepest recesses. The tour guides are extremely well informed about this cave and about caves in general. At one point along the way, in the belly of the cave, all lights are turned out—an eerie experience that gives new meaning to the word "black." This is not the largest cave around, but it is certainly one of the most dazzling. Visitors should be aware that the subterranean temperature is a constant fifty-four degrees, and there is a steep spiral staircase to climb at the end of the fifty-five-minute, $1/3$-mile tour.

Topside, you can visit an operating gristmill rebuilt on the original foundation used by Squire Boone, watch the miller at work, and buy his products. A cluster of log cabins near the cave's entrance houses various crafts shops, an art gallery, a homemade-candy store, and a restaurant; the craftspeople who work here are as authentic as the log cabins that

Trivia

The Edwardsville Railroad Tunnel near Corydon is Indiana's longest tunnel. Completed in 1881, the 4,311-foot-long passageway cost nearly $1 million to build.

shelter them. Children can get acquainted with farm animals at a petting zoo, uncover fossils at the Fossil Dig, pan for gold and gems, and learn something about earth science at the Rock Shop.

Although it's small in size and limited in menu, the restaurant serves some of the finest homemade soups, sandwiches, salads, and desserts in southern Indiana. Even the coffee and iced tea are exceptional, and the restaurant itself is bright, airy, clean, and cheerful.

To reach Squire Boone Caverns and Village, go south from Corydon on State Road 135 for about 10 miles, then turn east on Squire Boone Caverns Road for another 3 miles; look for signs. Guided one-hour-long cave tours start daily every thirty minutes from 10:00 A.M. to 5:00 P.M. when the village is open and at 10:00 A.M. and noon, 2:00, and 4:00 P.M. the rest of the year; closed major winter holidays and weekdays in January and February. Village activities from 10:00 A.M. to 6:00 P.M. daily from Memorial Day weekend through mid-August, Saturday and Sunday from August 21 through Labor Day. Cave tours only (at 10:00 A.M., noon, and 2:00 and 4:00 P.M.) the rest of the year; closed major winter holidays. The gristmill, which lies just outside the cave-village complex, is open, free of charge, when the village is open. Write P.O. Box 411, Corydon 47112; or call (812) 732–4381 or (502) 425–2283.

Trivia

On March 28, 1859, a meteorite fell on tiny Buena Vista. One recovered fragment is now in the British Museum; another is at Harvard. More pieces still lie buried in the Harrison County countryside.

Back in Corydon at the *Zimmerman Art Glass Factory* you can observe a process that is now nearly extinct. Brothers Bart and Kerry Zimmerman handblow every piece of glassware they make, and no two pieces are identical. The Zimmermans specialize in paperweights—clear crystal balls, large and small, that enclose unfolding blossoms—but will try just about anything that tickles their fancy. Their glass menagerie includes trays of glass fruits, sugar bowls and creamers, an assortment of baskets, lamps, vases, and perfume decanters—some clear, some in exquisite color.

Many customers order items made to their specifications. An example is the lady from Australia who dropped by to describe the lamp she wanted and asked the partners to send it to her home—the shipping charges cost more than the lamp.

Although small, the company is nationally known, and its artistic wares are displayed in many museums, including the Smithsonian Institution.

You're welcome to drop in and watch these skilled craftspeople breathe life into molten glass; free glass-sculpting demonstrations are given from 9:00 A.M. to 3:00 P.M. Tuesday through Friday. The factory, open from 8:00 A.M. to 4:00 P.M. Tuesday through Saturday except major holidays, is housed in a green, corrugated-metal shed at 395 Valley Road NW, right next to the Hudson Foods poultry-processing plant on the south edge of Corydon; (812) 738–2206.

The *Louisville, New Albany & Corydon Railroad* is one of the shortest railroads in the nation—its entire track is just under 8 miles in length. Established in 1883, "The Dinky," as it's affectionately known to local residents, has been hauling freight from Corydon to Corydon Junction ever since. Railroad enthusiasts can accompany the engineer and crew on a 16-mile round-trip by special arrangement. The depot at Walnut and Water streets in Corydon displays antique railroad equipment; (812) 738–3171. Each weekend from spring through fall the *Corydon 1883 Scenic Railroad* embarks from the depot on $1^1/_2$-hour round-trip tours through southern Indiana hill country. For additional information contact the railroad at the LNAC Railroad Station, 210 West Walnut Street, Corydon 47112; (812) 738–8000.

Henry County

In Indiana it's known as "Hoosier Hysteria"; to the rest of the world it's known as basketball. Almost anyone, after spending about five minutes in Indiana, can tell you that basketball holds a special place in the hearts of Hoosiers. It is not unheard of, for instance, for whole towns—gas stations, restaurants, and shops included—to shut down totally so that everyone can go to the local high-school basketball game. After a short visit to the state, CBS news anchor Dan Rather was heard to remark that "a ball and a net would make a perfect state flag" for Indiana. The world's record attendance for an indoor basketball game occurred in 1984, when 67,596 persons attended an exhibition game between the National Basketball Association All Stars and the U.S. Olympic team in Indianapolis. In 1990 two Indiana teams playing for the state championship set a national record for attendance at a high school basketball game—41,046 persons showed up to cheer on their favorites. Eighteen of the twenty largest high school gyms in the country are in Indiana.

It should therefore surprise no one that there is an *Indiana Basketball Hall of Fame;* the citizenry would have it no other way. Previously located in Indianapolis, the Hall of Fame moved to newer and roomier quarters in New Castle in 1990. Within its walls visitors can see multimedia presentations, use computers to research the basketball history of state schools, play a trivia game, try to outwit a mechanical guard, have the opportunity to make the winning shot as a clock counts down the last five seconds of a game, and learn basketball lore in abundance. The museum stands, appropriately, next door to the New Castle High School gym—the largest high school gym in the world. It's located at One Hall of Fame Court; there's a nominal admission fee. Open 10:00 A.M. to 5:00 P.M. Tuesday through Saturday and noon to 5:00 P.M. Sunday; closed major winter holidays; (765) 529–1891.

Few people realize that the older half of the famous Wright Brothers was born in Indiana. Wilbur Wright's extraordinary life began in the town of Millville, a small town near New Castle, on April 16, 1867. Although the Wright family lived here for only six months, the town pays homage to Wilbur's memory with the **Wilbur Wright Birthplace and Museum.**

Most people would agree that few events in the past one hundred years surpass in importance that defining moment when Wilbur and Orville first flew their airplane above the sand dunes of Kitty Hawk, North Carolina, in 1903. The Wright Flyer housed in the museum building is an exact replica of that plane and is believed to be the only one other than the original that is flightworthy. Parked outside the museum building, in stark contrast to the Flyer inside, is an F–84 jet fighter.

The house in which the future inventor was born burned down some time ago, but the small, two-story white frame dwelling has been reconstructed on the home's original foundation, and the smokehouse behind it is the original structure used by the Wright family.

Tour guides humanize the brothers with fascinating true stories about their personal lives. Among them are anecdotes about their numerous

It is a legend carved from dreams, a tale of a mystical tree that poets have sung about in every language in every land. Ross Lockbridge, Jr., wrote about it in his classic Civil War novel, Raintree County: *"Luck, happiness, the realization of dreams, the secret of life itself—all belong to he who finds the raintree. Stand beneath its rain of golden blossoms and discover love."*

The beautiful and exotic raintree about which he wrote, it is said, grows somewhere in Indiana's Henry County, its exact location obscured in the mists of time. Its seed may have been brought here by Johnny Appleseed, who wandered the Midwest in the first half of the nineteenth century planting apple orchards in what was then wilderness. With him, he carried one special seed—the seed of the golden raintree—searching for the one place where the seed might take root and flourish. Somewhere in Henry County, as legend has it, he found that place, and somewhere in Henry County, it endures to this day.

failed business ventures, Orville's proclivity for practical jokes, and Wilbur's attempts at cooking.

To reach the birthsite, go east from New Castle on State Road 38 to Wilbur Wright Road, turn north, and follow the signs. It's open from 10:00 A.M. to 5:00 P.M. Monday through Saturday and 1:00 to 5:00 P.M. Sunday, April through October, and by appointment the rest of the year. A small admission fee is charged. For additional information contact the Wilbur Wright Birthplace and Museum, 1525 North County Road 750 East, Hagerstown 47346; (765) 332–2495.

Vera's Little Red Doll House Museum is a child's fantasy world brought to life by Vera and Bob Sanders. Located next to the Sanders's home in Middletown, it contains two large rooms. One room overflows with every kind of doll imaginable and all the furniture any doll could ever want or need. The second is inhabited by more than 1,600 stuffed animals, collected over the years by the Sanders's daughter Amy. Admission is free. The museum is located at 4385 West County Road 850 North. Open daily 10:00 A.M. to 5:00 P.M., but please call before visiting; (765) 533–3453.

Jackson County

The heavenly aroma that sometimes tantalizes the nostrils in Brownstown is a vanilla bean on its way to becoming vanilla extract. This metamorphosis takes place each working day at the **Marion-Kay Spice Company** plant, which turns out an array of spices and seasonings. You can learn about the whole process, as well as the history of spices, on a free tour. The Marion-Kay plant is located at 1351 West U.S. Highway 50 on the western edge of town. Open 8:00 A.M. to 4:30 P.M. Monday through Friday; call (812) 358–3000 or fax (812) 358–3400 for tour hours.

Indiana's **Skyline Drive** meanders across a series of knobs for some 6 miles through the **Jackson-Washington State Forest** and offers spectacular hilltop vistas. The poorly surfaced road is hilly and treacherous, so plan on taking your time. To reach the drive, head south from Brownstown on South Poplar Street and follow the signs. Write the Jackson-Washington State Forest, 1278 East State Road 250, Brownstown 47220, or call (812) 358–2160, for information about the drive and the many recreational opportunities elsewhere in the forest.

Vallonia was established circa 1811, making it Jackson County's oldest community. Its longevity may be attributed in part to the fact that it has its own guardian angel.

Made of French marble and soaring to a height of more than 15 feet, the **Angel on Angel Hill** has stood atop a pedestal in a small family cemetery just south of town since 1887. The daughter of a prominent local businessman, who wanted to memorialize her father with a very special monument, had the sweet-faced angel shipped from Paris to New York. There she was placed aboard a train to Seymour and then carted on a log wagon to her permanent home in Vallonia, where she has been a lure ever since for both tourists and locals.

The cemetery over which she stands guard, wings unfurled and right arm extended, is atop a small rise in the midst of a soybean field along State Road 135 South. A narrow path leads through the field to the graveyard and its angel.

Jackson County has the finest collection of long covered bridges in the state. Three of them span the East Fork of White River. To view what's billed as one of the longest covered bridges in the world, head east from Medora for 1 mile on State Road 235. The 434-foot-long span, built in 1875, is certainly the longest in Indiana. It carried traffic across the river until 1974, when it was bypassed by a new bridge. Sadly, the old **Medora Bridge** is slowly falling into decay—the cost to preserve it has thus far been out of reach.

The 325-foot-long **Bell's Ford Bridge** is the only triple-burr-arch covered bridge in Indiana and the only known Post truss bridge in existence anywhere. Erected in 1869, the Post truss represents a period when bridges were evolving from all-wood into all-metal or concrete structures. Its sides and floor feature iron rods and straps covered with wood. The bridge is located on State Road 258, 3 miles west of Seymour.

The **Shieldstown Covered Bridge,** constructed in 1876, is 331 feet long. To visit it go southwest from Seymour on U.S. Highway 50 for about 6½ miles, then turn northwest onto a country road leading to Crane Hill and proceed about 1 mile; look for signs along the way.

For additional information about the county's bridges, contact the Greater Seymour Chamber of Commerce, 105 South Chestnut Street, P.O. Box 312, Seymour 47274; (812) 522–3681.

Wildlife lovers will want to stop at **Muscatatuck National Wildlife Refuge,** located 3 miles east of Seymour on the south side of U.S.

Highway 50. Covering more than 7,700 acres, it's Indiana's only such refuge and was established primarily as a sanctuary for wood ducks. Each spring and fall thousands of migrating waterfowl pause to rest on the open water and are occasionally joined by flocks of sandhill cranes. White-tailed deer and wild turkeys make their homes here all year long. The refuge is open daily year-round, from dawn to dusk; there's a nominal admission fee. Contact the Muscatatuck National Wildlife Refuge, Route 7, Box 189A, Seymour 47274; (812) 522–4352.

Jefferson County

The late Charles Kuralt once called **Madison** the most beautiful river town in America. The curator of a Michigan museum, when he first saw Madison, said, "Put a fence around the entire town and don't let anyone touch anything in it!" During World War II the Office of War Information selected Madison as the "typical American town" and made movies of it in thirty-two languages to distribute around the world and to remind our troops what they were fighting for. *Life* magazine chose Madison as the most pleasant small town in the country in which to live. Its nineteenth-century architecture, a mix of several styles, has been praised as the most beautiful in the Midwest, and its setting on the banks of the Ohio River, against a backdrop of wooded hills and limestone bluffs, is equally lovely. Obviously, if you're going to tour Indiana, Madison is one place you shouldn't miss.

Once Madison was a thriving river port and the largest town in the state. When railroads arrived on the scene, the river traffic departed, and Madison, in keeping with the times, built its own railroad. What no one foresaw was that nearly everyone would get on the train and leave town. For many years no one came to replace the populace that had moved on, and 133 blocks of buildings thus survived an era when it was fashionable to tear down anything old and replace it with something new in the name of progress. It is this legacy of architectural splendor that can be seen today.

The most notable building is the **Lanier Mansion** at 511 West First Street, a palatial home built in the 1840s for about $50,000—quite a chunk of money in those days. Its owner, James Lanier, was an astute banker whose loans to the state government during the Civil War helped Indiana avert bankruptcy. Facing a broad lawn that rambles down to the Ohio River, the Lanier Mansion is an outstanding example of the Greek Revival style. Its two-story portico is supported by tall

A Monument to Courage

*F*ew people know the story behind the decaying structure that sits atop a hill in rural Jefferson County, but its new owners plan to change that. When the building was first erected about a century and a half ago, it was known as Eleutherian College, and what went on there when it was first established was illegal.

The college was quietly set up in the rural community of Lancaster to educate blacks, the first college in Indiana to do so. The name it bears is a Greek word meaning "freedom" and "equality."

Although the exterior of the three-story building is made of stone, its floors and ceilings are rotting away. Remnants of cupboards and benches remain, along with a couple of long-abandoned pianos. A cast-iron bell in the belfry still rings as true as the first day it was placed there.

Only fragments of the college's history are known at this point, but the not-for-profit organization that recently purchased it for restoration is delving into its past. One bit of lore claims that two of the children born to Thomas Jefferson and Sally Hemings attended school here.

The members hope to restore the building and present its story in concerts and seminars. One far-distant dream is that Eleutherian will someday be the centerpiece of a national park. At present, the restorers will have to settle for the college's designation as a National Historic Landmark, an honor that was bestowed upon it at a dedication ceremony in October 1997.

The building is not yet open to the public, but it can be viewed on the south side of State Road 250, just east of Lancaster.

Corinthian columns and hemmed in by wrought-iron grillwork. Inside, a spiral staircase climbs three stories, unsupported except by its own thrust, and each of the rooms is decorated with period furniture and accessories. Now a state memorial, the five-acre estate is open free of charge year-round. Hours are 9:00 A.M. to 5:00 P.M. Wednesday through Saturday and 1:00 to 5:00 P.M. on Tuesday and Sunday; closed Monday, Thanksgiving, and Christmas; (812) 265–3526.

Among the other attractions in Madison's historic district are the *office and private hospital of Dr. William Hutchings,* with all the original medications and possessions of the late-nineteenth-century doctor still intact; a restored *pioneer garden* with vintage roses and other period plantings; and the *Francis Costigan House,* home of the architect who designed Lanier Mansion. Everywhere in Madison you'll see elaborate ornamental ironwork reminiscent of New Orleans but forged locally (as was much of New Orleans's ironwork). *"Little Jimmy,"* a locally famous weathervane, sits atop the firehouse bell tower.

If the **Delta Queen,** an old stern-wheeler that carries passengers on nostalgic journeys up and down the Ohio and Mississippi rivers, happens to be in port during your visit, the aura of yesteryear will be even more overwhelming. The majestic old boat can be toured when it's docked.

Maps and guides for walking tours are available from the Madison Area Convention and Visitors Bureau at 301 East Main Street, just across the street from the Jefferson County Courthouse; (812) 265–2956 or (800) 559–2956. '

Railroad buffs will want to take a look at one of the world's steepest noncog train tracks. Cut through limestone bluffs in 1835, it climbs 413 feet in little more than a mile. Eight-horse teams drew the first trains up the incline but were eventually replaced by a wood-burning steam engine. The tracks can be viewed from State Road 56 at the west edge of town.

Madison is located in the heart of burley tobacco country, and each year from about Thanksgiving through January, auctions are conducted in local *tobacco warehouses.* It's a fascinating scenario, set to the music of the auctioneer's lyrical but unintelligible (to the layperson) lingo. Two warehouses welcome visitors: Ford, 748 Scott Court, (812) 273–4184; and Morrow, 740 Clifty Drive, (812) 273–3610. Check locally for varying hours.

Not far west of Madison you can stay at the *Clifty Falls State Park Inn.* Recently renovated, it features guest rooms for $49 to $89 per night for two; some rooms have private balconies that overlook the Ohio River valley. The dining room serves three meals a day for reasonable rates. Write Clifty Inn, 1501 Green Road, P.O. Box 387, Madison 47250; (812) 265–4135.

Noted for its natural beauty, *Clifty Falls State Park* sprawls over 1,360 hilly acres. The prettiest area, *Clifty Canyon State Nature Preserve,* is accessible only on foot. The great boulder-strewn canyon is so deep that sunlight can penetrate it only at high noon. Mosses, lichens, and ferns cling to the precipitous cliffs along Clifty Creek. In the spring, when the water is running fast, there are spectacular waterfalls; Big Clifty Falls, the granddaddy of them all, drops 60 feet. The park also offers an Olympic-size swimming pool, a modern campground, a nature center, an exercise trail, and breathtaking views from atop a 400-foot bluff. Contact Clifty Falls State Park, 1501 Green Road, Madison 47250; (812) 265–1331.

Canaan is a really fowl place. In fact, there may be more fowl than people—and of more types than you ever knew existed. Schoolteacher Gale Ferris calls his poultry farm the *United Nations of the Poultry*

World. Forty rare breeds populate his farmyard, including silver spangled hamburgs from Germany, black cochin bantams from Asia, bearded mottled houdans from France, and the blue-skinned Chinese silkies, as fluffy as powder puffs. The unusual araucanas from South America actually lay colored eggs.

Mr. Ferris is happy to share his wealth of knowledge—both about fowls and about Jefferson County. Early April, when all the redbuds are in bloom and baby chicks and ducks are about, is the recommended time to visit. From mid-November to mid-April it's best to come on weekends or evenings. To make sure Mr. Ferris will be there when you visit or to arrange group tours, call (812) 839–4770. The Ferris farm is located 15 miles northeast of Madison and 3 miles east of Canaan on State Road 62.

Also on the Ferris farm, housed in a little red barn, is a display of old tools and utensils dating from the early 1800s to the early 1900s, including a copper kettle, liquor jugs more than a hundred years old, and dippers for molten bullet metal. Nearby stands a miniature one-room schoolhouse that the Ferris family built from brick. It contains several pieces from an old Canaan school that was razed a few years back, including the cornerstone, coal tongs, blackboard, and school bench; other items on display are authentic antiques. Both attractions are open to the public free of charge, but donations are appreciated.

Mr. Ferris is also one of the chief organizers of Canaan's annual Fall Festival, which features a potpourri of such events as a frog-jumping contest, a bucksaw woodcutting contest, a greased-pole climbing contest, and the Chief White Eye painting contest. Held the second weekend in September, the festival has become known far and wide, however, for its unique *Pony Express Run.* Mail is specially stamped at Canaan, packed in authentic Pony Express mailbags on loan from the Smithsonian Institution in Washington, D.C., and delivered to the Madison post office by a rider on horseback. For further information contact Gale Ferris at 9713 North State Road 62, Canaan 17224, (812) 839–4770.

Jennings County

Each weekend from mid-April to mid-December, visitors trek to tiny Commiskey to enjoy the pleasures of *Stream Cliff,* Indiana's oldest herb farm. They come to wander through the flower gardens or to enjoy the salads, sandwiches, and teas served at the Twigs & Sprigs

Tearoom. They browse through the three arts and crafts shops to the accompaniment of dulcimer music. They sit beneath a shaded arbor or watch the goldfish glide by in the farm's two ponds. If they're so inclined and register in advance, they can take one of the many classes offered here. Various experts demonstrate such things as the uses of different herbs and how to create craft items. Whatever you choose to do, you will find a quiet and serene retreat in which to do it. Open 10:00 A.M. to 5:00 p.m. Friday and Saturday, noon to 5:00 P.M. Sunday. Located at 8225 South County Road 90 West; (812) 346–5859.

Every Labor Day weekend for close to forty years, the population of Vernon swells from 300 to 30,300. That's when the Jennings County Historical Society holds its annual *Antique and Collectibles Market.* Actually, it's one huge yard sale, and word has gotten around. Dealers and shoppers alike come from more than 1,000 miles away to sell or shop from sunrise to sunset. If time permits, visitors can explore the town of Vernon itself. It is rich in history and has preserved that history well. For additional information, call the Jennings County Visitors Center at (812) 346–4865 or (800) 928–3667.

Ripley County

Many a visitor, while traveling through the small town of Versailles, has stopped to stare in wonderment at the unusual-looking church on the corner of Tyson and Adams Streets. Known officially as the *Tyson United Methodist Church* and unofficially as the Tyson Temple, it is a continuous flow of rounded corners, arches, columns, windows, and roof. Its striking spire is a rounded, inverted cone of openwork aluminum. Inside, the altar is framed by columns that duplicate those in the Taj Mahal. The rounded ceiling above the pews is painted with the stars and constellations that appear over Indiana in October. To enhance the effect of a nighttime sky, the ceiling is illuminated by light reflected from wall fixtures. The dome over the choir loft is covered with gold leaf from Germany. Pulpit furnishings come from Italy, and the windows are from Belgium. The grand but small Tyson Church (it seats only 200 people) draws visitors from around the country. Free tours are offered by appointment; call (812) 689–6976.

In Batesville you can enter the Old World atmosphere of the **Sherman House** and enjoy some of the tastiest food in southern Indiana. Diners can select one of twenty moderately-priced entrees or the specialty of the day, but fresh Maine lobster from the restaurant's tank, chateaubriand, veal Cordon Bleu, prime strip steaks, and Hoosier-fried chicken are among the longtime favorites.

Batesville is the Casket Capital of the World. The origins of the Batesville Casket Company date back to the nineteenth century, when the area was forested with an abundance of oak, cherry, and walnut trees.

The Sherman House also offers overnight accommodations at a rate of $55 to $75 for two. Although the inn has undergone several renovations since opening in 1852, the 30-inch-square, 90-foot-long yellow poplar timbers used in the original structure are still in place and in perfect condition. Restaurant open 6:30 A.M. to 8:45 P.M. Monday through Thursday, 6:30 A.M. to 9:45 P.M. Friday and Saturday, and 6:30 A.M. to 7:45 P.M. Sunday; closed Christmas and New Year's; reservations recommended. Located at 35 South Main Street (State Road 229); (812) 934–2407 or (800) 445–4939.

When **Carl Dyer** moved to Friendship in 1982, he thought he was retiring from a long career of **moccasin making,** but relentless customers who demanded his products drew him back into the business. He also discovered that he loved his craft too much to give it up.

Dyer never advertises his mostly mail-order business—he doesn't have to. Even people from abroad somehow obtain his phone number and call to place their orders.

The son of an accomplished bootmaker (his father crafted the aviation boots that Charles Lindbergh wore on his historic flight across the Atlantic), Dyer learned his trade early. Today, he and his wife, Robin, along with three assistants, produce about 3,000 pairs of handmade moccasins in eight different styles each year. The double-soled, heavy leather, waterproof moccasins range in price from $64 to $175.

Dyer's customers, including celebrities and Fortune 500 company executives, rave about the molded-to-your-feet comfort. Interestingly, Dyer even took an order from Charles Lindbergh's grandson, who was unaware that he was ordering his moccasins from the same family that had made his grandfather's boots.

Because Dyer is sometimes on the road attending gun shows, he prefers that people contact him before showing up at his shop. Write him at P.O. Box 31, Friendship 47021, or call (812) 667–5442.

Home of the Thump Jumpers

The first international rope-jumping competition was held in Sydney, Australia, in 1997. When it was all over, the Indiana Thump Jumpers had emerged as the number one team in the world. They beat out teams from ten different countries and four other states.

Mind you, this is not child's play. Imagine, if you will, two ropes turning simultaneously so fast that competitors often jump as fast as 400 times a minute, while at the same time executing flips, spins, and somersaults. Competitive rope jumping combines the athleticism of gymnastics, the artistry of figure skating, and the endurance of marathon running. It is also one of the few sports in which men and women can be on the same team.

Indiana's five-member championship team (one male and four females) is rooted in Richmond, where elementary school teacher Lee Stienbarger put together what is believed to be the very first rope-jumping team in the early 1980s. At the time, the American Heart Association was promoting the activity for cardiovascular exercise.

Today, there is even a U.S. Amateur Jump Rope Federation that is promoting competitive rope jumping as an Olympic event.

Rush County

ichael Bonne's store in Knightstown gleams with the warm glow of copper. It reflects the owner's love and enthusiasm for the work he does.

Although Michael has always loved metal sculpting, it didn't seem a likely way to make a living when he was growing up in this part of rural Indiana, so he went to work in his father's construction business.

Fate had a different idea, though, and when Michael was injured in a construction accident in 1982, he decided to give metal sculpting a go. Because he loves antiques, he started his new career by recreating historical copper kitchenware. At first, he sold his creations at regional crafts shows, but now his customers come to him. Today, he claims, his business is the world's largest producer of copper birdbaths and cookie cutters.

Michael and the craftspeople who work with him sculpt their wares behind an observation window so that tour groups and other visitors can observe them. By calling ahead, visitors can arrange to craft their own copper pieces to take home with them.

Although Michael frequently designs something new and different, his basic housewares continue to be his best-sellers. Michael believes that people love the warmth of copper in their kitchens. Certainly Martha Stewart does. The cooking and gardening maven favors Michael's cookie cutters and is one of the coppersmith's biggest customers.

For additional information, contact Michael at 102 East Main Street, Knightstown 46148; (765) 345–5521.

The first newspaper in Rushville, the Dog-Fennel Gazette, was reportedly printed on one side of a single sheet of paper. When subscribers finished reading it, they returned the paper to the Gazette's office so that the next issue could be printed on the blank side.

Wayne County

very state has one, and in Indiana it's in Wayne County. The distinguished (at least to Hoosiers) spot sits in the middle of a bean field and is marked by a pile of rocks with a stick in it. Officially known as **Hoosier Hill**, it soars to 1,257 feet above sea level and is the highest point in Indiana.

It's a lonely site. In a good year, it lures about 200 visitors from around the country. Many are members of The National Highpointers Club, a group dedicated to visiting the highest point in each of the United States.

The current high point has not always been the highest point in Indiana. Originally that honor belonged to a spot approximately 200 yards to the southwest. But when that spot was resurveyed by satellite a decade or so ago, it was discovered that the original high point had shrunk. The popular belief is that it was done in by the repeated attacks of a manure spreader. That fate will not soon befall the current high point. It was purchased in 1982 by Kim Goble, a resident of nearby Richmond, so that its unique status could be preserved. For additional information, contact Ms. Gobel at 136 Southwest Ninth Street, Richmond 47374; (765) 966–5674.

Getting to Hoosier Hill is an adventure in itself. The noted landmark is located in the northeastern corner of Wayne County, not far from the small town of Bethel. From Bethel, go north on State Road 227 for about $1\frac{1}{4}$ miles to Randolph County Line Road (also known as Bethel Road) and turn west. Go west 1 mile and turn south onto Elliot Road. Proceed about $\frac{1}{4}$ mile to an access road on the west. Park on the access road, climb over the adjacent fence on a stile provided by some Highpointers Club members, and walk about 100 feet to the pile of rocks that sits atop the hill.

All That Jazz

The sounds emanating from the small town of Richmond in the 1920s were some of the sweetest on earth. Musicians from all over the country came here during that decade to a tiny recording studio perched on the banks of the Whitewater River.

Our country was in the throes of the Jazz Age then, and many now-legendary jazz artists signed their first recording contracts at Gennett Studios. Among them were Fred "Jelly Roll" Morton, Bix Beiderbecke (his Rhythm Jugglers featured Tommy Dorsey on the trombone), King Oliver, Duke Ellington, and the incomparable Louis Armstrong.

Hoagy Carmichael made the first recording of Stardust here, but it was nearly lost to posterity when a Gennett employee almost threw it in the trash. Thankfully, the error was caught in time. Although that original version was recorded in an upbeat dance tempo, Stardust has evolved into a more mellow rendition that the world now regards as one of the most beautiful love songs ever written.

Blues musicians also recorded at Gennett, and the recordings of a young Gene Autry introduced old-time country music to the world. Billy Sunday, a popular preacher of the day, and poet James Whitcomb Riley, a native Hoosier, added the spoken word to Gennett's repertoire. The company also produced copies of William Jennings Bryan's famous 1896 "Cross of Gold" speech; they were taken to Tennessee and sold outside the courthouse where Bryan was participating in the 1925 Scopes trial.

From 1916 to 1934 the studio produced thousands of recordings, featuring any recorded sound that had or could have a market. All this was accomplished despite the fact that the studio had no electricity until 1926 and had to halt recording every time a train came by on the railroad track next to the building.

Unfortunately, like many other businesses of the day, the Gennett label was done in by the Great Depression, but Richmond has not forgotten its rich heritage as the "cradle of recorded jazz." Visitors can currently learn more about the Gennett studio at the Wayne County Historical Museum, and plans are under way for a new museum devoted solely to the history of the "label of legends."

There may or may not be a sign marking the spot. The signs keep getting stolen. There may or may not be a visitors' sign-in book in a waterproof box hanging from a tree. The book is sometimes stolen, too.

Although it may seem an unlikely location for such an enterprise, **Richmond** boasts one of the largest rose-growing industries in the world. **Hill Floral Products, Inc.,** pioneers in greenhouse rose growing since 1881, annually ships more than thirty million cut roses to midwestern and southern states. The famed American Beauty Rose was developed here, and new hybrids continue to be produced each year. Free tours are conducted during the annual Richmond Area Rose Festival each June; free tours for groups of ten or more are available year-round by appointment. Located at 2117 Peacock Road; call (765) 935–8687 or (800) 828–8414.

The luxurious **Hill Memorial Rose Garden** in Glen Miller Park, which displays more than 1,600 rosebushes, was established in tribute to the local flower industry. Located at 2200 National Road East, the park is also the site of the All-America Rose Garden, the German Friendship Garden, and a small zoo. The park is open 6:00 A.M. to 11:00 P.M. daily; (765) 935–8687.

Trivia

Liberty native Ambrose E. Burnside, a Union officer during the Civil War, was noted for his magnificent side whiskers. Today, his unique hairstyle is known as "sideburns."

At the **Hayes Regional Arboretum,** a 355-acre botanical preserve, you can view regional plant species—all labeled—on a 3½-mile auto tour. Also on the grounds are Indiana's first solar-heated greenhouse, a fern garden, a wild bird sanctuary, 10 miles of hiking trails (one of which passes an Indian mound), and a nature center housed in a barn some 180 years old, where a telephone line permits you to eavesdrop on a colony of bees busily at work making honey. The arboretum is open 9:00 A.M. to 5:00 P.M. Tuesday through Saturday and 1:00 to 5:00 P.M. Sunday, year-round. The nature center is open 9:00 A.M. to 5:00 P.M. Tuesday through Saturday and 1:00 to 5:00 P.M. Sunday, April through November; the arboretum is closed major winter holidays. Admission is free. Contact the Hayes Regional Arboretum, 801 Elks Country Club Road, Richmond 47374; (765) 962–3745.

Following a disastrous gas explosion and fire in 1968 that destroyed much of the downtown business district, Richmond covered its physical scars by building an unusual **Downtown Promenade.** The 5 blocks of flowing fountains, soft music, and unique specialty stores have been nationally acclaimed for their beauty. You'll find the promenade on Main Street between Fifth and Tenth Streets; (765) 962–8151.

The **Wayne County Historical Museum,** not far from the promenade area, is generally recognized as one of the best county museums in the state. Its diverse collection ranges from vintage cars made in Richmond to a Japanese samurai warrior's uniform, from a nineteenth-century general store to a 3,000-year-old mummy (X rays of the mummy taken by two local physicians can be seen by visitors). Open 9:00 A.M. to 4:00 P.M. Tuesday through Friday and 1:00 to 4:00 P.M. Saturday and Sunday, early February through mid-December; closed the

OFF THE BEATEN PATH

Trivia

The Ohio County Courthouse in Rising Sun, built in 1845, is the oldest Indiana courthouse in continuous use.

rest of the year and major holidays. There's a nominal admission fee. Contact Wayne County Historical Museum, 1150 North A Street, Richmond 47374; (765) 962–5756.

Although every other sport takes a backseat to basketball in Indiana, the state has also produced some football heroes. They're all honored in the *Indiana Football Hall of Fame,* located at 815 North A Street. Among the inductees are O. J. Simpson, Bart Starr, and Jim Thorpe, all of whom once played football in the Hoosier State; Knute Rockne, the legendary coach of Notre Dame; and Weeb Ewbank, a local great who coached the Baltimore Colts and New York Jets. Tony Hulman, whose name is synonymous with the Indianapolis 500, is remembered here as an All-American end on the undefeated Yale University team of 1923. Open Monday through Friday, 10:00 A.M. to 4:00 P.M., May through October and 10:00 A.M. to 2:00 P.M. the rest of year; closed holidays. There's a nominal admission fee; (765) 966–2235.

Earlham College, located on the south side of U.S. Highway 40 just west of downtown Richmond, is the home of the *Joseph Moore Museum of Natural Science.* Such wonders as a prehistoric mastodon, an extinct giant beaver, and authentic *Allosaurus* skeletons are displayed, along with Ordovician fossils, arthropods, live snakes, Indiana birds of prey, and a mummy. The museum is open, free of charge, from 1:00 to 4:00 P.M. Monday, Wednesday, and Friday, September through November and January through May; also open 1:00 to 5:00 P.M. Sunday year-round and other times by appointment. A planetarium that is part of the Moore Museum presents free shows at 1:30, 2:30, and 3:30 P.M. each Sunday. Contact Earlham College, West National Road (U.S. Highway 40), Richmond 47374; (765) 983–1303.

Whitewater Gorge Park, which borders the Whitewater River in the heart of Richmond, is one of only two known places in the United States where a unique type of limestone is exposed to the surface. Geologists, paleontologists, and amateur collectors have been coming to this site for more than a century to examine the abundance of fossils in the gorge's 425-million-year-old rock formations. The park also contains an Audubon bird sanctuary, Thistlethwaite Falls, Middlefork Reservoir, and some scenic fossil collection sites. A 3$^1/_2$-mile-long footpath leads through the gorge, but it's necessary to hike the entire length of it. Trail maps and additional information can be obtained by contacting the Richmond Parks and Recreation Department, Administration Office, 2200 National Road East, Richmond 47374; (765) 983–7274; or the

Richmond–Wayne County Convention and Tourism Bureau, 600 Promenade, Richmond 47374; (765) 935–8687 or (800) 828–8414.

Centerville, about 5 miles west of Richmond on U.S. Highway 40, claims to have the greatest concentration of antiques shops in the United States. *Webb's Antique Mall* alone covers approximately two acres and boasts some 300 dealers. Contact the mall's office at 200 West Union Street in Centerville; (765) 855–5551.

Fountain City is the home of the *Levi Coffin House,* known as "the Grand Central Station of the Underground Railroad." Levi and Catharine Coffin, Quakers who were opposed to slavery, opened their 1839 Federal-style home to approximately 2,000 fugitive black slaves during the Civil War era. You may know the Coffins better as Simeon and Rachel Halliday, characters in *Uncle Tom's Cabin.* Eliza Harris, the heroine of the same book, was a refugee who stayed with the Coffins for several days. The house, located on U.S. Highway 27 North, is open to the public from 1:00 to 4:00 P.M. Tuesday through Sunday, June through mid-September, 1:00 to 4:00 P.M. Saturday and Sunday only the rest of September through October; closed July 4; there's a nominal admission fee. Contact the Levi Coffin House, P.O. Box 77, Fountain City 47341; (765) 847–2432.

Since Guy Welliver bought his Hagerstown restaurant in the 1940s, he has increased its seating capacity from about 50 to 500—and still customers stand in line. They do so patiently, secure in the knowledge that what awaits them at *Welliver's Smorgasbord* is well worth it. Regular patrons include the 2,000 or so lucky people who live in Hagerstown and don't have far to go, as well as diners from all over central Indiana and neighboring Ohio. What lures them is the specialty of the house—an elaborate but reasonably priced buffet that features steamed shrimp in all-you-can-eat quantities. The homemade bread and salad bar are also highly recommended. Welliver's Smorgasbord, located at 40 East Main Street, is open 5:00 to 8:00 P.M. Thursday, 5:00 to 9:00 P.M. Friday, 4:30 to 9:00 P.M. Saturday, and 11:00 A.M. to 8:00 P.M. Sunday (no shrimp on Sunday); (765) 489–4131.

> **Trivia**
>
> *Indiana was the first state in the country to commercially produce wine. The industry began in Vevay in 1802.*

A short distance away, at 498 South Washington Street, some thirty employees of *Tedco, Inc.,* make about 30,000 gyroscopes a month for worldwide distribution. One of the toy factory's biggest customers is the Smithsonian Institution. Other popular toys are also produced here. Parents will be pleased to learn that all Tedco toys retail for $2.50 to $10.00. Call (765) 489–4527 to arrange a free tour.

Abbott's Candy Shop, the oldest continuous business in town, uses old family recipes to turn out a cornucopia of confections that are sold at a store in Hagerstown and by mail throughout the country. Its specialty and most popular sweet is the caramel, but many other varieties await visitors, too. Located at 48 East Walnut Street; open 9:00 A.M. to 5:00 P.M. Monday through Friday; also open 9:00 A.M. to 5:00 P.M. Saturday from Thanksgiving to Christmas Eve. Call (765) 489–4442 to arrange a free tour (yes, free samples *are* included).

The redbrick storefront in Dublin gives little hint of the treasure trove inside. Owner Patricia McDaniel is an antiques dealer extraordinaire. She is also one of Hollywood's aces-in-the-hole.

It all began in 1987, when movie director John Sayles needed some props for *Eight Men Out,* a baseball movie that was filmed partly in Indiana. McDaniel was able to supply them; the word spread, and Hollywood has beat a path to her door ever since. Her period props, many of them hard to find elsewhere, have appeared in such movies as *Legends of the Fall, Avalon, This Boy's Life,* and *A League of Their Own.*

McDaniel's store is amazing to behold. Something appears to occupy every centimeter of shelf space and very nearly all of the floor space. Yet McDaniel knows her stock. She always knows *where* something is, even if she's not sure *what* it is. A case in point is an item called Stop and Go. She originally thought it was a laxative but later learned it was a vitamin.

McDaniel's shop, called **Old Storefront Antiques,** is located at 2191 East Cumberland Street. Store hours are from 1:00 to 5:00 P.M. Monday through Saturday and at other times by chance or appointment; (765) 478–4809.

PLACES TO STAY IN SOUTHEAST INDIANA

BETHLEHEM
Inn at Bethlehem
101 West Walnut Street
(812) 293–3975

BROOKVILLE
Duck Creek Farm
12246 State Road 1
(765) 647–4575

The Mill Street Inn
500 Mill Street
(765) 647–2974

CENTERVILLE
Historic Lantz House Inn
214 West Main Street
(765) 855–2936
(800) 495–2689

COLUMBUS
The Columbus Inn
445 Fifth Street
(812) 378–4289

Country Chalet
624 North Hickory
Hills Drive
(812) 342–7806

Ruddick-Nugent House
1210 16th Street
(812) 379–1354

CONNERSVILLE
Maple Leaf Inn B&B
831 North Grand Avenue
(765) 825–7099

The Over House Bed
and Breakfast
1826 Indiana Avenue
(765) 825–2371

CORYDON

Kintner House Inn
Capitol Avenue and
Chestnut Street
P.O. Box 95
(812) 738–2020

HAGERSTOWN

Teetor House Inn
300 West Main Street
(765) 489–4422
(800) 824–4319

JEFFERSONVILLE

1877 House Country Inn
2408 Utica-Sellersburg
Road
(812) 285–1877
(888) 284–1877

The Old Bridge Inn Bed &
Breakfast
131 West Chestnut Street
(812) 284–3580
(800) 484–6507

KNIGHTSTOWN

Main Street Victorian
130 West Main Street
(765) 345–2299

Old Hoosier House
7601 South Greensboro
Pike
(765) 345–2969
(800) 775–5315

LAWRENCEBURG

Folke Family Farm
18406 Pribble Road
(812) 537–7025
(888) 593–6358

Victoriana Bed
and Breakfast
212 Short Street
(812) 537–5877

MADISON

Cliff House Bed
and Breakfast
122 Fairmount Drive
(812) 265–5272

Clifty Inn
Clifty Falls State Park
1501 Green Road
P.O. Box 387
(812) 265–4135
(877) 925–4389

Main Street Bed
and Breakfast
739 West Main Street
(812) 265–3539
(800) 362–6246

Roth's Get-Away Cottages
203 Walnut Street
(812) 265–6636

Schussler House Bed
and Breakfast
514 Jefferson Street
(812) 273–2068
(800) 392–1931

Stonefields Dream Bed
and Breakfast
411 West First Street
(812) 265–6856

METAMORA

Gingerbread House Bed
and Breakfast
19074 Clayborn Street
P.O. Box 28
(765) 647–5518

The Grapevine Inn
10083 Bridge Street
(765) 647–3738

Thorpe House Country Inn
19049 Clayborne Street
P.O. Box 36
(765) 647–5425
(888) HAPPY DAY

MIDDLETOWN

Cornerstone Guest House
705 High Street
(765) 354–6004
(800) 792–6004

Maple Hill B&B
9909 North County Road
600 West
(765) 354–2580

MILAN

Milan Railroad Inn
Main and Carr Streets
(812) 654–2800
(800) 448–7405

NEW ALBANY

Honeymoon Mansion
B&B and Wedding Chapel
1014 East Main Street
(812) 945–0312
(800) 759–7270

NEW CASTLE

Country Haven Inn
395 North County Road
300 West
(765) 533–6611

La Casa di' Maroni
5835 West County Road
200 South
(765) 785–2810

Mulberry Lane Inn
5256 North County Road
75 West
(765) 836–4500

NORTH VERNON

North Vernon's
Railroad Inn
302 Summit Street
(812) 346–2398

OSGOOD

Victorian Garden B&B
243 North Walnut Street
(812) 689–4469

RICHMOND
Hilltop Hide-A-Way
Log House
1088 Boston Township
Line Road
(765) 935–5752

The Historic Clarion
Leland Hotel
900 South A Street
(765) 966–5000

Norwich Lodge
920 Earlham Drive
(765) 983–1575

Philip W. Smith Bed
and Breakfast
2039 East Main Street
(765) 966–8972
(800) 966–8972

RISING SUN
Jelley House Country Inn
222 South Walnut Street
(812) 438–2319
(877) 429–0695

Mulberry Inn and Gardens
118 South Mulberry Street
(812) 438–2206
(800) 235–3097

VERNON
Raymers Bed and Breakfast
10 East State Street
P.O. Box 361
(812) 346–5658

VEVAY
Rosemont Inn
806 West Market Street
(812) 427–3050

**PLACES TO EAT IN
SOUTHEAST INDIANA**

AURORA
Applewood by the River
215 Judiciary Street
(812) 926–1166

The Steamboat Clinton
301 Second Street
(812) 926–0304

The Tree House
10768 Gatch Hill Road
(812) 926–3737

BATESVILLE
The Sherman House
35 South Main Street
(812) 934–2407
(800) 445–4939

BETHLEHEM
Inn at Bethlehem
101 West Walnut Street at
Riverview
(812) 293–3975

BROOKVILLE
The Case House
801 Main Street
(765) 647–3463

CENTERVILLE
Jag's Cafe
129 East Main Street
(765) 855–2282

CLARKSVILLE
Texas Roadhouse
757 East State Road 131
(812) 280–1103

COLUMBUS
Grindstone Charley's
2607 Central Avenue
(812) 372–2532

Peter's Bay Restaurant
310 Commons Mall
(812) 372–2270

Ribeye Steak and Ribs
2506 Twenty-fifth Street
(812) 376–6410

Zaharako's Confectionery
329 Washington Street
(812) 379–9329

CONNERSVILLE
Miller Cafeteria
704 North Eastern Avenue
(765) 825–6821

The Willows Downtown
Restaurant
522 North Central Avenue
(765) 825–5552

GREENSBURG
Cattlemen's Inn
1703 North Lincoln Street
(812) 663–2411

Heritage Acres
Call-Ahead Restaurant
5084 West State Road 46
(812) 663–1088
(888) 663–1088

Storie's Restaurant
109 East Main Street
(812) 663–9948

GUILFORD
Chateau Pomije
25060 Jacobs Road
(812) 623–3332
(800) 791–9463

HAGERSTOWN
Welliver's Smorgasbord
40 East Main Street
(765) 489–4131

JEFFERSONVILLE
Ann's by the River
149 Spring Street
(812) 284–2667

Frank's Steak House
520 West Seventh Street
(812) 283-3383

Inn on Spring
415 Spring Street
(812) 284-5545

Jenny Lind Tea Room
249 Spring Street
(812) 283-4832

Parrella's Italian Restaurant
3014 Sherman Drive
(812) 283-7933

Rocky's Sub Pub
1207 East Market Street
(812) 282-3844

KNIGHTSTOWN
Mel's Diner
132 East Main Street
(765) 345-7688

LAWRENCEBURG
Taverne on the Lake
19325 Schmarr Drive
(812) 537-9000

Whisky's
334 Front Street
(812) 537-4239

MADISON
Nex-Dor Restaurant
and Lounge
Best Western Inn
700 Clifty Drive
(812) 273-5151

Upper Crust
209 West Main Street
(812) 265-6727

The Wharf Restaurant
and Lounge
375 West Vaughn Drive
(812) 265-2688

METAMORA
Hearthstone Restaurant
18149 U.S. Highway 52
(765) 647-5204

MILAN
Milan Railroad Inn
Main and Carr Streets
(812) 654-2800
(800) 448-7405

The Reservation
1001 North Warpath Drive
(812) 654-2224

Villa Milan Vineyard
7287 East County Road 50
North
(812) 654-3419

NEW ALBANY
Creekside Outpost Cafe
614 Hausfeldt Lane
(812) 948-9118

Hoosier Pizza
2152 State Street
(812) 948-2229

Mancino
330 Grant Line Road
(812) 949-7777

Ranch House
1736 Millerwood Drive
(812) 949-7717

OLDENBURG
Brau Haus
22170 Wasserstrasse
(812) 934-4840

Wagner's Village Inn
22171 Main Street
(812) 934-3854

RICHMOND
Connie's House of Marker
1500 North "E" Street
(765) 966-2016

Country Rib Eye
Steakhouse
725 Progress Drive
(765) 966-4902

Damon's Clubhouse
4700 National Road East
(765) 962-5555

Jade Palace
Chinese Restaurant
4340 National Road East
(765) 935-4575

Olde Richmond Inn
138 South Fifth Street
(765) 962-2247

Pedro's Cactus Cantina
540 West Eaton Pike
(765) 966-1330

Pizza King
203 West Main Street
(765) 966-1541

Taste of the Town
1616 East Main Street
(765) 935-5464

RUSHVILLE
Pizza King
211 North Perkins Street
(765) 932-2212

SEYMOUR
Larrison's Diner
200 South Chestnut Street
(812) 522-5523

STARLIGHT
Joe Huber's Family
Restaurant
2421 Scottsville Road
(812) 923-5255

VERNON
Old Tunnel Inn
Restaurant
114 Pike Street
(812) 346-9760

VEVAY
The Ogle Haus
1013 West Main Street
(812) 427–2020

Brookville/Franklin County
Chamber of Commerse
440 West Main Street
P.O. Box 211
Brookville 47012
(765) 647–3177

Clark/Floyd Counties
Convention and
Tourism Bureau
Southern Indiana
Visitor Center
315 Southern
Indiana Avenue
Jeffersonville 47130-3218
(812) 280–5566
(800) 552–3842
Fax: (812) 282–1904

Columbus/Bartholomew
County Visitors Center
506 Fifth Street
P.O. Box 1589
Columbus 47202
(812) 378–2622
(800) 468–6564
Fax: (812) 372–7348

Connersville/Fayette
County Chamber
of Commerce
504 Central Avenue
Connersville 47331
(765) 825–2561

Dearborn County
Convention, Visitor, and
Tourism Bureau
555 Eads Parkway East,
Suite 175
P.O. Box 344
Lawrenceburg 47025
(812) 537–0814
(800) 322–8198
Fax: (812) 537–0845

Greensburg/Decatur
County Chamber
of Commerce
325 West Main Street, Suite 2
Greensburg 47240
(812) 663–2832
(800) 210–2832
Fax: (812) 663–4275

Harrison County Chamber
of Commerce
310 North Elm Street
Corydon 47112
(812) 738–2137
(888) 738–2137
Fax: (812) 738–3609

Henry County Convention
and Visitors Bureau
3900 South Memorial
Drive, Suite B
New Castle 47362
(765) 593–0764
(800) 676–4302

Jackson County Visitor and
Convention Bureau
357 Tanger Boulevard,
Suite 231
(Tanger Outlet Center)
Seymour 47274
(812) 524–1914
(888) 524–1914
Fax: (812) 524–1915

Jennings County Visitors
Center
325 North State Road 7
P.O. Box 415
Vernon 47282-0415
(812) 346–4865
(800) 928–3667
Fax: (812) 346–8928

Madison/Jefferson County
Convention and
Visitors Bureau
301 East Main Street
Madison 47250
(812) 265–2956
(800) 559–2956
Fax: (812) 273–3694

Richmond/Wayne County
Convention and
Visitors Bureau
5701 National Road East
P.O. Box 18595
Richmond 47374
(765) 935–8687
(800) 828–8414

Rushville/Rush County
Chamber of Commerce
315 North Main Street
Rushville 46173
(765) 932–2880

Ripley County Tourism
Bureau
102 North Main Street
P.O. Box 576
Versailles 47042
(812) 689–6654
Fax: (812) 689–3044

Southwest Indiana

enerally described as the most beautiful part of the Hoosier State, southwest Indiana is filled with uninterrupted stretches of dense forests, jutting cliffs, and clear streams. Scenic highways wind through hills lush with greenery in the spring and summer and blazing with color in the fall. Where the Wabash River, which forms much of the state's western border, meets the Ohio River, which bounds the state on the south, there are misty bayous and cypress swamps reminiscent of the Deep South.

The banks of the Ohio River are dotted with small towns in which historic sites and nineteenth-century architecture have been carefully preserved. Beneath the earth's surface lies Indiana's world-famous limestone belt, laid down by an ancient sea 300 million years ago.

This is the land that shaped a young Abraham Lincoln. It is the place the founders of New Harmony viewed as Utopia. In the 1920s and 1930s, movie stars and gangsters came here to relax and rejuvenate themselves in the waters of the region's abundant mineral springs. It is still a place where life plays out in its own sweet time, a place that invites the visitor to explore and discover.

Brown County

Things don't change much in Brown County. The population today is nearly the same as it was in 1880. Each morning the mists rise from hills still draped with forests. Log cabins, hemmed in by split-rail fences, nestle in isolated hollows. Like as not there's a woodpile in the yard, and on cool days fingers of wood smoke spiral up from stone chimneys. Narrow, twisting country roads lead to picturesque places with picturesque names—Gnaw Bone, Bean Blossom, Scarce O'Fat Ridge, Bear Wallow Hill, Milk-Sick Bottoms, Slippery Elm Chute Road, and Booger Holler. No billboards mar your view along the way—they're not allowed in Brown County. No air pollution muddies the landscape and offends your nostrils—Brown County has no industry.

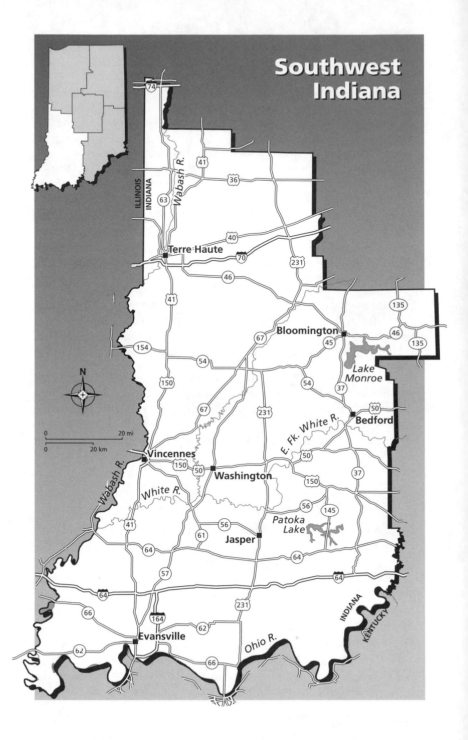

Southwest
Indiana

And if you're in a hurry, you're out of luck—Brown County doesn't cater to people in a hurry.

Nashville, the county seat and largest town in the county, normally has a population of about 700 people, but on October weekends that figure swells to more than 100,000. Brown County is best known for its dazzling fall color. Most folks head for **Brown County State Park,** some 15,000 acres of natural beauty near Nashville. Each year it ranks as one of the top-ten most-visited parks in the nation—and the other nine are all *national* parks! **Yellowwood State Forest** in western Brown County and a portion of the southern part of the county offers equally spectacular and less-crowded panoramas.

In spring Brown County is glorious with the blossoms of redbud and dogwood trees and myriad wildflowers. In summer the woods offer a cool green retreat, and for wintertime visitors there are cross-country ski trails and a downhill ski resort.

Author's Favorite Attractions/ Events in Southwest Indiana

Brown County State Park, *Nashville;*
(812) 988–6406

Gasthof Amish Village, *Montgomery;*
(812) 486–3977

Greene County Viaduct, *near Solsberry;*
(812) 384–8995

Lilly Library of Rare Books
and Manuscripts,
Indiana University, Bloomington;
(812) 855–2452

New Harmony (entire town);
(812) 682–4488

West Baden Springs Hotel, *West Baden;*
(317) 639–4534 or (800) 450–4534

Wyandotte Cave,
Leavenworth; (812) 738–2782

Bluegrass Hall of Fame and
Uncle Pen Day Festival,
Bean Blossom; September
(812) 988–6422 or (800) 414–4677

Limestone Heritage Festival,
Bedford; July
(812) 275–4493

Mennonite Relief Sale,
Cannelburg; September
(812) 486–3281

Mushroom Festival,
Mansfield; April
(765) 653–4026

Parke County Covered
Bridge Festival,
Rockville; October
(765) 569–5226 or 569–5372

Spirit of Vincennes Rendezvous,
Vincennes; May
(812) 886–0400 or
(800) 886–6443

Turkey Trot Festival,
Montgomery; September
(812) 486–3649

Brown County first gained fame as a mecca for artists and craftspeople, who have been inspired by the peace and beauty of these hills since the 1870s. Today many open their studios to the public. The *Brown County Craft Gallery,* the *Brown County Art Guild,* and the *Brown County Art Gallery,* all in Nashville, are among the galleries that exhibit some of their works.

Nashville is the hub of activity in Brown County—a potpourri of some 250 shops, museums, and restaurants. Craftspeople make and sell quilts, pottery, wood carvings, metal sculptures, hand-carved candles, leather goods, silver and gold jewelry made to order, stained-glass wares, dollhouses, teddy bears, handblown art glass, dulcimers, and much more. At many shops you can watch the artisans at work. On summer days, the beautifully handcrafted Melchior Marionettes delight onlookers at an outdoor theater on South Van Buren Street; call (317) 535–4853 or (800) 849–4853 for schedule and ticket information.

Trivia

Freshwater jellyfish are known to exist at twenty-five sites in Indiana. About the size of a nickel or dime, they are clear or translucent white and consist of more than 90 percent water. One of their known habitats is Yellowwood Lake, which lies within Yellowwood State Forest in Brown County.

With no chair more than ten rows from the stage, the *Brown County Playhouse* in the heart of Nashville doesn't have a bad seat in the house. This is Indiana's oldest professional stock theater; performers are from the Theatre and Drama Department at Indiana University in nearby Bloomington (see Monroe County). Actors Kevin Kline, Patricia Kalember, and Jonathan Banks, as well as the late Howard Ashman, the Academy Award–winning lyricist of the Disney films *Aladdin, Beauty and the Beast,* and *The Little Mermaid,* are just a few of the people who have honed their skills on this stage before going on to bigger things. Showtime is at 8:00 P.M., with nights of performance varying from Wednesday through Sunday during summer and fall months. For an exact schedule and other information, contact the Indiana University Auditorium, Bloomington 47405; (812) 855–1103. In season you can also write the Brown County Playhouse, P.O. Box 1187, Nashville 47448; or call (812) 988–2123 from 10:00 A.M. to 5:00 P.M. daily and from 10:00 A.M. to 8:30 P.M. on days of performance.

A complex of authentic nineteenth-century buildings just northeast of the courthouse in Nashville is known collectively as the *Brown County Historical Museum.* Carding, spinning, and weaving are demonstrated in an old log barn. You'll also see a country doctor's office, a blacksmith's shop, and a log cabin home, all complete with furnishings, and an unusual log jail that claims the distinction of being the only one in the state that ever permitted a prisoner to be his own keeper. While serving a sentence for bootlegging, the prisoner went wherever he wanted to during the day, locked himself up at night, acted as a guide for tourists, and once aided the sheriff in making an arrest. Open 1:00 to 5:00 P.M. Saturday, Sunday, and holidays, May through October. There's an admission fee. The buildings can always be viewed, however, from the outside.

To bluegrass music fans, the late *Bill Monroe* is a legend and Bean Blossom is a bluegrass mecca. Monroe held annual festivals on his sprawling Bean Blossom property starting in the mid-1960s, making this the locale of the longest-running bluegrass festival in the country. The thousands of devotees who still come here from all over the country and beyond say the *Bean Blossom bluegrass festivals* have an ambience unlike any other in the world. When professional musicians aren't playing on stage, amateur musicians in the audience are playing in their own impromptu groups. It's a rare moment when there's no music to be heard anywhere.

Most people stay on the festival grounds for the three or four days a festival is held. A campground on the property offers both modern and primitive campsites. In 1992 Monroe brought his extensive collection of bluegrass and country music memorabilia to Bean Blossom and opened the *Bluegrass Hall of Fame and Museum.* Recognized as the father of

Annual Events in Southwest Indiana

Cherry Blossom Festival,
Washington; April (812) 254–2740

Lotus Dickey Hometown Reunion,
Paoli; June (812) 723–4769

Shoals Catfish Festival,
Shoals; July (812) 247–2828

Jasper Strassenfest,
Jasper; July/August (812) 482–6866

Riverfest,
Evansville; July/August (812) 424–2986

Amish Quilt Show and Auction,
Cannelburg; August (812) 486–3491

Knox County Watermelon Festival,
Vincennes; August (812) 886–0400
or (800) 886–6443

Mosquito Fest,
Zoar; August (812) 536–2920

Schweizer Fest,
Tell City; August (812) 547–2385

Native American Days Festival,
Evansville; September
(812) 853–3956

Persimmon Festival,
Mitchell; September (812) 275–7637
or (800) 798–0769

Lotus World Music and Arts Festival,
Bloomington; September/October
(812) 336–6599

Herbstfest,
Huntingburg; October (812) 683–5699

The Thousand-Year Storm

*T*ornadoes, nature's most destructive storms, occur more frequently in the United States than in any other country on earth. Seventy-five percent of the world's tornadoes take place in the United States, and the vast majority of those strike our country's midsection. As residents of that tornado-prone heartland, Hoosiers are well acquainted with these violent whirlwinds (Indiana experiences an average of twenty-three tornadoes each year). Few people today, however, remember that Indiana was one of three states devastated by the single most destructive tornado in recorded history.

The weather forecast for much of the Midwest on March 18, 1925, called for "rains and strong shifting winds." It was a common forecast for a spring day in that part of the world. Midwesterners went about their business as usual but kept a wary eye on the sky, aware at all times how violent a spring storm could suddenly become.

No one, however, expected the unprecedented fury of the tornado that dropped from the skies that day. The Tri-State Tornado, as it is known in the record books, is the one tornado that stands apart from all others— before and since..

The tornado was born at 1:01 P.M. in the Missouri Ozarks. From there it raced northeastward across the Mississippi, through Illinois, and into Indiana, hugging the ground with a vengeance for three and one-half hours. It did not lift, skip, or, until the last few miles of its life, veer from its straightforward path. When it finally dissipated, it had traveled 219 miles at forward speeds of more than 70 miles per hour. Its winds at times were in excess of 300 miles per hour. Its width varied from $1/2$ mile to more than 1 mile wide. (By way of comparison, the average tornado lasts a few minutes, travels 5 miles at a forward speed of 30 miles per hour, produces winds of 150 miles per hour or less, and averages 220 yards in width.)

When the storm crossed the Wabash River and entered Indiana at about 4:00 P.M., it headed straight for Griffin, a small village located approximately 3 miles from the river in northwestern Posey County. It took less than three minutes for the twister to obliterate the entire town. Not a single structure was left standing. Stunned survivors could only guess where they had once lived.

Still the twister raced on, turning slightly northward toward Owensville and Princeton. Although narrowing in width, it increased its forward speed to nearly 75 miles per hour—faster than its top speed in either Missouri or Illinois. It created havoc in Owensville and swept away half of Princeton before finally exhausting itself about 3 miles southwest of Petersburg.

As survivors came together in the aftermath of the storm, tales of bizarre phenomena surfaced. The river mud that had been sucked up into the tornado by the time it reached Griffin left people there with mud so thoroughly imbedded in their skin that they were unrecognizable. A baby, completely covered with mud, *was dug from a ditch after its cries were heard; no one in the area had a baby, and its rescuers never learned if its parents had been found. At the site of one house, only a carton of eggs and a remnant of the floor on which it was sitting were found intact. A cow was found standing and chewing her cud, seemingly unperturbed, although the barn around her had been lifted up and carried away. An office in Princeton was razed to the ground, but a bundle of paychecks that had been stored in an office cabinet was found undamaged 55 miles away.*

Property damage wrought by the storm was estimated at $16.5 million

in 1925 dollars (equal to $159 million today). The storm had completely annihilated four towns and 15,000 homes, severely damaged six more towns, and injured 2,027 people. Most significant of all, there were 695 confirmed deaths, still a record for a single tornado.

On average, 800 to 1,000 tornadoes occur in the United States each year. Nearly 1,200 tornadoes were reported in 1999. But to this day, the 1925 Tri-State Tornado remains the deadliest tornado in history, a rare storm that some weather historians say comes along once in a thousand years.

bluegrass, Monroe accumulated his collection throughout more than sixty years of entertaining.

One of the fourteen rooms in the 5,000-square-foot museum is filled with Bill Monroe's personal mementos. Country music artifacts include items once owned by Johnny Cash, Dolly Parton, and Dottie West. On the grounds near the museum is a cabin that was moved here log by log from Nashville, Tennessee. Known as Uncle Pen's Cabin, it belonged to a relative who took young Bill Monroe into his home when Monroe's parents died. Fans will recognize the name from a song Monroe wrote about his uncle. (It was recorded by Ricky Skaggs and Porter Wagoner.)

The museum, campground, and festival park are located on the east side of State Road 135 in Bean Blossom, about 5 miles north of Nashville. Open daily spring through fall; hours may vary. For additional information call (812) 988–6422 or (800) 414–4677.

A little farther east of Nashville on State Road 46 is the northern entrance to **Brown County State Park,** accessible via Indiana's only divided, two-lane covered bridge (circa 1838). Enjoy 27 miles of scenic roads, hiking and bridle trails, a nature center, campgrounds (including one for horseback riders), an archery range, an Olympic-size swimming pool, a lodge with a restaurant, and rustic rental cabins. A nature trail leads through **Ogle Hollow State Nature Preserve,** noteworthy for its rare yellowwood trees. Open year-round during daylight hours; there's a vehicle entrance fee April through October. Contact Brown County State Park, P.O. Box 608, Nashville 47448; (812) 988–6406. For lodge and cabin reservations contact Abe Martin Lodge, P.O. Box 547, Nashville 47448; (812) 988–4418 or (877) 265–6343.

Continuing east from the park on State Road 46, you'll come to State Road 135, which leads south into a secluded and little-known part of Brown County. Follow State Road 135 to an area referred to locally as *Stone Head,* so called because of the unique monument by the side of the highway that serves as a road sign—a white stone head atop a stone pillar. Every once in a while a prankster makes off with the carving, but an outraged community has always managed to recover it.

Proceed on State Road 135 to the tiny community of *Story.* Virtually unchanged since its founding in the 1850s, the peaceful hamlet exudes the charm of a Brown County that was—a long-ago Brown County whose rural serenity and beauty first lured artists and craftspeople to these forested hills. Here, amid a cluster of tumbledown buildings that bear mute testimony to old dreams, the *Story Inn* offers food and shelter so pleasing that the Indiana Division of Tourism bestowed its Best Bed-and-Breakfast in the State award on it. On the outside, the tin-faced, tin-roofed building resembles the general store it once was. On the inside, antiques and knickknacks line the walls of the dining room, and a potbellied stove stands ready to serve on cold winter days. The food, however, is pure gourmet. Such offerings as rabbit New Orleans, chicken Provençal, and Greek spinach pie appear on a menu that changes weekly but always features fresh fish and a pasta dish. No matter what entree you decide on, save room for dessert—the turtle cheesecake, with its chocolate graham cracker crust and thick caramel topping, is to die for. Guests who spend the night can stay in one of the inn's five upstairs bedrooms or in one of the renovated village cottages nearby; a full country breakfast is included in the inn's room rates of $76 to $90 or the cottages' rates of $82 to $104 per night for two. All rooms have private baths and air-conditioning but no television or telephone. The inn serves three meals a day; prices are moderate to expensive. Advance reservations are recommended for dinner and are required for overnight accommodations. Contact the Story Inn at 6404 South State Road 135, Nashville 47448; call (812) 988–2273 or (800) 881–1183.

To experience a bit of splendid solitude and delve into a mystery that has defied a solution for decades, continue southwest from Story on Elkinsville Road to *Browning Mountain.* The journey is an adventure in itself. The paved road soon gives way to a graveled one. Hills and ridges rise above you, and Salt Creek meanders across the valley floor. The road becomes rougher, the bridges narrower. Eventually, you'll drive through rather than over dry creek beds. Then, approximately 4 miles after leaving Story, at the juncture of Elkinsville and Combs Roads, the mountain appears before you.

The mountain, of course, is actually a hill, but once you have ascended the steep path that leads to its summit you'll understand why it has come to

Other Attractions Worth Seeing in Southwest Indiana

BEDFORD

Antique Auto and Race Car Museum,
Junction of U.S. Highway 50 and State Road 37; (812) 275-0556

BLOOMINGTON

Indiana University Art Museum,
*Fine Arts Plaza, East Seventh Street;
(812) 855-5445*

Mathers Museum,
*416 North Indiana Avenue;
(812) 855-6873*

EVANSVILLE

Evansville Museum,
*411 Southeast Riverside Drive;
(812) 425-2406*

FERDINAND

Monastery Immaculate Conception,
200 Hill Tenth Street; (812) 367-1111

GENTRYVILLE

**Colonel William Jones
State Historic Site,**
RR 1, Box 60D; (812) 937-2802

HELMSBURG

Fig Tree Gallery and Coffee Shop,
*4865 Helmsburg Road,
(812) 988-1375*

JASPER

Indiana Baseball Hall of Fame,
1436 Leopold Street; (812) 482-2262

Saint Joseph Church,
*Thirteenth and Newton Streets;
(812) 482-1805*

NASHVILLE

Fourth Dimension Hologram Museum,
*90 West Washington Street,
(812) 988-8212*

T. C. Steele State Historic Site,
RR 1, Box 256; (812) 988-2785

TERRE HAUTE

**C.A.N.D.L.E.S. Holocaust Museum
and Education Center,**
*1532 South Third Street;
(812) 234-7881*

**Children's Science and
Technology Museum,**
*523 Wabash Avenue;
(812) 235-5548*

Native American Museum,
*5050 East Poplar Drive;
(812) 877-6007*

Sheldon Swope Art Gallery,
25 South Seventh Street; (812) 238-1676

VINCENNES

Indiana Military Museum,
4305 Bruceville Road; (812) 882-8668

**Lincoln Memorial Bridge and
USS Vincennes Monument,**
*West Vigo Street at the Wabash River;
(812) 886-0400 or (800) 886-6443*

be popularly known as a mountain. Atop the hill is the mystery you are seeking—Indiana's own version of Stonehenge (the world-famous site near Salisbury, England, where huge stone blocks arranged in an orderly fashion have stood for nearly 1,000 years). No one is sure how the enormous slabs at Stonehenge could have been transported there so long ago, just as no one is sure how the scattering of giant hunks of limestone atop Browning Mountain made their way there. One theory is that a bed of limestone was laid down long ago when Brown County was covered by an ancient sea, then broken up and tossed about by natural forces when the sea waters receded. Another theory is that the stones once marked a place sacred to Native Americans. It is true, however, that these huge rocks must weigh many tons each, and some look as though they might have been cut to size and placed in some sort of significant arrangement.

Over the years, attempts were made to quarry the stones, but so many accidents occurred that all further attempts were abandoned. This gave rise to the legend of an Indian spirit watcher who makes sure no one disturbs the stones and to tales of the ghosts of men who died when they disturbed this spot and are condemned to roam the area forever.

If the solution to the mystery evades you, you're in good company. A few years ago, a party of scientists journeyed here from South America to examine these stones, but they couldn't determine an answer either. Like them, you will come away from Browning Mountain with more questions than answers, but the journey that takes you there, through one of the most beautiful and unspoiled areas of Indiana, will likely be so rewarding you won't mind at all.

Another mystery in Brown County, just recently come to light, also beggars a solution. It was discovered by a hunter who was tracking a wild turkey in Yellowwood State Forest on a cold February morning in 1998. He found his turkey in a most unlikely spot—perched atop a huge, refrigerator-size rock that was cradled in the limbs of an oak tree about 35 feet above the ground.

Any explanation as to how the rock got there is purely speculative. No heavy equipment could have placed it there. The area is so remote and so densely forested that any activity involving heavy equipment would be easily spotted. Another theory is that the rock might have been flung there by blasting in a nearby area, but there has been no nearby blasting. Perhaps the most logical suggestion thus far is that a tornado deposited the rock in the branches, but there's no sign of any tornado damage anywhere else in the vicinity. And of course there are a few people who hint at UFO involvement.

Whatever the explanation, **Gobbler's Rock,** as it has been officially named, is firmly entrenched in its treetop perch. Word of the strange sight has spread, and the forest office has been getting inquiries about its exact location. If you would like to view the rock yourself and are willing to walk a bit to see it, stop by the forest office and pick up a map. The office is located at 772 Yellowwood Lake Road; take State Road 46 west from Nashville for about 6 miles and turn north at the YELLOWWOOD STATE FOREST sign; call (812) 988–7945 for office hours.

The highest point in Brown County is on State Road 46 southwest of Nashville where there is a respectable downhill ski, snow tubing, and snow-boarding area that offers all the makings for a fine winter holiday—eight slopes and trails with a vertical drop of 250 feet, a bunny slope for beginners, chairlifts, rope tows, a lodge, a ski shop, and dining facilities. **Ski World** also hosts the annual **Brown County Winter Fest,** held in early February. Activities during the rest of the year include an Alpine Slide, one of only a handful in the United States (riders slide down one of two twisting concrete tracks in carts). Visitors will also find two 60-foot-high water slides, go-cart and bumper boat rides, bank shot basketball, batting cages, and, during spring through fall weekends, live entertainment. Open 10:00 A.M. to 10:00 P.M. Monday through Thursday; 10:00 A.M. to 4:00 A.M. Friday; 9:00 A.M. to 4:00 A.M. Saturday; and 9:00 A.M. to 10:00 P.M. Sunday during ski season; noon to 8:00 P.M. weekends and holidays in the spring and fall; 11:00 A.M. to 10:00 P.M. daily in the summer (weather permitting); closed Christmas Eve. New trails, attractions, and activities are constantly being added, and hours may vary. For up-to-date information, contact Ski World, P.O. Box 445, Nashville 47448; (812) 988–6638.

Tourists, as well as armies, travel on their stomachs. The most popular of the many fine eateries in Nashville is **The Nashville House,** located on the corner of Main and Van Buren Streets in the center of town. Its charming, rustic atmosphere is enhanced by antique furniture, checkered tablecloths, and a huge stone fireplace. The menu lists such Hoosier favorites as fried ham steak, baked ham, barbecued ribs, roast turkey, country-fried chicken, and hot or iced sassafras tea, but the highlight of any meal has to be the fried biscuits. These delicious deep-fried dough balls, served with baked apple butter, could make an addict of anyone. Owner Andy Rogers says they were invented by his father, Jack Rogers, around 1947. The Nashville House is no place for dieters—not only is everything sinfully fattening, but unless you're a lumberjack you might be hard put to eat everything that's placed in front of you. Although the menu is limited, the food is country cooking

Indiana is on top of several earthquake faults. The largest concentration, known as the Wabash Valley fault system, lies in the southwestern part of the state. Most earthquakes centered in Indiana are relatively minor events, but recently discovered evidence indicates that a quake of magnitude 7.5 occurred near Vincennes about 5,000 years ago.

at its finest. Prices range from $6.00 to $10.00 for lunch and from $12 to $20 for dinner; there's a children's menu. Open 11:30 A.M. to 8:00 P.M. Sunday through Thursday and 11:30 A.M. to 9:00 P.M. Friday and Saturday in October; closed Tuesday the rest of the year; also closed for two weeks during the Christmas season. Reservations are accepted except during October; (812) 988–4554.

The entrance to the Nashville House is through the *Old Country Store,* a pleasant place to browse if you have to wait for seating in the restaurant. It's just what the name implies—a delightful clutter of goods that includes many hard-to-find items from yesteryear.

Need a cup of hot brew and a pleasant corner in which to relax a spell? Drop in at *The Daily Grind.* You'll find it in Nashville's Calvin Place, a cluster of shops on the southwest corner of Franklin and Van Buren Streets. Although coffeehouses have dropped from the scene in many places, this one is alive and well, thank you. No one gets sticky about it, but from the moment you lift the latch and walk through the heavy wooden door you feel welcome here. Your main problem will be making a decision. There are about twenty different gourmet coffees from all over the world and fifty varieties of tea—all served in stoneware mugs. Go-withs include salads, sandwiches, soups, bagels, and pastries. Belgian waffles, sausages, and croissants filled with ham, eggs, and cheese are popular breakfast fare. Stored on the mantel of the stone fireplace is a selection of such games as chess, checkers, and backgammon—help yourself. Read one of the newspapers lying about or play a game of darts. The country store area offers coffee beans, apothecary jars filled with tea leaves, coffee mugs, spices, teapots, and coffeemakers. The Daily Grind, which fills mail orders, is open year-round 8:00 A.M. to 6:00 P.M. Sunday through Thursday, and 8:00 A.M. to 10:00 P.M. Friday and Saturday. Live entertainment is featured on Friday and Saturday nights at 7:00 P.M. Hours may vary in the winter. Contact The Daily Grind, P.O. Box 607, Nashville 47448; (812) 988–4808.

Overnight facilities in and near Nashville range from resort inns to motels, from bed-and-breakfast rooms in private homes to furnished log cabins with equipped kitchens. Many are booked up as far as two years in advance, especially on weekends from spring through fall and the week before Christmas, so plan ahead.

For more information about Brown County and its attractions, contact the Brown County Convention and Visitors Bureau, P.O. Box 840, Nashville 47448; (812) 988–7303 or (800) 753–3255; fax (812) 988–1070.

While in Nashville buy a copy of the **Brown County Democrat,** which has been honored as Indiana's finest weekly newspaper more times than anyone can remember. The "Sheriff's Log" therein is a Brown County classic. You'll find such entries as:

Man called and said he just put on a pot of coffee if any officers are in the area and want coffee.

Girl at restaurant requests a conservation officer. An owl is sitting on the pizza oven.

Trouble reported at the city dump. Someone abandoned a person there.

A coon is asleep on the shelf [of a local shop] with a teddy bear.

Man wants deputy [any deputy] to meet him so that he can borrow $5 or $10.

Man requests Nashville town marshal go to restaurant and check the stove to see if he left a pot of beans on.

Caller says someone has been cow tipping. His cows were asleep in the field and someone tipped them over.

Woman reports that a white space ship with an El Camino on the back of it has been going into her neighbor's house. The man driving the space ship has been dead for several years.

Man wants to know if the sheriff would like to come watch his snakes eat.

Cancel burglar alarm. A grouse flew through a window, setting off the alarm, but the house cat ate the grouse.

Wild cow reported in Fruitdale.

Three UFOs hovering over house near Bean Blossom. Keep changing colors and shapes.

Woman wants to know what she has to do to get arrested so she can spend Thanksgiving weekend in jail with her sister.

Man says a naked woman walked into his house.

Like the mythical sheriff's office in Mayberry, North Carolina, made famous by a television series, this one's run with a lot of heart.

Crawford County

ost spelunkers are aware of the subterranean wonders that exist in the Hoosier State, but few other people know that there is a proliferation of caves in southern Indiana. Several of those open to the public are in Crawford County.

Thanks to being mentioned in both *Ripley's Believe It or Not* and the *Guinness Book of World Records,* **Wyandotte Cave** has become world-famous for its Monument Mountain—the highest underground mountain in any known cave on earth. It stands 135 feet tall, the focal point of an awe-inspiring room known as Rothrock's Cathedral, which is approximately 185 feet high, 360 feet long, and 140 feet wide. Your tour guide may introduce you to the ghost of Chief Wyandotte, a weird and entertaining play of shadows at the top of the cathedral. Superlatives apply elsewhere in the cave, too: an area $1/2$ mile in circumference and 200 feet high is the largest subterranean room known anywhere in the world, and a resplendent stalagmite 35 feet high and 75 feet around is believed to be the world's largest formation of its kind. With some 25 miles of known passages explored, the cave itself is among the earth's largest. You'll also see delicate and exquisite formations called helictites that are extremely rare. A two-hour walk covers $1^1/2$ miles; if you're the rugged type, opt for a five- or eight-hour tour during which you'll not only walk but crawl, climb, descend a pole once used by Indians, and, in places, travel by lantern light.

Just south of Wyandotte Cave is **Little Wyandotte Cave,** which can be toured in about thirty minutes. This cave is much more ordinary but is enjoyable for those who've never been in a cavern.

To reach the caves travel west from Corydon on State Road 62 for about 12 miles and turn north on a blacktop road; signs point the way. There are admission fees; reservations are necessary for the five- and eight-hour tours. Although available all year, tours are conducted more frequently in the summer. Nature provides a constant temperature of fifty-two degrees all year long for both caves. The caves and a visitor center are open daily Memorial Day through Labor Day; closed Monday the rest of the year. Contact Wyandotte Caves, Route 1, Box 85, Leavenworth 47137; (812) 738–2782.

The state-owned caves are part of a larger recreation area known as the *Harrison-Crawford Wyandotte Complex.* Besides the caves it includes the *Wyandotte Woods State Recreation Area* and the *Harrison-Crawford State Forest,* both of which straddle the Harrison-Crawford county line. Wyandotte Woods offers developed campsites, hiking and bridle trails, a nature center, views of the Ohio River, and an Olympic-size swimming pool. For those who enjoy roughing it, Harrison-Crawford State Forest has primitive campsites and overnight backpacking trails. To reach both, travel west from Corydon on State Road 62 for about 8 miles to State Road 462 and turn south; State Road 462 runs through the forest and ends in Wyandotte Woods. For information about both the forest and the recreation area, contact Harrison-Crawford State Forest, 7240 Old Forest Road, Corydon 47112; (812) 738–8232.

Not far north of Wyandotte Caves is *Marengo Cave,* discovered in 1883 by a young brother and sister exploring a sinkhole. The cave, a comfortable fifty-four degrees at all times, has been open to the public ever since, and its beauty has been acclaimed throughout the world. Concerts were once held in a subterranean room noted for its acoustics, and an early-day evangelist preached his fiery message from Pulpit Rock. Underground weddings and dances were regular occurrences throughout the years, and a square dance is still held in the Music Hall Chamber each July.

Two tours are offered. The highlight of the 1/3-mile tour is Crystal Palace, acknowledged by speleologists as one of the ten most beautiful cavern rooms anywhere. A 1-mile tour through a different part of the cave features totem pole stalagmites and a cavern possibly big enough to build a highway through. Above the cavern is a 112-acre park, complete with campsites and trail rides atop horses from the park's stables. There's a separate fee for each tour and a special combination price for both. The cave is open daily year-round, except Thanksgiving and Christmas; 9:00 A.M. to 6:00 P.M. Memorial Day to Labor Day and spring and fall weekends; 9:30 A.M. to 5:30 P.M. spring and fall weekdays; 9:00 A.M. to 5:00 P.M. the rest of the year. Marengo Cave is just northeast of the town of Marengo; go east from Marengo on State Road 64/66 and follow the signs. Contact Marengo Cave Park, Marengo Cave Road, 360 East State Road 64, P.O. Box 217, Marengo 47140; (812) 365–2705 or (888) 70–CAVES.

Twisting its way southward through Crawford County is the lovely, spring-fed *Blue River,* Indiana's first officially designated natural and scenic river and an ideal canoe stream. Several outfitters offer trips, ranging from 7 to 58 miles in length; on longer trips you spend the night on the river. Depending on the trip you take, you'll float quiet waters and shoot rapids; pass caves, springs, limestone bluffs, and walls of trees; or make your way around rock gardens and through narrow gorges. The fishing is some of the best in the Midwest, producing catches of bass, crappie, bluegill, and catfish, and the serenity can be well-nigh incredible. In its lower stretches, just before it joins the Ohio River, the Blue River turns sluggish—perfect for tubing. Rates for canoeing range from $7.50 to $21.00 per person and include paddle, life jacket, and shuttle service; there are special rates for children. The season is usually April through October, but water levels are best for canoeing before mid-July. For names of outfitters in the area, contact the Crawford County Chamber of Commerce, Route 1, Box 224D, Marengo 47140; (812) 365–2174 or (800) 742–6763.

About 5 miles south of Milltown is one of Indiana's most curious landmarks—a white oak known locally as the *Shoe Tree*. Most days, more than 150 pairs of shoes of all shapes, sizes, and colors can be seen dangling from its branches. No one seems to know exactly when the custom started, but it dates back some thirty-five years. Local folks speculate that someone thought of his shoes as longtime friends that had served him faithfully and well and deserved a better fate than to be unceremoniously dumped in the garbage, so he decided to display them in a permanent place of honor.

Although one sees old shoes hanging from many places these days, the folks in Milltown, who refer to this tree as the town's "branch office," will tell you that their Shoe Tree is the original. In fact, they claim, they've even copyrighted it. Inquire in Milltown for directions; the tree stands at the junction of two gravel roads that aren't shown on most maps.

Just west of Milltown, on the north side of State Road 64, is an *old limestone quarry* with an intriguing maze of tunnels dug into the side of a hill. Inside the cavernous excavations, eerie echoes bombard your ears— the flutter of birds' wings, dripping water, your own footsteps. Ceilings at least 20 feet high, supported by great stone buttresses, and the silent halls they enclose create the impression that you are entering some ancient catacombs or perhaps a cathedral, now hushed and still, whose days of glory have been lost in the mists of time. Explore at your own risk.

The little town of Leavenworth on the Ohio River likens its history to that of Noah and the ark—the oldest establishments in town date back to just after the flood. The granddaddy of all floods on the Ohio occurred in 1937, and most of the riverside town of Leavenworth was washed away to points south. Undaunted, residents moved up to a blufftop and started over. Lack of money, like politics, can make for strange bedfellows,

Trivia

Forty-two species of orchids are native to Indiana. Hawaii is home to only three native species.

so a small cafe and a grocery store shared the second floor of a chicken hatchery. From those humble beginnings has evolved a family restaurant called *The Overlook,* which now occupies the entire building. Through the years the restaurant has specialized in good home cooking and reasonable prices, and people go out of their way to stop here. Even if the food weren't so good, it would be worth stopping at The Overlook just for the view—a sweeping panorama of forested hills and the broad Ohio River as it arches around a horseshoe bend. The Overlook, located on the south side of State Road 62 in Leavenworth, is open 8:00 A.M. to 9:00 P.M. daily year-round, except Christmas, for breakfast, lunch, and dinner. Dinner prices range from $7.00 to $16.00. Contact The Overlook, P.O. Box 67, Leavenworth 47137; (812) 739–4264.

Also on State Road 62, not far from The Overlook, is a shopping experience not to be missed. You can find most anything imaginable at *Stephenson's General Store and Museum,* even though it may take a while to find it. There are craft items, antiques, groceries, furniture, and hardware items—in no discernible order. Some mole traps, rusty though they may be, do not detract from the exquisite beauty of the pottery shelved near them. Cookie mixes are on a shelf below sleigh bells, and slabs of bologna are found behind a display of ball gloves. The museum mentioned in the eighty-year-old store's name, a bit worse for years of wear, is housed in the basement; among the exhibits is a rare wicker casket. Wander the aisles and browse a bit, and you'll find that, as much as anything, Stephenson's contains memories. Open 10:30 A.M. to 5:30 P.M. Monday through Saturday year-round; also 1:00 to 5:00 P.M. Sunday, April through December. For additional information call Stephenson's at (812) 739–4242.

Daviess County

Along about 1972 the local folks decided they needed a unique attraction to put Daviess County on the map, and their idea brought them fame that exceeded their wildest expectations. They combined Indiana's best-known event, the Indianapolis 500, with Daviess County's best-known product—turkeys—and gave birth to the *Turkey Trot Festival.*

Come September, turkeydom's finest make their way to Montgomery Recreation Park in Montgomery for four days of the most laughable racing imaginable. Because there are about forty turkeys to every human being in Daviess County (with a noticeable but temporary change in the ratio just after the Thanksgiving and Christmas holidays), there can be a lot of birds to face off. This requires many preliminary heats, and only the cream of the crop survive the grueling schedule to race in the final championship run.

On the last, fateful day, anxious jockeys lead their tethered birds to the starting line, eager to put weeks of training to the test. Some raw talent is always on hand, too, since many owners believe that training a bird with a brain the size of a thumbnail is a waste of time. Onlookers cheer their personal favorites—such racing greats as Dirty Bird, White Lightning, and Turkey Lurkey.

On signal, the turkeys head down a 213-foot-long straightaway track toward a finish line that, for a top turkey trotter, is approximately twenty seconds away. Alas, prima donnas are inevitable. Some refuse to start at all. The more befuddled go sideways or backward. Still others tire along the way and pause to peck at whatever turkeys like to peck at. Some even take to the air, disdainfully rising above it all. Eventually, however, one galloping gobbler manages to cross the finish line and is declared the grand champion.

Another big event is the best-dressed turkey contest, which inspires elaborate costumes. One winner devastated the judges when she modeled her stunning powder-blue bikini, then further charmed them by coyly batting her false eyelashes.

And if you think they don't take all this seriously in Daviess County, consider the fact that these are the only turkey races in the world sanctioned by the National Turkey Federation. The races have received national attention from the day of their inception, and stories about them have been translated into a half dozen languages and printed all around the globe. Spectators come from all over.

Although the turkeys are obviously the main attraction, the festival also features mud volleyball, a demolition derby, tractor pulls, and entertainment by top country music stars. For additional information contact the Daviess County Visitors Bureau, 1 Train Depot Street, P.O. Box 430, Washington 47501; (812) 254–5262 or (800) 449–5262.

Montgomery is located in the heart of southern Indiana's Amish country, a fact that until recently was little known beyond the borders of Daviess County and its immediate neighbors. To celebrate this heritage, the sixty-five-acre *Gasthoff Amish Village* is being constructed on the Henry Wittmer farm near Montgomery. At this writing, visitors will find **Der Deutsche Gasthof,** a restaurant that features authentic Amish cooking; a gift shop that sells items handmade by Amish craftspeople; an outdoor flea market (Tuesday and Wednesday, May through October); and a year-round farmers' market. Future plans include the addition of an inn, an auction barn, and shops that will house various Amish businesses. Located just north of Montgomery on County Road 650E, the village is open 8:00 A.M. to 8:00 P.M. Monday through Thursday and 8:00 A.M. to 9:00 P.M. Friday and Saturday during summer months; 11:00 A.M. to 8:00 P.M. Monday through Thursday, 11:00 A.M. to 9:00 P.M. Friday, and 8:00 A.M. to 9:00 P.M. Saturday the rest of the year. Call (812) 486–3977.

Guided tours of the surrounding area are available for groups of fifteen or more; visitors are taken to Amish communities and to such Amish businesses as a quilt shop, a buggy factory, a candy factory, and a country store. Tours, which include a meal at the village's restaurant, are offered at 9:00 A.M. and 1:00 P.M. Monday through Saturday year-round; reservations must be made at least ten days in advance. For tour reservations and updated information about the village, contact the Daviess County Development Company, Inc., P.O. Box 7, Montgomery 47558; (812) 486–3354.

The **Graham Farms Cheese Company** at Elnora has been producing cheese for Hoosiers since 1928. Visitors are invited to stop by this family-owned business and watch the entire process. The free tour is accompanied by free samples. All finished products, including unique Indiana University, Purdue University, and State of Indiana cheeses, can be purchased on the premises. Open 8:00 A.M. to 6:00 P.M. Monday through Saturday and noon to 5:00 P.M. Sunday. Located on State Road 57 North; call (812) 692–5237 or (800) 472–9178.

Greene County

No matter what you've read or been told, there is no way to fully prepare you for your first glimpse of the **Greene County viaduct.** One minute you're driving along an isolated rural road that winds through wooded hills and hollows; the next minute you're suddenly confronted with an open valley and the massive railroad trestle that spans it—one of the most spectacular sights in the state.

Completed in 1906 as part of the Illinois Central Railroad line, the viaduct is 180 feet high and 2,295 feet long—the second longest in the world. (To see the longest, you'll have to travel to Cantal, France.) Park beneath the massive steel girders that support it, and climb a well-worn path up the hill at the north end for a sweeping view.

The viaduct is located just south of a road that links Solsberry and the hamlet of Tulip. Head west from Solsberry on the country road that parallels the railroad tracks. After driving about 5 miles, you'll come to County Road 480E, which turns off to the south and leads beneath the trestle.

It's best to stop at the general store in Solsberry and ask for exact directions. Roads are not well marked hereabouts, and besides, it's great fun to listen to the yarns being spun by any occupants of the store's "liar's bench." Maybe they'll tell you the one about the man wearing gum rubber boots who fell off the viaduct while it was being constructed and bounced for three days. He finally had to be shot to keep him from starving to death. For additional information contact the Bloomfield Chamber of Commerce, 6 East Main Street, P.O. Box 144, Bloomfield 47424; (812) 384–8995.

In the vast, dense forest that covered most of Indiana during the last century, there grew a *huge sycamore* that was the largest tree in the eastern half of the United States. Naturalists and historians advised everyone to go to Worthington and see this wonderful tree, which stood 150 feet high, spread its branches to a length of 100 feet, and measured more than 42 feet in circumference at 5 feet above the ground.

In 1920 a storm toppled it, and the town of Worthington decided to preserve one of its limbs in a place of honor. That limb, more than 23 feet in circumference and larger than the trunks of most trees in Indiana today, can be seen in Worthington's City Park at the north end of town. You can't miss it—it's the only tree in the park with a roof over its head.

The town of Linton was the birthplace of the late bandleader and show business personality Phil Harris, who never forgot his Indiana roots. For many years, he and his late wife, movie actress and singer Alice Faye, returned to Linton for the annual Phil Harris Festival. Ms. Faye reportedly loved this small town, and she and Harris donated their collection of numerous show business memorabilia to the town's public library. A virtual history of show business, the *Harris-Faye collection* includes photographs, awards, scrapbooks, letters, and trophies. Also seen here are souvenirs from well-known personalities in the fields of entertainment, sports, and government. The collection can be seen almost anytime the town's library is open. The library is located at 110 Northeast Vincennes Street; call (812) 847–4635. If you'd like to visit the library and enjoy the festival at the same time, come in June; call (812) 847–4846 for the exact dates.

Knox County

Vincennes, Indiana's oldest city, has a colorful history, and the town abounds with monuments to its past. George Rogers Clark came here during the American Revolution to battle the British, and his deeds are memorialized in the twenty-four-acre *George Rogers Clark National Historical Park,* located at 401 South Second Street (open 9:00 A.M. to 5:00 P.M. daily, except major winter holidays). Within a magnificent round stone structure are seven murals depicting Clark's campaigns. Living-history programs, featured on some summer weekends, re-create camp life with military drills and firearm demonstrations. There's a nominal admission fee for memorial building, but the visitor center is free; (812) 882–1776.

At the *Indiana Territory State Historic Site,* at the corner of First and Harrison Streets on the western edge of the Vincennes University campus, is a two-story white frame building that served as the capitol for the Indiana Territory from 1811 to 1813. Nearby is the **Western Sun Print Shop** where the territory's first newspaper was published on July 4, 1804; the wooden printing press seen by today's visitors is the same type as the original. Legend has it that Abe Lincoln, a faithful reader of the *Sun,* came here as a young man to study a printing press in operation and actually helped print the Saturday, March 6, 1830, edition of the paper on the day of his visit. Donations are accepted. Open 9:00 A.M. to 5:00 P.M. Wednesday through Saturday, 1:00 to 5:00 P.M. Sunday, mid-March through December. Contact P.O. Box 81, Vincennes 47591; (812) 882–7472.

Grouseland, an early-nineteenth-century Georgian mansion, was the home of William Henry Harrison when he served as the first governor of the Indiana Territory. (He later became the ninth president of the United States and was the grandfather of the twenty-third.) As part of his official duties, he once invited Indian Chief Tecumseh to his home to discuss their differences. Tecumseh refused to come inside, saying he preferred to sit on the Earth, his mother, and so the two men held council in a walnut grove on the front lawn. Located at 3 West Scott Street; (812) 882–2096. Open daily, 9:00 A.M. to 5:00 P.M., March through December, except Thanksgiving and Christmas; 11:00 A.M. to 4:00 P.M. January and February, except New Year's Day. There's a nominal admission fee.

Grouseland

The boundaries of the Indiana Territory first encompassed the present-day states of Indiana, Illinois, Michigan, and Wisconsin and part of Minnesota, and later the lands included in the 1803 Louisiana Purchase. So tiny Vincennes, with Harrison at its helm, was for a while the seat of government for most of the United States from the Alleghenies to the Rockies.

Harrison also served as one of the first trustees of *Vincennes University.* Founded in 1801, it is the oldest university west of the Alleghenies.

St. Francis Xavier Cathedral, dating back to 1702, is the oldest Catholic church in Indiana. The present redbrick building is actually the fourth church to stand on this site; its first two predecessors were built of logs, while the third, also a brick structure, was built in 1826 and rebuilt later the same year after a storm nearly destroyed it. Rich, dark cedars shelter the serene grounds of the *Old French Cemetery* adjacent to the cathedral, where priests, parishioners, natives, soldiers, and African slaves lie buried, many in unmarked graves. The first interment was in 1741, the last in 1846. The cathedral is located at 205 Church Street; open 7:00 A.M. to 4:00 P.M. daily. Call (812) 882–5638 or 886–1141.

Behind the cathedral, housed in a modern redbrick building, is *Brute Library,* the oldest library in Indiana, containing more than 11,000 rare books and documents. Bishop Simon Brute (1779–1839), the first Bishop of Vincennes, assembled the collection in France and brought it with him to the wilderness that was the Indiana Territory. He was called by President John Quincy Adams "the most learned man of his day in America."

A papal bull of Pope John XXII, dated 1319 and written on heavy parchment, is the oldest manuscript in the library. The oldest book, dated 1476, glows with the lustrous colors of hand illumination, and the parchment still bears the holes made by the pins that held the pages in place while the illuminating was done. Another interesting volume contains the Lord's Prayer in 250 different languages. In addition, there are old maps, letters, and a certified copy of a license issued on March 6, 1833, to Abraham Lincoln and William Berry, permitting them to operate a tavern in New Salem, Illinois. There's a nominal admission fee. The library is open 11:00 A.M. to 4:00 P.M. daily, May through August; (812) 882–5638.

Built about 1806, the **Brouillet French House** at 509 North First Street is one of the few remaining upright log-and-mud houses in North America. Inside are the original fireplace and warming oven, along with authentic period furnishings. The house is open 1:00 to 5:00 P.M. Tuesday through Sunday; admission is free. Call (812) 882–7886.

A remnant of prehistory, the 140-foot-high **Sonotabac Indian Mound** was constructed about 300 B.C. You can journey even further back in time within the museum at the mound's base, where exhibits and artifacts date back to 8000 B.C. There's a nominal admission fee. Open daily 10:00 A.M. to 4:00 P.M. (Sunday 1:00 to 4:00 P.M.) May through September and weekends in October. Call (812) 882–7679. The grounds are open daily,

The Marrying Man

*U*ntil his demise on June 10, 1997, at the age of eighty-eight, Glynn "Scotty" Wolfe was acknowledged to be the world's most-married man. Reportedly, until the day he died, he was still chasing women at the nursing home in which he was living—even though he was by then confined to a wheelchair.

Wolfe, who lived in California at the time of his death, was a native of Knox County. Between 1927 and 1996, he married twenty-nine times. His longest marriage lasted six years, his shortest just nineteen days. The flamboyant Wolfe claimed that he left one of his wives because she ate sunflower seeds in bed and walked

out on another because she used his toothbrush.

According to the man himself, his colorful life included stints as a Baptist minister, a pilot in Britain's Royal Air Force, a sailor on the USS Arizona (before it was bombed and sunk at Pearl Harbor), and a bodyguard for Al Capone.

Wolfe is survived by his several children (believed but not confirmed to be nineteen in number) and his twenty-ninth wife—Linda Essex-Wolfe of Anderson, Indiana, who married twenty-three times and is the world's most-married woman.

dawn to dusk; admission is free. The mound is located on the south side of Wabash Avenue about $^1/_2$ mile east of Thirteenth Street; look for signs. Several other mounds lie to the east and south of Vincennes.

The late Red Skelton, the beloved comedian, was born in Vincennes at 111 West Lyndale Avenue. A sign in front of the house commemorates the occasion. When Red was just ten years old he joined the Hagenbach-Wallace Circus (which wintered in Peru, Indiana) as a clown.

For additional information contact the Vincennes Area Chamber of Commerce, 27 North Third Street, Vincennes 47591; (812) 882–6440 or (800) 886–6443.

Lawrence County

For more than one hundred years, many of the great public edifices in this country and elsewhere have been constructed with Indiana limestone. Architects favor it because it lends itself easily to carving and the most delicate tracery when first quarried, then becomes hard and durable when exposed to atmospheric agents. Just a few of the structures that are built at least partly of oolitic limestone (so called because of its granular composition, which suggests a mass of fish eggs) from the Bedford area are the Empire State Building (it withstood King Kong, you know) and Rockefeller Center in New York City; Washington National Cathedral (eighty-three years in the making, it was completed on September 29, 1990, when a crane placed a 1,000-pound chunk of intricately carved Indiana limestone atop one of the church's towers); the Pentagon; the Lincoln Memorial; Chicago's Merchandise Mart; and the University of Moscow.

The *limestone quarries* are quite impressive to see—great gaping cavities in the earth from which are extracted immense blocks of stone that average 4 feet in thickness, 10 feet in width, and from 50 to 100 feet in length. Before being removed from the quarry floor, they're broken into small blocks for easy transportation to a processing mill. To view the quarries, go north from Bedford on State Road 37 through Oolitic; the quarries are about $^1/_2$ mile north of Oolitic.

When you pass through Oolitic, stop and meet one of the town's residents—the limestone *statue of Joe Palooka,* which stands in front of the town hall on Main Street. A famous comic strip character from the not-too-distant past, Joe was at the peak of his popularity in the 1940s. A paragon of good, Joe was an earthbound Superman of sorts who championed democracy and decency and was an inspiration to the youth of his day. He was also a boxer, and he is depicted—7 feet tall and weighing more than ten tons—wearing trunks and boxing gloves.

A few years ago, the Bedford Industrial Development Foundation, a non-profit financial arm of the Chamber of Commerce, opened a twenty-acre limestone demonstration center that overlooks the two largest quarries. A museum was built, displays of machinery and tools were set up, and construction was begun on the two main attractions—a ⅕-scale limestone reproduction of the Great Pyramid of Cheops and a 650-foot duplication of a segment from the Great Wall of China. The project was eventually abandoned due to lack of funds, but every once in a while someone decides to have a go at reviving it—thus far to no avail. Known locally as "the pyramid," the park-to-be now consists of a rusting Quonset hut that was meant to serve as the museum, a jumble of limestone boulders, and signs that proclaim this to be the *LIMESTONE TOURIST PARK*. For current information on the on-again, off-again tourist attraction, which lies on a fifteen-acre lot about 9 miles north of Bedford via State Road 37, contact the Lawrence County Tourism Bureau, 1116 Sixteenth Street, P.O. Box 1193, Bedford 47421; (812) 275–7637 or (800) 798–0769.

Bedford stone, another name for local limestone, is sometimes used for gravestones, and many fine examples can be seen in *Green Hill Cemetery,* 1202 Eighteenth Street in Bedford; (812) 275–5110. The monument for Louis Baker, a twenty-three-year-old apprentice stonecutter who died suddenly in 1917, was carved by his grieving fellow workers; they reproduced his workbench, fully detailed even to actual size, exactly as he had left it for the last time. The statue of Michael F. Wallner preserves his doughboy uniform down to the most minute crease. Also seen in the cemetery are some of the tree-trunk carvings that were popular around the turn of the century, including one adorned with high-button shoes and a straw hat that memorializes a seven-year-old girl who died in 1900. These and other Green Hill's monuments have been featured on several national television shows. Free walking-tour maps of the cemetery are available from the Lawrence County Tourism Bureau (see the preceding paragraph for the address and phone numbers).

On the south side of State Road 158, about 3 miles west of Bedford, you can visit *Elliott Special Products, Inc.,* a small limestone milling operation that creates many unique items from local limestone. A combination showroom/gift shop on the premises is open seasonally; call for hours. A rugged, ¼-mile-long, self-guided walking path leads visitors past the stacking yard of a working quarry and an abandoned quarry; the path is accessible when the showroom is open. Contact

Elliott Special Products, Inc., P.O. Box 1267, Bedford 47421; (812) 275–1900, for additional information.

Visitors can explore the history of the area's limestone industry at the **Land of Limestone Heritage Exhibit,** housed in a historic limestone building at the Bedford campus of the Oakland City University. Archival and architectural photographs, historical news accounts, and official records document the area's role in building the nation. It's located at 405 I Street in Bedford; admission is free. Open 8:00 A.M. to 5:00 P.M. Monday through Friday and 9:00 A.M. to noon Saturday. For further information contact the Lawrence Country Tourism office at (812) 275–7637 or (800) 798–0769.

At Purdue University's **Feldun Purdue Agricultural Center,** you can roam the 449 acres of the Moses Fell Farm. Mr. Fell donated the farm to Purdue University in 1914, and it has been used ever since for experimental purposes. The center is located on State Road 458, which runs north off State Road 158, 3 miles west of Bedford; signs point the way. Open daily year-round, 6:30 A.M. to 5:30 P.M. Monday through Saturday and 6:30 A.M. to 4:00 P.M. Sunday; admission is free. Contact Feldun Purdue Agricultural Center, Dark Hollow Road, RR 10, Box 122, Bedford 47421; (812) 279–8554.

Southwest of Bedford the longest "lost river" in the United States flows through a startling subterranean world. More than 20 miles of passageways currently have been explored at **Bluespring Caverns,** one of the world's ten longest, and most of those miles are wet ones—inundated by a system of underground streams. Visitors descend a stairway into a sinkhole entrance room, then venture 4,000 feet into the yawning depths aboard flat-bottomed boats that glide silently through a world of total darkness. The rare white fish and crayfish that live in these waters are blind, having adapted themselves over the years to a habitat where sight is of no use. Lights mounted on the bottom of the tour boat create shifting shadows on fluted walls and provide unique glimpses of water-sculpted formations on the mirrorlike surface of the stream. By prior arrangement you can also participate in a "wild tour," which includes exploration of some of the dry portions of the cave, crawling, climbing, and an underground slide show.

This is one place where weather will never surprise you—the temperature is a constant fifty-two degrees year-round. To reach Bluespring Caverns Park from Bedford, go south on U.S. Highway 50 for about 6 miles, then turn west on County Road 4505 for about $\frac{1}{2}$ mile; signs point the way. Open 9:00 A.M. to 6:00 P.M. daily, May through September;

Saturday and Sunday, April and October. Last tour leaves at 5:00 P.M. There's an admission fee. Campsites with water and electricity are available in the park. Contact Bluespring Caverns Park, RR 11, Box 988, Bedford 47421; (812) 279–9471.

The many attractions at *Spring Mill State Park* span a time period from the early 1800s to the threshold of the space age. As a boy growing up in nearby Mitchell, Virgil I. "Gus" Grissom loved this park. Grissom grew up to become one of the seven original astronauts and, in 1965, the second American in space. Two years later he was dead—one of three astronauts killed in a tragic spacecraft fire at Cape Kennedy. A *Gemini III* capsule like the one he once piloted now rests, along with his spacesuit and other items related to space travel, in the *Grissom Memorial Visitor Center,* P.O. Box 376, Mitchell 47446; (812) 849– 4129. Open daily year-round.

Nestled in a small valley among the park's wooded hills is a *pioneer village* that was founded in 1814. Its sawmill, meetinghouse, apothecary, hatmaker's and weaver's shops, water-powered gristmill, general store, tavern, distillery, post office, and log cabin homes have all been restored, and from April through October they are alive with inhabitants who go about their daily routine just as their long-ago counterparts did. You can purchase cornmeal ground at the old gristmill and products from the weaver's looms, and, on occasion, you can participate in candlelight tours of the tiny settlement.

Plants in the *Hamer Pioneer Gardens* are the same as those grown by the village's original occupants; some were used for medicine, some for cooking, and some simply to add beauty to a life that was often harsh. Uphill from the village is a pioneer cemetery that dates back to 1832. The stone markers provide a genealogical history of the town below.

During the spring and summer, nearly every variety of wildflower and bird indigenous to Indiana is found here, and to protect some of the 1,300-acre park's finest natural features the state has set aside two areas as nature preserves. A 2½-mile-loop hiking trail, the most beautiful in the park, winds through *Donaldson's Woods State Nature Preserve,* an outstanding seventy-six-acre virgin forest dominated by giant tulip trees and white oaks. Six acres surrounding the mouth of *Donaldson Cave,* reached by another trail, have also been designated a state nature preserve. The scene that meets your eye here—a small stream flowing from the cave's entrance and through a gorge whose slopes are thick with hardwood trees—is one of the loveliest in the state.

Park naturalists conduct walking tours into Donaldson Cave and also into *Bronson Cave.* At *Twin Caves* you can take a short ride on the underground river while a naturalist tells you about the tiny blind cave-fish swimming beneath you. To reach the park go east on State Road 60 from Mitchell for about 3 miles; the park is on the north side of State Road 60—signs point the way. Contact Spring Mill State Park, P.O. Box 376, Mitchell 47446; (812) 849–4129.

Spring Mill Inn is a combination of rustic charm and modern conveniences. Constructed in 1939 of native limestone and remodeled in 1976, the buff-colored building is located in the heart of the park. Guest rooms are decorated with Colonial furniture, and the dining room serves three meals a day. Dinner usually features cornsticks made from meal ground in the park. Swimming is a year-round activity in the unique indoor-outdoor pool. Rooms cost from $49 to $89 per night year-round, and rollaway cots are available for $5.00 each. Dinner prices range from $6.00 to $10.00, with breakfast and lunch considerably cheaper. Contact Spring Mill Inn, P.O. Box 68, Mitchell 47446; (812) 849–4081.

The greatest concentration of Indiana's several earthquake faults is located in Posey County in the southwestern corner of the state, but the longest fault occurs in south central Indiana. Known as the *Mt. Carmel Fault,* it extends 50 miles southeastward from the Morgan-Monroe county line into Washington County. One of the few places in the state where a fault can actually be seen on the surface of the land is alongside State Road 446, 2$\frac{1}{2}$ miles south of the Monroe-Lawrence county line, where ancient movements along the Mt. Carmel Fault have uplifted the land. (It may be reassuring for visitors—and nearby residents—to know that no movement of this fault has been recorded in modern history.) For additional information visit the Indiana Geological Survey (IGS) at 611 North Walnut Grove Avenue in Bloomington, where detailed maps showing the location of the Mt. Carmel Fault are on open file. The IGS also can provide information about other faults in Indiana; it's open from 8:00 A.M. to 4:30 P.M. Monday through Friday; (812) 855–9350 or 855–7636.

Nearby Heltonville is the home of the *Turner Doll Factory,* where Virginia and Boyce Turner began producing porcelain dolls in the mid-1980s. Because the dolls are collectibles, each doll is made in limited numbers ranging from 20 to 500. The Turner factory added vinyl dolls to its output in 1993, limiting each model to 2,500 or fewer dolls. Visitors may watch the production process free of charge from 9:00 A.M. to 3:00 P.M. Monday through Friday; call (812) 834–6692 or (800) 887–6372 for directions and, if you're bringing more than one carload, to make an appointment.

Martin County

There's silver in them thar hills, if legend be truth! Since the first Europeans came to these parts, tales have abounded about the lost Indian treasure cave of **McBride's Bluffs.** For nearly one hundred years the Choctaw Indians lived in the bluffs area north of Shoals, taking shelter in one particular cave during severe weather. Absalom Shields, one of the first white settlers, told of the time when the natives blindfolded him and took him to this cave, where he was shown a fabulous amount of silver crudely molded into bricks. Shortly after their disclosure to Shields, the natives were forced to flee the area so hastily that they could not take the silver with them. They did, however, seal the entrance to the cave. When one of their tribe was later sent to claim the treasure, the trees he was to use as landmarks to guide him to the cave had been cleared away and he was never able to find the silver. Since then a few isolated bars of silver have been found above ground, but the whereabouts of the cave remains a secret to this day. It's not for lack of trying, though—people still search for the silver.

The precipitous cliffs known as McBride's Bluffs, which soar 175 feet above the East Fork of White River, are riddled with small caves. Because country roads may be unmarked, it's best to ask locally for exact directions to the bluffs, which lie approximately 5 miles north of Shoals and are shown on the official state highway map. Start out from Shoals going northwest on U.S. Highway 50/150, then turn north onto State Road 450. Continue north to a side road about 1^1/$_2$ miles north of Dover Village and turn east toward the White River; a single-lane gravel road winds along the riverbank at the base of the bluffs.

Martin County is one of the best places in the state for shunpiking (driving the backroads). Meandering country lanes lead past little-known havens of beauty—rugged hills, dense woodlands, sheer sandstone cliffs—that are even more beautiful when wildflowers color the spring landscape and trees don their autumn hues.

Jug Rock, a striking sandstone monolith that is the focal point of a state nature preserve, is a product of centuries of erosion. Although it stretches to a height of 60 feet and is more than 15 feet in diameter, it is difficult to see when the surrounding trees are heavy with foliage. The bottle-shaped rock stands on the north side of U.S. Highway 50/150 a little to the northwest of Shoals, about a mile beyond the White River bridge and some 200 yards downhill from the Shoals Overlook Rest Park. Stop at a small roadside pull-off on a high point along the highway and look for a large, flat slab that tops this unusual formation. To gain a better perspective of Jug Rock's dimensions, walk to its base along a 60-yard-long woodland path. For additional information contact the Division of Nature Preserves, Indiana Department of Natural Resources, 402 West Washington Street, Room W267, Indianapolis 46204; (317) 232–4052.

Directly west of Shoals you can see the bluffs of *Beaver Bend,* noted for the rare species of ferns that cling to the cliff and grow nearby. Beaver Bend is a sharp curve in the East Fork of White River where Beaver Creek flows into it. These cliffs reach their loftiest height at Spout Spring, where water emerges from a pipe driven into the solid rock wall. The honeycombed cliff that overhangs the spring is layered with ocher and yellow rocks that soar 400 feet into the air. Ask for directions locally; an old country road passes near the base of the bluffs.

A few miles downriver from Beaver Bend you can explore the picturesque *Hindostan Falls* area. In the early 1800s the thriving community of Hindostan stood on the banks of White River. It was abandoned in 1828, at the height of its prosperity, when a mysterious disease began killing its citizens. Only 6 feet high but nevertheless impressive, Hindostan Falls extends from one bank of the river to the other, creating scallops of white foam along the uneven path it follows. The power produced by the tremendous volume of water that passes over it each day was harnessed by the people of Hindostan to power their mills, while a large sandstone ledge below the falls provided the rock for the mill's foundations. Still evident today are the large square holes from which the rock was hewn, but the ledge is now used primarily by picnickers and fishermen looking for solitude. The pools below the falls teem with catfish, drum, crappie, white and smallmouth bass, buffalo, shad, and suckers. Officially designated a state fishing area, the site also offers a free concrete boat-launching ramp and some free primitive campsites. Do use caution here, though—the current is both strong and dangerous at times. To reach Hindostan Falls go south from Shoals on U.S. Highway 50/150 to State Road 550, turn west, and follow the signs to the falls area on the south side of State Road 550. The area is open at all times; admission is free. Contact the Regional Access Manager, Public Access South, Hindostan Falls State Public Fishing Area, RR 2, P.O. Box 140, Montgomery 47558; (812) 644–7731.

Hoosier National Forest, just east of Hindostan Falls, occupies the southeast corner of Martin County. A drive along forest roads reveals a seemingly endless panorama of some of nature's most stunning handiwork: huge rock bluffs, woods, waterfalls, streams, and box canyons. For additional information contact Hoosier National Forest

Headquarters, 811 Constitution Avenue, Bedford 47421; (812) 275–5987.

Northeast of Shoals, bordering the north side of U.S. Highway 50, is *Martin State Forest,* one of the nicest surprises in the state forest system. Within its 6,132 acres you can climb a fire tower, visit an arboretum, or tour one of five demonstration areas to learn about forest management practices. The most spectacular hike in the forest takes you over a rugged 3-mile trail that leads to Tank Spring, where water tumbles down 150 feet over moss-covered sandstone; come here in the spring when the greens are newborn and lustrous. Shady campsites atop a breezy ridge make this a great place to spend warm-weather days. The forest is open at all times; admission is free. Contact Martin State Forest, P.O. Box 599, Shoals 47581; (812) 247–3491.

James "Doc" Counsilman of Bloomington is the oldest person to swim the English Channel. He accomplished his feat at age fifty-eight in September 1979. During an illustrious thirty-three career as the varsity swim coach at Indiana University (1957–1990), he coached fifty-nine Olympians. One of them was Mark Spitz, who won an unprecedented seven gold medals at the 1972 Summer Olympics in Munich.

Monroe County

Indiana University, which sits in the heart of *Bloomington,* enrolls nearly 33,000 students from around the world. The diverse cultures they represent have given rise to a cuisine that is international in scope and truly extraordinary for a town this size (52,000 people, sans students). Eateries specialize in Irish, French, Greek, Mexican, German, Italian, Ethiopian, Middle Eastern, Malaysian, Indonesian, African, Thai, Tibetan, Japanese, and all styles of Chinese foods. Of course, American dishes and that staple of every college town in the country—pizza—are also available.

More than twenty pizza parlors thrive in Bloomington. One serves a pizza chosen by *People* magazine as the fourth best in the United States. You can try it for yourself at *Mother Bear's* (1420 East Third Street; 812–332–4495) or just down the street at *Bear's Place* (1316 East Third Street; 812–339–3460). The former is your basic pizzeria, just for eating; the latter serves pizza only after 4:45 P.M., but it offers big-screen television, a classic movies series, and live entertainment on the side. The sauce that brought Mother Bear's its fame is a bit on the spicy side, so arm yourself with lots of liquids.

Located in a quaint old home at 412 East Sixth Street is a small cafe/restaurant known as *The Runcible Spoon,* where patrons can sit upstairs, downstairs, or outside in a Japanese garden. A 300-gallon aquarium occupies a dominant position on the main floor; more fish reside in a bathtub in the rest room. Jeff Danielson, the owner, likes to think that this relaxing atmosphere brings out the philosopher in everyone. The cuisine, ranging from Seoul barbecue to African ground-nut soup to Indian mulligatawny, can only be described as eclectic. Freshly roasted gourmet coffee is the lifeblood of the cafe, luring a mix of customers that's as varied as the cuisine, and the homemade bagels produced in the in-house bakery are an exclusive in Bloomington. One thing diners won't find here is an ashtray, not even in the garden; the Runcible Spoon is a nonsmoking establishment. The restaurant is open 8:00 A.M. to 2:30 P.M. and 5:00 to 8:00 P.M. daily; the cafe is open 8:00 A.M. to 12:30 A.M. Monday through Saturday and 8:00 A.M. to 11:00 P.M. Sunday. The Spoon also serves a Sunday brunch; (812) 334–3997.

For gyros unsurpassed anywhere stop in at *The Trojan Horse* on the southeast corner of Kirkwood and Walnut Streets. Paper-thin slices of beef and lamb are garnished with tomato slices, onion rings, and zaziki sauce, then served on pita. Have a Greek salad on the side, and top it all off with a Greek pastry. Open 11:00 A.M. to 11:00 P.M. Monday through Thursday; 11:00 A.M. to midnight Friday and Saturday; 3:00 to 9:00 P.M. Sunday; (812) 332–1101.

Before professional basketball player Michael Jordan soared with the National Basketball Association's Chicago Bulls, he soared with the 1984 gold medal–winning U.S. Olympic basketball team. Since Indiana University's Bobby Knight served as the team's head coach that year, team trials were held in Bloomington. It didn't take long for Jordan to develop a taste for the *Peterson's* Smoothie, a taste he indulged every day he was in town. Years later, he recalled those days when he sent an autographed poster of himself to Jay Twomey, owner of Peterson's (a deli-style restaurant and bakery), with an inscription praising the Smoothie. Isaiah Thomas, no slouch at basketball himself, attended Indiana University and helped its basketball team win the 1981 NCAA championship before joining the NBA's Detroit Pistons. While an IU student, Thomas was such a devotee of the Smoothie that Peterson's staff let him stand behind the counter and make his own. Jordan and Thomas are not alone in their enthusiasm. Many IU graduates stop in for a Smoothie every time they return to campus because, they tell Twomey, it's the one thing they can't get anywhere else.

The fabled Smoothie is a fruit-flavored yogurt shake with a distinctive taste that Twomey achieves by using a special brand of low-fat frozen yogurt made in California. Not only is the shake a frosty, thirst-

quenching delight that has been called Bloomington's favorite summertime drink, but it contains only half the calories and fat of milk
shakes. Purchasers of Smoothies get their choice of yogurt flavors
along with the fresh fruit and fruit juice they want blended with it.
Peterson's, which is located at 1811 East Tenth Street in the Crosstown
Shopping Center, is open 11:00 A.M. to 9:00 P.M. Tuesday through Sunday;
(812) 336–5450.

Bloomington also boasts the **Snow Lion,** one of only a few Tibetan
restaurants in the country. The Bloomington restaurant, however, has a
connection with Tibet that is one-of-a-kind. Jigme K. Norbu, who owns
the Snow Lion, is the nephew of the Dalai Lama, the Buddhist priest-
king who is Tibet's political and spiritual leader. Although Norbu adjusts
his recipes somewhat to appeal to the American palate (Tibetan food
features plenty of liver, mutton, barley, and fat), he achieves an authentic
flavor by using traditional spices and herbs from Tibet. The menu
includes such offerings as Phingtsel (beanthread sautéed with mixed
vegetables), Thukpa Shamic (fried egg noodles sautéed with shrimp and
vegetables), and Tasha Ngopa (Indian chicken curry with Tibetan seasonings served on a bed of rice). All entrees are served with a cup of
Tibetan tea and a salad with a house dressing that's so popular many
people come here just to eat the salad. The only dessert offered is Deyse,
a dish of steamed sweet rice with raisins that's topped with cold yogurt.

In addition to serving food, the restaurant introduces diners to the
culture of Tibet. The Tibetan national flag, which features two snow
lions grasping an iridescent jewel, hangs near the door. Tibetan music
is interwoven with the classical selections that play softly in the background, and several Tibetan hand paintings representing good luck
adorn the walls. The Snow Lion, located at 113 South Grant Street, also
offers cuisine from other parts of the Orient; prices are moderate.
Open for lunch from 11:30 A.M. to 2:00 P.M. Monday through Friday
and for dinner from 5:00 to 10:00 P.M. daily; carryout's available all day.
Call (812) 330–0035.

Tibet is a small, peace-loving nation that lies in a remote mountainous
area along the southwestern border of China proper. The region has
been intermittently governed by China through the centuries, last
achieving independence in 1911. That status endured until 1950, when
China once again asserted its rule. Since then some 1.2 million Tibetans
have died in the struggle to regain their country's freedom, and the Dalai
Lama has set up a government in exile in India. Thubten J. Norbu, a
retired Indiana University professor who is the father of Jigme Norbu
and the older brother of the Dalai Lama, was motivated by the plight of

his homeland to found the *Tibetan Cultural Center* (TCC) in Bloomington. In 1987 the Dalai Lama came to Bloomington to consecrate the then-new *Jangchub Chorten,* the only Tibetan chorten in the United States and the cornerstone of the TCC. Rising 35 feet above its pastoral surroundings, the copper-topped, white, concrete monument to peace memorializes Tibetans who have died under Chinese rule. Sealed within the chorten are such religious artifacts as Buddhist scriptures, bits of clothing worn by ancient monks and saints, and hair clippings from thirteen Dalai Lamas (the current Dalai Lama is the fourteenth). Just prior to another visit by the Dalai Lama in 1999, a second monument was added to the center. Known as the *Kalachakra Stupa,* it is dedicated to world peace and harmony. The chorten and stupa, located on the TCC's ninety-acre property at 3655 South Snoddy Road, can be seen free of charge during daylight hours. A nearby building houses a museum, library, and workshop. For further information and a schedule of special cultural events sponsored by the TCC, contact the Center at P.O. Box 2581, Bloomington 47402; (812) 334–7046.

Bloomington is also home to the *Dagom Gaden Tensung Ling.* Established in 1998, it is the only Tibetan Buddist monastery in the country. The public is welcome to visit and to attend the many classes and meditation sessions led by the monks who live there. Located at 102 Club House Drive; call (812) 339–0857 for additional information.

Among the more unusual attractions on the Indiana University campus is the *Lilly Library of Rare Books and Manuscripts,* a repository of more than 400,000 books and six million manuscripts. Among its most recent acquisitions are the original scripts from the popular television show *Star Trek: The Next Generation.* (The library also has scripts from the original *Star Trek.*) The library draws on its vast holdings to set up a series of changing exhibits throughout the year, but such treasures as a Gutenberg Bible, George Washington's letter accepting the presidency of the United States, Thomas Jefferson's copy of the Bill of Rights, four Shakespeare folios, and a major Lincoln collection are on permanent display. Admission is free; the library is open during the school year from 9:00 A.M. to 8:00 P.M. Monday through Thursday, 9:00 A.M. to 5:00 P.M. Friday and Saturday, and 1:00 to 5:00 P.M. Sunday (shorter hours during summer months). Call (812) 855–2452.

Although Indiana University's School of Music is famous throughout the world for its excellence, Bloomington-born songwriter Hoagy Carmichael earned a law degree here. Music was always his passion, however, and passion would eventually have its way. One night in 1926, while sitting alone on a spooning wall at the edge of campus thinking of the two girls then in his life, Carmichael looked up at the starry sky and began whistling a tune. Unable to get the song out of his mind, he dashed over to use the piano at a local hangout. A few minutes later the proprietor closed up and tossed Hoagy out. Fortunately for the world, the song remained on Hoagy's mind—it ultimately became "Stardust."

Hoagy died in 1981 at age eighty-two, and is buried in Rose Hill Cemetery on Bloomington's west side (see page 196). In 1986 Hoagy's family donated a large collection of the composer's memorabilia to Indiana University, and the school established a **Hoagy Carmichael Room** in which to display it. The composer's piano, a jukebox, photographs of Carmichael with numerous Hollywood stars, and the original manuscript of "Stardust," signed and dated by its composer on January 15, 1952, are just a few of the mementos visitors will see. Located in Room 006 of the **Archives of Traditional Music** in Morrison Hall, the Hoagy Carmichael Room is open free of charge by appointment. Other rooms of the archives the largest university-based ethnographic sound archives in the country—house such varied holdings as tapes of 350 spoken languages from around the world, the music of the Tupi Indians of Brazil,

The Puzzlemeister from Indiana

*I*n 1974 Indiana University in Bloomington awarded what was believed to be the world's first degree in enigmatology. The young man upon whom it was conferred, a native of Crawfordsville, Indiana, designed the degree himself through IU's Individualized Major Program. When he first approached his adviser with the idea for such a degree, she was lukewarm, but the young man persisted and was eventually given the go-ahead to pursue the degree of his dreams. In 1993, at the age of forty-one, that man became the youngest puzzle editor ever at the New York Times.

Although Will Shortz went on to earn a law degree from the University of Virginia, he never practiced law.

Instead, he went straight to an editing job at a puzzle magazine and by 1989 was editor of Games magazine. Then it was on to the New York Times.

Shortz has also authored or edited fifteen books of puzzles, founded and served as director of the American Crossword Tournament, and founded the World Puzzle Championship. He lives in New York City and collects what else?—puzzles and puzzle magazines. Among his prized possessions is the first "word-cross" puzzle ever invented; it was published in the December 21, 1913, New York World, a Christmas gift for the ages.

Those folks at IU who allowed Shortz to pursue his dream now have an alumnus to be proud of.

and recordings of blues artists of the 1940s. The public is welcome to visit the archives and listen to its collections from 9:00 A.M. to 5:00 P.M. Monday through Friday; admission is free. Call the Hoagy Carmichael Room at (812) 855–4679 or the archives librarian at (812) 855–8631.

At the *Indiana University Cyclotron Facility* on Milo B. Sampson Lane at the campus's eastern edge, you can enter the world of nuclear physics. The variable-energy light-ion cyclotron is used by scientists from around the world to explore the mysteries of the atomic nucleus, as well as to conduct research concerning astrophysics and the application of space devices. A major upgrade equipped the facility with particle beams of unconventional and superior characteristics. If all this "tech talk" is a bit difficult to understand, the guides who lead free tours through the facility will be happy to clarify things. For a tour schedule call the facility at (812) 855–9365.

You can obtain more information about the attractions of Indiana University by contacting the Indiana University Visitor Information Center in the Carmichael Center on the corner of Indiana and Kirkwood Avenues in Bloomington; (812) 855–GOIU.

If the campus looks familiar, it may be because you saw the award-winning movie *Breaking Away.* It was filmed in Bloomington and featured the university's *Little 500 Bicycle Race,* held here each spring. The swimming hole in the movie was one of the water-filled limestone quarries you can see in the surrounding countryside.

On the western edge of Bloomington lies beautiful *Rose Hill Cemetery*— as much a sculpture garden as a graveyard. Many of the memorials that mark its graves are works of art. In the oldest part of the cemetery are stones adorned with carvings of weeping willows, a symbol of grief that was popular when these markers were carved in the period from 1830 to 1865. These earlier tombstones are made primarily of marble, brought here from Vermont before the growth of the Indiana limestone industry. The image of willows and the use of marble to create them appear to have lost favor about the time the Civil War ended, replaced by the striking tree trunk memorials carved from the more enduring limestone. Other materials have gained favor in later years, but the limestone markers of Rose Hill still stand today as visible reminders of a unique art that once brought worldwide fame to this part of Indiana.

The cemetery also serves as the final resting place for some of Bloomington's most renowned citizens. Composer Hoagy Carmichael is buried here, as is Alfred Kinsey, who established his groundbreaking sex research institute on the nearby campus of Indiana University. The university's first president also lies here, along with a former governor of the state and a Civil War general. Near the Elm Street entrance to the cemetery is a monument that honors the memory of a former resident who isn't even buried here. John B. Crafton was on a trip to Europe in the early part of this century when, overwhelmed by homesickness for his family in Bloomington, he decided to return home early. The wealthy businessman canceled his reservation on a German liner and booked an earlier passage on another ship. His decision cost him his life. The year was 1912; the ship was the RMS *Titanic*.

Rose Hill Cemetery extends westward from the corner of Fourth and Elm Streets; call (812) 349–3497.

Farther west, at 6370 West May Road, master gardener Sherry Brunoehler welcomes visitors to her **Great Geode Gardens West.** A favorite of local rockhounds, geodes are odd-looking rocks that range in size from tiny to tremendous. The smallest are no bigger than a walnut, while two whoppers in Brunoehler's gardens weigh 300 and 400 pounds each. Irregularly rounded and lumpy, the drab exteriors of geodes conceal a crystalline interior of exquisite beauty.

> ### Trivia
>
> *David V. Buskirk of Monroe County, whose height has been estimated from 6 feet, 10 inches, to 8 feet, was the tallest man to serve in the Union Army during the Civil War. The company in which Captain Buskirk served numbered 101 soldiers, 67 of whom were more than 6 feet tall.*

Relatively rare in Indiana, geodes are generally found along a line that extends southeast from Monroe County to the banks of the Ohio River in Floyd County. It is a line formed by the southernmost boundary of the great glaciers of the Ice Age.

Brunoehler, who also sells plants from her gardens, is happy to share her knowledge of geodes with visitors. Her gardens are open to the public, free of charge, from 10:00 A.M. to 6:00 P.M. Thursday and Friday and from 1:00 to 4:00 P.M. Saturday from early spring through September. For additional information, call (812) 825–8419.

Seven miles north of Bloomington on State Road 37, **Oliver Winery,** Indiana's oldest and largest, offers a free tour, free wine tasting, and, on Saturday evenings in June and July, outdoor concerts (most of which are free) on the parklike grounds. Owner Bill Oliver, a law professor at Indiana University, started his vineyards in 1971 and now produces 40,000 gallons of wine a year. Several of the fifteen or so varieties have won gold and silver medals in competitions throughout the country. If you're in the mood for lunch, you can have "a jug of wine, a loaf of bread," and your own "thou" beside you at a picnic table outside or at a table in the cozy tasting room inside. Cheeses, summer sausage, fruits, popcorn, maple syrup, and unique limestone gifts are also available. Open 10:00 A.M. to 6:00 P.M. Monday through Saturday and noon to 6:00 P.M. Sunday; closes at 8:00 P.M. Friday and Saturday in June and July and at 5:00 P.M. daily January through March; tours available Saturday and Sunday or by appointment. Contact Oliver Wine Co., Inc., 8024 North State Road 37, Bloomington 47404; (812) 876–5800.

Morgan-Monroe State Forest wanders over 23,916 acres, most of which occupy northeastern Monroe County. Nestled in a clearing in the midst of the woods is a rustic log cabin where a true get-away-from-it-all experience awaits you. *Draper's Cabin* is described by the state as primitive, and the description is apt. There's no electricity, all water has to be carried in, heat is provided by a stone fireplace, and you make your bed on the floor. The forest provides plenty of wood for the fireplace, but it's up to you to gather it and carry it in. Only dead material can be used, and no saws are allowed. You can cook in the fireplace or, if you bring your own grill, on a concrete slab outdoors. The cabin contains nary a stick of furniture, but two picnic tables are just outside the door. A few yards away a small stream sometimes trickles by and sometimes doesn't—it depends on the rainfall.

Draper's Cabin is the only such cabin on any state-owned land, and you can rent the whole thing for $10.50 a night, including tax. The maximum stay is fourteen days. Available by advance reservation from April to November through the Property Manager, Morgan-Monroe State Forest, 6220 Forest Road, Martinsville 46151; (317) 342–4026.

To reach the forest go north from Bloomington on State Road 37 to Forest Road, the main entrance road, which runs east off of State Road 37 into the forest just before you reach the Morgan-Monroe county line. If you go in the spring or fall, you probably won't be able to resist a hike through the woods. Brochures for the trails—which include 9- and 7-mile loops, a ³⁄₄-mile pathway through the *Scout Ridge State Nature Preserve,* and a 1-mile-square orienteering course called the Pathfinder Trail—are available at the office building. If you do your walking during hunting season, it's best to wear bright colors.

Orange County

When Larry Bird first burst on the professional basketball scene in 1979, he was promptly dubbed "the hick from French Lick" by many sportswriters across the nation. Larry Bird went on to establish himself as the very heart of the Boston Celtics, and the sports world learned two things: He sure could play basketball, and, shyness and Hoosier dialect aside, he was no hick. What's more, Bird's hometown of French Lick, although small, is also the home of one of the most luxurious all-season resorts in the nation.

French Lick came into being because of some rich mineral springs that flowed from the hillsides. In 1837, to accommodate the hordes of people who flocked here to "take the waters," the French Lick Springs Hotel opened. Around the turn of the century, the hotel was purchased by Thomas Taggart, a nationally known political figure who served as mayor of Indianapolis and as U.S. senator from Indiana. Taggart, who juggled his two careers, was named chairman of the National Democratic Party in 1904. His national prominence came at a time when spas were at the height of their popularity, and the elite of society and politics from all over the country descended on French Lick to drink the waters from its springs and to partake of the mineral baths.

Gambling was added, luring even more visitors, including both celebrities and gangsters. In 1932 several state governors met here and decided to back Franklin Delano Roosevelt for president. The Vanderbilts, Morgans, and Whitneys came here to play, followed later by such stars as Lana Turner, Roy Rogers, Dale Evans, and Gene Autry.

Today the gambling is long since gone, and the opulent era of the spas has drawn to a close. But the hotel, as lovely as ever with its tall white pillars, crystal chandeliers, and plush carpeting, still operates as the *French Lick Springs Resort.* It stands in the midst of 2,600 acres of hills, woodlands, landscaped lawns, and formal gardens, a gracious queen who has splendidly survived the test of time. Although the springs are still there, guests come today to relax in the peaceful setting and to enjoy a full range of activities—golf on two eighteen-hole courses, tennis on indoor or outdoor courts, two swimming pools (one indoors for year-round use), skeet and trap shooting, horseback riding, bicycling, and such games as bowling, shuffleboard, badminton, volleyball, horseshoes, and miniature golf. There's even a modern-day version of the spa—a health and fitness center. From approximately December to March, you can go skiing on six nearby slopes or skate on the hotel's ice rink.

As impressive as it all is, what you'll most likely remember as much as anything is the food served at *Chez James,* the resort's gourmet restaurant. Such delights as New England codfish cakes, Spanish omelettes, braised capon, South African lobster tail, peach Melba, strawberries Romanoff, and baked Alaska Vesuvius may appear on the menu, along with favorite Hoosier foods. The hotel's six other restaurants serve a variety of food in more casual surroundings.

Most facilities, many special activities, and transportation to and from French Lick Airport are included in the rates, which range from $150 to $225 per night for two people (breakfast and dinner included). There are also seasonal rates and many special packages. Contact French Lick Springs Resort, 8670 West State Road 56, French Lick 47432; (812) 936–9300 or (800) 457–4042.

Railroad buffs will be intrigued by the *Indiana Railway Museum,* located just north of French Lick Springs Resort's parking lot on State Road 56. Operated as a nonprofit corporation, the museum has its headquarters in the old Monon Railroad station, where several steam locomotives, a rare railway post office car, and a 1951 dining car are among the memorabilia on display. Visitors can also board the *French Lick, West Baden & Southern Railway* for a one-and-three-quarter-hour, 20-mile, round-trip ride between French Lick and Cuzco, Indiana. A diesel locomotive pulls 1920s-era passenger cars away from the station and plunges into the wooded terrain of Hoosier National Forest, offering its passengers views of rugged Orange County backcountry where no roads penetrate. Along the way the train passes through a 2,200-foot tunnel, one of Indiana's longest. Children are especially delighted by the train robberies staged on holiday and various other weekends. Trains depart at 10:00 A.M., and 1:00 and 4:00 P.M. each Saturday, Sunday, and holiday April through November. For additional information write the Indiana Railway Museum, P.O. Box 150, French Lick 47432; (812) 936–2405 or (800) 748–7246.

The museum also operates a 2-mile round-trip trolley ride between French Lick and West Baden. At the latter, visitors see all that remains of the *West Baden Springs Hotel.* The architectural masterpiece, once known as the "most unique hotel on earth" and the "Carlsbad of America," was world-famous in the early 1900s, but through the years it did not fare as well as French Lick's resort.

Begun in October 1901, construction on the West Baden Springs Hotel was completed eight and a half months later—an astonishing accomplishment in any day but truly extraordinary given the technology of the time. Its imaginative owner, Colonel Lee Sinclair, had conjured up visions of a sumptuous hotel that established architects of the day said was impossible to build. Urged on by his daughter Lillian, Colonel Sinclair finally found an enterprising young architect who accepted the challenge not only to build the hotel but to do so for $414,000—with a

$100-a-day penalty clause if construction took longer than the agreed-on 200 working days.

When finished, the dome above the immense central atrium, larger than the dome at St. Peter's Cathedral in Rome, was regarded as the "eighth wonder of the world." Two hundred feet in diameter, 130 feet above the floor, ribbed with twenty-four steel girders mounted on rollers to accommodate expansion and contraction, it remained the world's largest self-supporting dome until the Houston Astrodome was completed in 1965. The atrium floor was covered with twelve million Italian marble tiles, and the elaborate sunken gardens were planted with rare flowers from Europe and the Orient. Circling the atrium and its gardens were 708 guest rooms on six floors.

West Baden Springs Hotel thrived for thirty years, attracting an illustrious clientele that included General John J. Pershing, J. M. Studebaker, and Diamond Jim Brady, as well as the likes of Al Capone. In 1932, however, it became a casualty of the Great Depression.

Subsequently it served as winter headquarters for the old Hagenbach-Wallace Circus, as a Jesuit school, and as the home of Northwood Institute, a college that trained its students for employment in the hotel restaurant field. During the Jesuits' tenancy the face of the old hotel was altered forever. Some of the grander touches, they felt, were unseemly for their austere lifestyle. And so the Roman-style baths were wrecked and hauled away, the gardens were left untended, the lavish furniture was sold, the beautiful Moorish towers were removed from the roof, and the arabesque brickwork atop the building was straightened. The hotel was allowed to deteriorate for years until funds were recently acquired to begin its restoration. A gorgeous garden features fountains and brick pathways, and the Moorish towers have been replaced. The one-of-a-kind building, designated a National Historic Landmark, may be seen on special tours that are conducted on the hour from 10:00 A.M. to 3:00 P.M. Monday through Saturday and noon to 4:00 P.M., from April through October. Special twilight tours with a light show are available on the first Saturday of the month. Tours are also offered at 1:00 P.M. Wednesday through Sunday from November through March. Admission fees are applied to renovation costs. Call (317) 639–4534 for further information, or contact the French Lick/West Baden Chamber of Commerce, P.O. Box 347, French Lick 47432; (812) 936–2405 or (800) 450–4534.

No visit to Orange County would be complete without a stop at Punkin Center, 8 miles southeast of Orleans in the heart of the county's Amish country. The tiny hamlet is listed on the official state road map as

Pumpkin Center, but don't you believe it. The late Add Gray always said so, and since he lived here all his life, he should know.

On Halloween Day in 1922, Add opened the **Punkin Center General Store** with $327.28 worth of groceries he'd purchased from a wholesaler in Orleans. That store evolved into **Add's Museum of All Sorts of Stuff**—a combination home, general store, and barn—which now is presided over by Add's charming widow, Mabel. Although the general store is no longer open for business, it is still a repository for many of the Grays' relics and antiques. Swords, bells, plates (both dining and upper), saddles, sleighs, wagons, a crank-style telephone and the operator's switchboard, Colorado sagebrush, Indiana tickleweed, Spanish moss, Utah tumbleweed, a baby casket, an antique baseball uniform, an old-fashioned soda fountain, a roulette wheel, several scarecrows, a cast-iron chandelier from a Louisville, Kentucky, funeral home, a spring-operated churn, a collection of Indiana license plates that date back to 1913 (including the only one ever made in the state with the number 1,000,000), a wooden Santa Claus suspended from the barn roof who waves his hand and jingles some sleigh bells at the flick of a switch—this list just skims the surface. Add, who claimed he hadn't thrown any-thing away since 1917, gave new meaning to the term "pack rat."

When you arrive at Punkin Center, you might spot a sign that says COME ON IN. WE WERE EXPECTING YOU. EVERYTHING ELSE HAS GONE WRONG TODAY. Ignore it. It's just Add's delightful sense of humor at work. Although Add is gone now, Mabel likes nothing better than to welcome visitors and show them through the mind-boggling accumulation of goods.

Be sure to ask Mabel about the yarns Add used to spin—yarns about folks like old Ma Hollis, for instance, who made wine and beer for the local farmers and occasionally took a few swigs herself. When Pa Hol-lis died suddenly, she said he fell and hit his head on the pine floor—but it was hickory bark they found in his forehead. Or Rough Tedrow, who could shinny up a tree and catch a coon bare-handed. During the Great Depression he charged traveling salesmen 10 cents to watch him catch snapping turtles by the head. The biggest night in Punkin Center's history occurred in 1926, when Ray Trinkle dropped by the store carrying a lighted lantern and walked a mite too close to the gas tank. And many's the night the local folk stopped in to watch Bob McCoy spit on the store's potbellied stove from clear across the room. His accuracy was uncanny.

The Punkin Center museum is open most anytime Mabel is home, but please call ahead to announce you're coming. Mabel's phone number is

(812) 723–2432. To get to Punkin Center, take State Road 56 east from Paoli to a narrow, blacktopped lane known as Potato Road (the locals call it Tater Road). Take Potato Road north for about 2 miles, cross a bridge over Stamper Creek, and you'll be in Punkin Center. Follow these directions carefully, for there are two Pumpkin Centers shown on the Indiana map—the other one lies just a few miles to the east in adjoining Washington County.

Although the name Punkin Center conjures up pictures of Halloween, you might want to journey here in the spring and make a visit to Orleans at the same time. Orleans has been the official *Dogwood Capital of Indiana* since 1970, a few years after Mr. and Mrs. C. E. Wheeler

Birthplace of the Slider

*M*ost people who travel to and through Orleans know it as the small Orange County town that's the self-proclaimed Dogwood Capital of Indiana. Very few know that it is also the birthplace of the White Castle hamburger, affectionately called the slider by its legions of afficionados. (It's known by a few other names, too, mostly descriptive of the way in which the little burger affects one's digestive system.)

Until 1992 a downtown factory was the only supplier of White Castle burgers in the United States. Approximately three million of the square, five-holed patties were produced here each week. Because of increasing demand, the company has since built a new Orleans facility with twice the production capacity and added a second facility in Lebanon, Indiana. There are currently more than 300 White Castle restaurants, and ten to fifteen new outlets are added each year. Unfortunately for the part of the nation that's excluded, White Castle shops are found only in a limited area, bound by New

York on the east, Kansas on the west, Minnesota on the north, and Tennessee on the south.

The burger's reputation, though, has no boundaries. Visitors from White Castleless parts of the country scorn other more expensive and certainly more luxurious restaurants to dash to the nearest White Castle outlet. Not long ago, a couple of transplanted midwesterners were married in Arizona. The food of choice for the wedding reception was the White Castle burger, several thousand of which were transported across country in a refrigerated semi rented for the occasion by the bride and groom.

White Castle restaurants also have a reputation for cleanliness. A recent inspection of all Indiana restaurants, from the most to least expensive, chains and nonchains, revealed that White Castle kitchens tied with one other restaurant chain (Bob Evans) as the cleanest in the state. Apparently, when they're not cooking at White Castle, they're cleaning.

started planting dogwood trees along State Road 37, one of the town's main thoroughfares. It was a labor of love for the Wheelers, who believed that the dogwood's pink and white blooms had no equal for beauty. Today the trees cover a 12-mile stretch between Mitchell on the north and Paoli on the south, and more trees are added each year in what is now a communitywide project. They're usually in full bloom in late April and early May.

Orange County is also the site of two of the Hoosier State's most unusual natural landmarks. On the southern edge of Orangeville, which lies about 7 miles southwest of Orleans via country roads, you can view the *Orangeville Rise of the Lost River.* An underground river surfaces here as an artesian spring, flowing from a cave into a 220-foot-wide rock-walled pit at the base of a limestone bluff. The three-acre preserve is well marked, and there's a pull-off for parking. For additional information contact The Nature Conservancy, Indiana Field Office, 1330 West Thirty-eighth Street, Indianapolis 46208; (317) 923–7547.

Not far from Paoli, on the edge of Hoosier National Forest, is an eighty-acre tract of virgin woodland known as *Pioneer Mothers Memorial Forest,* whose magnificent trees are from 150 to 600 years old. Its crown jewel is the Walnut Cathedral, a moist cove that, according to the U.S. Department of the Interior, contains the finest black walnut trees of their kind in the entire country. From Paoli go south on State Road 37 for about 1¼ miles to the Pioneer Mothers State Wayside on the east side of the road. From this picnic area you can follow marked trails for a short distance into the Memorial Forest. Contact the Forest Supervisor, Hoosier National Forest, 811 Constitution Avenue, Bedford 47421; (812) 275–5987.

Owen County

The *Barn House,* a 70-foot-tall, 135-foot-long structure that defies description, rises from a hillside near Vandalia and regularly startles passersby. Begun in 1972 and completed a decade later, the house is a monument to recycling. James Pendleton, its builder, razed eleven barns and seven houses to collect the materials he needed to construct his one-of-a-kind house. Its forty-one rooms, no two of which are the same shape or size and no two of which are perpendicular to each other, cover more than 7,200 square feet of floor space. Access to the rooms is provided by fifteen stairways and ladders, with a few hidden passageways thrown in for good measure. Rising five levels in some places and four levels in others, the unique house also features seventy-four different roof angles and twin rooftop towers. Pendleton, who once lived in the house but now occupies a smaller residence on the same property, is happy to give tours of the Barn House to anyone who stops by when he's at home. On the average, that adds up to about twenty persons per week. Pendleton's guest book reveals that his visitors have come not only from this country but from such faraway places as Russia, the Czech Republic, Thailand, Vietnam, India, and Japan. Each year on the first weekend of October, he hosts a festival at his home that's highlighted by Barn House tours. To reach the Barn House, go west from Vandalia on State Road 46 for about 4 miles to Bixler Road, and turn south (just before you come to Bixler Road, you'll pass the Garrard Chapel Church on the left side of State Road 46); the Barn House is the second house on the right (west) side of Bixler Road. You'll have no trouble recognizing the house once you see it, but since Bixler Road can be difficult to identify, you may want to inquire locally. James Pendleton has no phone, but you can write to him at RR 1, Bowling Green 47833.

Parke County

All of Parke County is a museum of *covered bridges.* Within its boundaries are more covered bridges than you'll find in any other county in the United States—more, in fact, than you'll find in most states. At last count, thirty-two of them remained intact. What's more, they're all authentic, with the two oldest dating back to 1856 and the youngster of the bunch to 1920. All thirty-two were placed on the National Register of Historic Sites in 1978.

Joe Sturm, a retired farmer and carpenter, has served as official bridge inspector for more than twelve years and can relate all kinds of interesting facts about them. He can tell you, for instance, that so many bridges were built because of the numerous zigzagging streams in the country, that the only metal used in constructing them is the bolts, and that the bridge at Mecca was built on dry ground and a nearby stream rerouted to pass under it.

Most of the bridges still support traffic, and the folks in Parke County have mapped out four automobile routes that provide access to most of them. A free map outlining each route is available at the Parke County Tourist Information Center, located in the old train depot on U.S. Highway 36 at the eastern edge of Rockville. It's open 9:00 A.M. to 4:00 P.M. daily Memorial Day weekend to the first weekend of November, and Monday through Saturday the rest of the year; (765) 569–5226.

Covered Bridge in Parke County

The northwest route leads you to **West Union Bridge,** 315 feet and the longest in the county. The community of Bridgeton, with its many unusual shops, is a highlight of the southernmost route. Standing on the bank of Big Raccoon Creek, next to the double-span **Bridgeton Bridge,** is the **Weise Mill.** It's been grinding meal since it was built in 1823, making it the oldest known gristmill west of the Allegheny Mountains that's still in service. Directly west of Rockville is the **Sim Smith Bridge,** which claims the distinction of being the county's only haunted bridge.

If you head northeast from Rockville, you'll come to **Turkey Run State Park,** noted for its steep ravines, its sandstone formations, and the **Rocky Hollow–Falls Canyon State Nature Preserve,** which protects a lush primeval forest. The **Narrows Bridge,** one of the most photographed in the county, crosses Sugar Creek in the park. A tree-shaded inn in the park offers overnight accommodations in fifty-two rooms and twenty-one nearby cabins, two swimming pools, and four tennis courts; call (765) 597–2211. Write Turkey Run State Park, Route 1, Box 164, Marshall 47859, or phone (765) 597–2635.

On U.S. Highway 41 north of Rockville, just before you reach the state park, stands **Gobbler's Knob Country Store,** where you can purchase nostalgic wares that revive memories of grandmother—penny candies in jars, pickles from a barrel, sassafras bark, country hams, sunbonnets, corncob jelly, and carnival glass; (765) 597–2558.

Follow U.S. Highway 36 east from Rockville for 1 mile, and cross Billie Creek Bridge into an early-twentieth-century village and farmstead where the crafts and skills of yesteryear are on vivid display. One of the finest living museums in the state, **Billie Creek Village** is open daily from mid-January to late December; hours vary. An admission fee is charged when craftspeople are in residence (generally Saturday, Sunday, holidays, and during the Covered Bridge Festival in October); admission is free at other times. Write Billie Creek Village, RR 2, Box 27, Rockville 47872; (765) 569-3430.

Although many Hoosiers have never heard of Mordecai "Three Finger" Brown, he has never been forgotten by his hometown of Nyesville and by diehard baseball fans. Brown, who was born in 1876, earned his nickname at age seven when his right hand was mangled in a corn-grinding machine. Undaunted, he started throwing baseballs at a barn wall and developed a unique curve ball that made him one of the greatest pitchers ever to play the game.

During his fourteen years in the major leagues, Mordecai won 239 games and had a lifetime 2.06 earned-run average that remains to this day the third best in baseball history. His greatest fame came during his 1905–1916 tenure with the Chicago Cubs. While in Chicago he won twenty or more games six years in a row. He won twenty-nine games in 1908 and that same year became the first pitcher ever to record four consecutive shutouts. As the team's star pitcher, Mordecai helped the Cubs earn four National League pennants and two World Series championships.

When the arrival of the year 2000 prompted the compilation of lists of the greatest athletes of the twentieth century, *USA Today* listed Mordecai as one of the five greatest from Indiana, and *Sports Illustrated* listed him in the state's top ten. The great Ty Cobb once called Mordecai's curve ball "the most devastating pitch I have ever faced." When asked how he could achieve so much with only three fingers, Mordecai replied, "All I know is I had all the fingers I needed." In 1949, one year after his death, Mordecai Brown became the first Indiana native to be inducted into the Baseball Hall of Fame in Cooperstown, New York.

Trivia
Paper coal is found in only two places in the world—Central Russia and Parke County, Indiana. A rare relic of the Coal Age, paper coal is so called because it resembles scorched paper. The fragments of seed ferns in Indiana's paper coal have been extinct for more than 200 million years.

Today his memory is honored with a monument in a cornfield near Nyesville, where his boyhood home once stood. Engravings on the 3-foot-high, black-and-gray-granite marker depict the image of Mordecai launching his famous curve ball and relate the remarkable achievements of a man who turned adversity into triumph. To see **Mordecai's monument,** go east from Billie Creek Village on U.S. Highway

36 a short distance to County Road 160 East (also known as the Nyesville-Judson Road); turn north and proceed to Nyesville. The monument can be seen near Nyesville, about 100 yards off the road. Ask locally for exact directions.

Parke County originally had more than fifty covered bridges, but several were lost to fire, flood, and natural deterioration before a preservation effort was begun. Each October since 1957, the county has celebrated its heritage with a ten-day *Covered Bridge Festival.* The nationally recognized event regularly lures some 500,000 visitors.

Another popular festival is the late-winter *Maple Fair,* which takes place when local sugar camps are producing maple syrup. For more information contact Parke County, Inc., P.O. Box 165, Rockville 47872; (765) 569–5226.

Perry County

esides its bountiful natural beauty, this Ohio River county is worth visiting for its array of unusual monuments.

If Tell City has a landmark, it is the life-size *statue of William Tell* and his son that serves as the centerpiece for the fountain in front of city hall. The statue is a reflection of the town's Swiss heritage and a tribute to the legendary Swiss hero from whom Tell City took its name. Town residents were delighted when, in 1974, plans were announced for the construction of the fountain that would honor the town's namesake, but they never dreamed it would cause such a fuss.

After the statue had been formed by Evansville sculptor Don Ingle, it was sent to a New York foundry to be cast in bronze. Ingle and his wife then personally picked up the 500-pound statue in New York, placed it in a rented U-Haul van, and headed home for the formal dedication. Imagine their horror when, after spending the night in an Ohio motel, they discovered that the van—statue and all—had been stolen as they slept. Everyone got into the act, with local police and the FBI cooperating in a frantic search and news media throughout the country warning everyone to be on the lookout for the kidnapped William Tell. The nationwide furor was such that the thief eventually abandoned his ill-gotten gain on a side street in Cleveland, and the statue was escorted the rest of the way home without further ado. You can see William Tell today in his place of honor atop the fountain—one arm holding his crossbow, the other arm around his son's shoulder, and not an apple in sight.

Poised above State Road 66 near Troy, a towering 19-foot statue of Christ overlooks the Ohio River, arms extended in an eternal blessing of all who gaze on it. Herbert Jogerst, a German artist, sculpted the statue when he was a prisoner of war in Indiana during World War II. It stands on a bluff once owned by Robert Fulton, of steamboat fame, and is now part of a summer camp for crippled children. Illuminated at night, the all-white *Christ of the Ohio* is always visible to travelers on land or water.

At St. Augustine's Church in Leopold stands the *Shrine of Our Lady of Consolation,* whose strange history dates back to the Civil War. Three young Union Army soldiers from Perry County, members of the church, were confined in the infamous prison at Andersonville, Georgia. They vowed to one another that if they lived through the horror of that experience they would donate a shrine to their church as a token of their gratitude. Miraculously they all survived, and one of them personally made a trip to Belgium to oversee the making of an exact reproduction of a shrine he remembered seeing in a small village church there.

Some historians claim that, unable to obtain the reproduction he desired, the young man stole the original and transported it back to Indiana, sparking an international incident between the governments of the two countries. It happened, however, that Leopold had been named for the Leopold who was then king of Belgium. The Belgian leader was so pleased to learn of his namesake that he allowed the shrine to remain there. It can be seen today, a statue of Mary and the infant Jesus, each wearing a white gown, a blue robe, and a crown of jewels. Call (812) 843–5143 for information.

One of the Hoosier State's finest historical landmarks is now a vast and silent structure—the huge, castlelike *Cannelton Cotton Mill.* From 1849 until 1965 the mill was a beehive of activity. Once the busiest industry in Indiana, it contained the most modern textile machinery, rivaling the better-known mills of New England. Some 400 laborers operating 372 looms spun raw cotton into thread and cloth, and a good worker in the old days could sometimes earn as much as $4.50 a day. Union Army uniforms were made here during the Civil War.

Often honored for its architecture and described as one of the most outstanding engineering feats of its time in the Midwest, the mammoth stone structure is 60 feet wide by 280 feet long and has 5-foot-thick interior walls. Two copper-roofed towers, each more than 100 feet tall, serve as landmarks for Ohio River traffic. One of the towers held water that could be used to flood each of the five floors in case of fire, a constant threat in a cotton mill. The second tower, besides serving as a fire escape, was designed to reduce the risk of fire; it contained five trap-doors that were opened twice each working day so that air could be drawn down through a chimney to remove accumulated lint.

It is a gaunt gray ghost now, but people still come—to view the mill from the road, to marvel at its unusual style, to photograph a treasured relic of the past that has outlived its days of glory. For information about the mill, located on Washington Street in Cannelton, contact the Perry County Chamber of Commerce, 123 Main Street, P.O. Box 82, Tell City 47586; (812) 547–2385.

Rising from a soybean field not far east of Cannelton is a grim reminder of one of Indiana's worst air tragedies. The *Air Crash Memorial Monument,* 9 feet tall and 12 feet wide, recalls a March day in 1960 when a

Gone, but Not Forgotten

*O*n August 21, 1865, the steamboat USS Argosy III *was transporting a group of mustered-out Civil War veterans up the Ohio River to Cincinnati. A sudden storm hurled the boat against some rocks near the Perry County town of Magnet (then known as Rono) and caused its boiler to explode. Ten Union soldiers, on their way home after surviving years of brutal warfare, either drowned or were scalded to death. The survivors and local farmers pulled the dead from the waters and buried them in a mass grave.*

The history of that accident and the mass burial site did not come to light until 1962. To commemorate the dead, the federal government supplied ten white stone markers that were anchored in a concrete base, and the Indiana Civil War Centennial Commission supplied a "Civil War Memorial Grave" marker. The names of the victims are carved into nine of the stones; the tenth bears the poignant message "Unknown U.S. Soldier." One day before

the centennial of the riverboat tragedy, a gathering of Perry County citizens and interested visitors officially dedicated the site.

The late Clyde E. Benner became the small cemetery's self-appointed caretaker, clearing and weeding the gravesite until his death in 1985. Today, his four daughters carry on the tradition. One, Pat Irwin, is the primary caretaker. She currently works at the Some Other Place restaurant, the only commercial business in Magnet, and says it's hard to believe how many people stop by there asking for directions to "that Civil War place around here."

There are no road signs to direct you there, but you can reach it by taking U.S. Highway 66 to the turnoff road for Magnet. Go east through Magnet and continue for about $1/2$ mile to the cemetery, nestled in a grove of maples, poplars, laurels, and cottonwood on the right. If you have difficulty finding it, stop by the restaurant and ask for Pat.

SOUTHWEST INDIANA

Northwest Airlines flight from Minneapolis to Miami plummeted to the ground at this spot. According to a witness, the plane's wings simply broke off in midair. The plane fell 18,000 feet straight down, literally burying itself in the ground. The impact killed all sixty-three persons on board and created a crater 20 feet deep and 30 feet wide. It took two weeks to complete the recovery operation. Investigators later blamed the crash on structural faults in the engine, which caused a flutter in the wings that caused them to snap off.

The Cannelton Kiwanis Club raised funds to erect the monument seen today at the crash site. Topped by a "torch of life," the granite memorial is inscribed with the names of each of the victims.

To reach the monument, head east from Cannelton on State Road 66 to State Road 166 and turn right. Follow 166 southeast about 1½ miles to Millstone Road. Turn left onto Millstone Road and proceed approximately 1 mile to the monument on the left side of the road.

Another monument, a tall obelisk in Tell City's **Greenwood Cemetery,** memorializes the same tragedy. Here an 1,800-square-foot plot was set aside in which to bury fifty-five of the crash victims, of whom only seventeen could be identified. The obelisk, inscribed with the names of the dead, was placed here by Northwest Airlines.

While in Tell City tour the **Tell City Pretzel Company,** which may be the only company in the United States and one of the few in the world that still produces pretzels the original way—by hand twisting them. A Swiss baker brought the recipe with him from Europe when he settled here more than one hundred years ago. Although the recipe is still a secret, passed down from owner to owner, visitors are welcome to watch the twisters at work each Monday through Friday from 7:00 A.M. until about 3:00 P.M. The 12,000 pretzels produced daily are sold on the premises and by mail order. Contact Tell City Pretzels, 632 Main Street, Tell City 17506, (012) 547 4631.

Posey County

In 1814 a group of German Lutheran separatists migrated westward from Pennsylvania to the verdant valley of Wabash River. There they purchased some 30,000 acres of land along the riverbank and carved from the dense woodlands the personification of a dream—a tiny communal settlement they named Harmony. An industrious people, the

Harmonists established a variety of successful industries that ranged from the making of fine silks to the distilling of whiskey, and their products were much in demand throughout the eastern United States. They developed prefabricated houses, dug tunnels beneath them, and used the cool air therein to air-condition their dwellings. Oranges were grown year-round in their greenhouses. Eventually they found themselves with enough leisure time to start bickering among themselves, and in 1825 their leader, Father George Rapp, sold the entire town to Robert Owen, a wealthy industrialist from Scotland.

Trivia

Three Hollywood movies were made in Huntingburg in the 1990s: A League of Their Own *(1992),* Soul of the Game *(1995), and* Hard Rain *(1998).*

Owen envisioned a utopia of a different sort, a commune that focused on innovative education and intellectual pursuits. His **New Harmony** lured scientists, social reformers, writers, and artists whose ideas and creations made a lasting impact on our country's history. America's first free public school system, kindergarten, day care center, free library, trade school, women's club, and civic dramatic club came to fruition here. One of Owen's sons became an eminent geologist and was commissioned to make the first survey of new government lands in the West. After that son was appointed U.S. Geologist in 1938, he ran the U.S. Geological Survey from New Harmony for seventeen years. Another of Owen's sons entered Congress, became an early crusader for the rights of women, and drafted the legislation that established the Smithsonian Institution. Yet another son became president of Indiana's Purdue University. Although many of the concepts developed at Owen's New Harmony have survived, the commune foundered in 1827. One reason for this was that its inhabitants did not possess the husbandry skills needed to feed its populace. While lofty ideas and ideals were being discussed inside, the hogs were invading the vegetables outside.

New Harmony was never deserted, however. Its reputation as an intellectual center gradually faded, but many residents stayed on, putting down roots that have kept the community alive to this day.

In the 1940s Jane Owen, wife of a direct descendant of Robert Owen, visited here and was so entranced by what she saw that she initiated a restoration project. Today New Harmony is a state historical site, and people come from all over the country to take a twelve-point tour that traces the history of the settlement from its original log cabins to some striking structures added in recent years.

Enclosed within the brick walls of the Harmonist cemetery at the west end of Granary Street are more than 200 unmarked graves—symbolic of continued equality in death—and several Native American burial mounds. The Labyrinth, a fascinating maze of paths and hedges on the south edge of town, represents the twists and turns and choices that confront each of us in our passage through life.

Completed in 1979, the stark white atheneum that rises from a meadow near the riverbank has garnered many honors for its architectural design. The visitor center within periodically shows a film entitled *The New Harmony Experience* and exhibits a scale model of the original town; (812) 682–4474.

Serving as the altar for the Roofless Church, a paved courtyard that's open to the sky, is a unique dome that's shaped like an inverted rosebud but casts the shadow of a full-blown rose. Its design was inspired by writer George Sand, who remarked that the sky was the only roof vast enough to embrace all of worshiping humanity. When he visited here in 1963, Paul Tillich, the world-renowned philosopher and theologian, was so impressed by the Roofless Church that he said it alone justified our century. When Tillich died not long afterward, his ashes were buried in Tillich Park opposite the church.

One of the most beautiful sights at New Harmony, however, is a seasonal event orchestrated by nature. The first golden raintree in the nation was planted at New Harmony, and today there is scarcely a lawn or street anywhere in town that does not boast at least one of these lovely trees. An ornamental tree that originated in the Orient, the golden raintree is unusually beautiful throughout the year but is most glorious around the third week in June when it bursts into full

> **Trivia**
>
> *Indiana was the first state to begin reforesting strip mines. The system was initiated in fall 1920, when thousands of trees were planted by coal companies operating in Clay County.*

bloom, then sheds its petals in a virtual shower of brilliant gold. There's no place in the United States where this tree grows in greater quantity, and New Harmony celebrates its beauty each June with a festival.

New Harmony is easily explored on foot. Historic New Harmony, Inc., has its headquarters at 506$^1/_2$ Main Street and offers general information as well as guided tours for nominal fees; contact the organization at P.O. Box 579, New Harmony 47631; (812) 682–4488.

Even the town's commercial district has a revitalized early-twentieth-century aura, and although it's not historic, the redbrick ***New Harmony***

Inn is a charming mix of traditional and modern design that blends well with its surroundings. Wood-burning fireplaces, rush-seated rockers, kitchenettes, living rooms, and spiral staircases that lead to sleeping lofts are all available. Trees march right up to glass walls that enclose a heated pool, and the sky is always visible through a sliding glass roof. The beautifully landscaped grounds share the shoreline of a placid lake with open fields and patches of forest laced with biking and hiking paths. Rates vary seasonally. Contact the New Harmony Inn, 506 North Street, P.O. Box 581, New Harmony 47631; (812) 682–4491.

Next door, a gourmet restaurant, the **Red Geranium,** serves lunch and dinner six days a week. The spinach salad with house dressing, warm homemade bread, and Shaker lemon pie are really special. Children's menus are available. Hours are 11:00 A.M. to 10:00 P.M. Tuesday through Thursday, 11:00 A.M. to 11:00 P.M. Friday and Saturday, and 11:00 A.M. to 8:00 P.M. Sunday; closed Monday and some major holidays; (812) 682–4431.

By driving south from New Harmony on State Road 69 for about 24 miles, almost to the Ohio River, you are suddenly confronted with a scene that might have been transported here from the Deep South. *Hovey Lake* resembles a southern swamp, particularly in the slough areas to the east of the lake. Its waters are studded with huge bald cypress trees—one noteworthy old patriarch has lived to about 250 years of age. Along the lakeshore are southern red oak, wild pecans, mistletoe, holly, and swamp privet.

Bird-watchers spot great blue herons, American egrets, double-breasted cormorants, and pileated woodpeckers. Osprey have been known to nest here, and white ibis, bald eagles, hawks, and owls frequent the area. In the autumn, usually beginning in the first week in October, some 500,000 ducks and geese arrive for the winter.

Hovey Lake, formed about 500 years ago, is an oxbow lake that occupies an old channel of the nearby Ohio River. It's now part of a 4,300-acre state fish and wildlife area, but even if you don't like to fish, you can rent a rowboat, glide among the majestic trees that rise from the surface of the water, and enjoy the serenity and seclusion of this lovely place. When seen through the mists of early morning, Hovey Lake takes on the aura of a dream.

Close to the launching ramp, you'll find an oak-shaded picnic area and forty-eight primitive campsites. Contact Hovey Lake State Fish and Wildlife Area, 1298 West Graddy Road, Mt. Vernon 47620; (812) 838–2927.

Putnam County

In the valley of Big Walnut Creek lies one of the most beautiful and unusual natural areas in Indiana. The clear waters of the creek calmly meander southward through steep ravines studded with limestone outcroppings. A great blue heron rookery that has been continuously occupied for more than sixty years shares the forest with the great horned owl and more than 120 other species of birds. What is thought to be the largest sugar maple in the world, as well as the two largest sassafras trees and the second biggest hemlock in Indiana, thrive within the preserve's confines. Located about 1½ miles northeast of Bainbridge, the **Big Walnut State Nature Preserve** lies primarily along that part of the creek between Pine Bluff Covered Bridge and Rolling Stone Covered Bridge. It's open daily, free of charge, during daylight hours. For additional information and exact directions, contact The Nature Conservancy, Indiana Field Office, 1330 West Thirty-eighth Street, Indianapolis 46208; (317) 923–7547; or the Greencastle Chamber of Commerce, P.O. Box 389, Greencastle 46135; (317) 653–4517.

Roachdale, a small village in the northern part of the county, is the site of one of the zaniest events held anywhere—an **annual race for cockroaches.** Each Fourth of July contestants adorned with brightly colored racing stripes line up in their appointed lanes atop a plywood course and await the official signal to start. Entrants with a tendency to wander at this critical time are kept in place with flypaper. At last someone calls out, in true Indianapolis 500 fashion, "Gentlemen and ladies! Start your cockroaches!" and the race is on. The rules permit owners to place edible enticements behind the finish line, and that's usually all a cockroach with any get-up-and-go needs to spur it on its way.

> ### Trivia
>
> *The first sorority in the nation, Kappa Alpha Theta, was founded at DePauw University in Greencastle in 1870.*

The rules are simple—any trainer with a live roach may enter. And how, you might ask, do you train a roach? One woman claims she taught her bug to do isometrics.

It's not unusual to see racers from faraway states, but recently the contest went international. One woman hand-carried her roach—a thoroughbred—all the way from England. It didn't win, but the officials ran up a British flag in its honor.

If you have a roach that's into racing or if you'd just like more information, contact Jim Holland, Roachdale Lions Club, RR 1, Box 110, Roachdale 46172; (765) 522–4244.

Spencer County

Poised majestically atop a hill, the *St. Meinrad Archabbey* emerges unexpectedly from the trees and hills of northeastern Spencer County. Your eyes are first drawn to the soaring twin spires of the Abbey Church, then to the entire complex of beautiful buildings that house a theological school, a college, a monastery, and such income-producing enterprises as a publishing company, a winery, and a meat-packing plant.

Trivia

As a child growing up in southern Indiana, Florence Henderson was inspired to become a singer when she heard the Gregorian chants sung by the Benedictine monks at the St. Meinrad Archabbey. The Dale native is best-known today for her portrayal of Carol Brady, mother to television's The Brady Bunch.

When the abbey was founded by immigrant missionaries from Switzerland in 1854, the monks themselves transported the sandstone from a quarry 1 mile distant, hand-chipped it into the desired shape, and erected buildings patterned after the European medieval style so vivid in their memories. Newer, more modern buildings appear among the old ones these days, but all interiors remain starkly simplistic in keeping with the order's dedication to a spiritual rather than materialistic lifestyle.

Visitors who roam the well-maintained grounds find themselves in the company of priests and brothers in simple black gowns—teachers, lay employees, and some 400 students who are training for the priesthood. Although silence is part of the Benedictine life, it is expected only from 9:00 P.M. through breakfast the following day and at all times in the halls of the monastery. Otherwise, the monks and brothers are fun-loving, hospitable people who enjoy conversing with visitors. There's even a campus bar and pizzeria called The Unstable that's open two hours each weekday night and three hours on weekends. Overnight accommodations are also available by reservation.

You're welcome to join the monks for a worship service; Mass is in English. Brochures for self-guided tours can be picked up at the Guest House Office from 9:00 A.M. to 4:00 P.M. Monday through Saturday and 1:00 to 4:00 P.M. Sunday. Free guided tours are available by advance

St. Meinrad Archabbey

appointment; contact St. Meinrad Archabbey, St. Meinrad 47577; (812) 357–6585. The abbey is located on State Road 62, just south of I–64, near the Perry-Spencer county line; follow the signs.

One of the happiest places in Indiana can be found near Dale. Just follow the giggles to **Dr. Ted's Musical Marvels,** and join in the toe-tapping, swinging, swaying, and stomping to the delightful sounds that emanate from this extraordinary collection of mechanical musical machines.

Among the music makers you'll see here are the Decap Belgian Dance Organ, one of the few in existence. Measuring 12 feet tall by 24 feet long and weighing 4,000 pounds, it is similar in operation to a player piano. With 535 pieces, two accordions, two saxophones, a snare drum, a bass drum, a wood block, a tempo block, and cymbals, all playing at the same time, it can very nearly substitute for an entire orchestra.

A Wurlitzer organ that dates to the early 1900s originally provided the music for merry-go-rounds. The KT Special is a nickelodeon with colored lights that flash on and off in time to the tunes it plays. There's also an air-drive calliope to evoke memories of the circus. And then there are the street organs, music boxes, player pianos, phonographs, and gramophones.

Dr. Ted's eclectic collection is open from 10:00 A.M. to 6:00 P.M. Monday through Saturday and 1:00 to 6:00 P.M. Sunday, Memorial Day through

Labor Day; group tours are given year-round by advance appointment. Located on U.S. Highway 231, about ¹/₂ mile north of I–64; nominal admission fee. For additional information, write Dr. Ted's at RR 2, Box 30–A, Dale 47523; (812) 937–4250.

It would be hard to miss *Megamaze.* The brilliant colors of its 7-foot-high vinyl walls virtually light up the landscape. The Midwest's first world-class maze, Megamaze was inspired by the "maze craze" that began in 1985 in Japan, where hundreds of thousands of participants test their maze-running skills each week.

At Megamaze, which sprawls over an acre of land, visitors are challenged to negotiate the mile-long maze as quickly as possible. Punch a time card when you enter the maze, then stamp it again at each of four 32-foot-tall towers within the maze and once more as you exit. The average time for finding your way through the maze is forty-five minutes, but veterans complete the labyrinth in five to ten minutes. Negotiate it in eight minutes or less and win a free game of miniature golf (the eighteen-hole course is in the center of the maze).

Because your admission fee lets you "do the maze" as often as you like for one full day, you can race through and try for a free game of golf or simply relax and dawdle along the way. You can also opt for an intergalactic battle. Don a headband, carry a laser gun that emits light beams, and take along a similarly equipped friend. It's quite an experience to feel your headband vibrate when you're hit. You can also give in to the kid in you and conduct a war of water with water balloon launchers.

Megamaze (also known as *Fun Island*) can be found just south of the interchange of U.S. Highway 231 and I–64 (exit 57) near Dale; just follow the signs. Special rates are available for children under twelve and seniors fifty-five and over; season passes are also available. Open daily 10:00 A.M. to 10:00 P.M. Memorial Day through Labor Day and on weekends in April, May, September, and October. Write Megamaze at Seven East Medcalf Street, Dale 47523, or call (812) 937–2020.

Two notable residents have made their homes in this county, and it would be tough to decide who is more famous—unless you are six years old or younger.

The U.S. Postal Service receives several million pieces of mail each Christmas addressed to Santa Claus, and it's all forwarded to Santa Claus's true domicile—a small town in southern Indiana. A few million more letters and packages are sent to the local postmaster with the request that they be stamped with the *Santa Claus, Indiana,* postmark before being sent on to their final destinations. Pretty heady stuff for a town with a population of about 500, give or take a few elves.

Although the town has borne its unusual name since 1852, it became world-famous only after Robert Ripley featured it in his *Believe It or Not* column in 1929. Such a hullabaloo followed that the annual Town Christmas Party had to be rescheduled for early October, when there was time to deal with such things. Today the **Santa Claus Post Office,** whose stone front resembles a castle, probably gets more visitors than any other post office in the country. Folks can't believe the stacks of mail they see there each year just before Christmas.

Elsewhere there's a city park where a 22-foot-tall statue of the jolly old man gazes down on the "little people of the world" to whom he is dedicated. Another Santa image sits atop a candy-striped water tower. The names of just about everything contribute to the aura of fantasy—Silver Bell Terrace, Donner Lane, Sled Run, Lake Rudolph, Lake Holly, Lake Noel, the Snowflake Drive-in, the Christmas Lake Village housing development, and a newspaper called *Santa's Country.* Some town shops carry out the Christmas theme in their architecture, and Santa Claus Land opened in 1946 as the first theme park in the nation.

Santa Claus Land has since been renamed **Holiday World,** but it still has all the attractions that endeared it to countless children—and adults—in the past. Santa's headquarters are there, of course, as are lots of toys; the animal farm where Santa's reindeer rest up for their arduous Christmas Eve journey; a variety of live musical, magical, and trained animal shows; a wax museum (the Hall of Famous Americans); antique toy and doll museums; a seventeen-acre water park that's the state's largest, a country music show; and a bevy of rides, including The Raven, recently voted one of the three best roller coasters in the world, and The Legend, the state's largest roller coaster. If you dismiss all this as child's play, you should know that there are senior citizens from all over who make regular visits here.

The one-price admission, extremely reasonable by today's standards, entitles a guest to ride all rides and see all shows and attractions; children two and under are admitted free. In general, Holiday World opens at 10:00 A.M. daily mid-May to mid-August and on weekends in April, early May, late August, September, and October; it closes at 10:00 P.M. mid-June through mid-August and around dusk at other times. Holiday World may also be open on weekends from late November through the last weekend before Christmas. Because hours vary from year to year, it is best to request a schedule in advance. Contact Holiday World,

P.O. Box 179, Santa Claus 47579; (812) 937–4401 or (800) 467–2682, or visit its Web site at www.holidayworld.com. Santa Claus, the village, is located on State Road 245 in the north central part of the county.

Spencer County's second famous resident is immortalized in the pages of history books. When people think of **Abraham Lincoln,** they usually think of the state of Illinois, but it was in Indiana that a young Abe went to school, worked the land, and grew to manhood. Abe's father, Thomas Lincoln, brought his small family here in 1816 and homesteaded 160 acres along the banks of Little Pigeon Creek. Indiana was a wilderness then, a forest of giant oaks, maples, and hickories where open views of even 200 yards were rare. Lincoln himself described it thus, in a poem he wrote many years after leaving the state.

When first my father settled here
'Twas then the frontier line.
The panther's scream filled the night with fear,
And bears preyed on the swine.

In 1818, when Abe was nine and his sister Sarah was eleven, their beloved mother died, and little more than a year later a lonely Thomas married Sara Bush Johnston. A widow with three children, she raised Abe and Sarah as though they were her own, lavishing such love and affection on them that she forever tarnished the image of the wicked stepmother. She recognized the intimations of future greatness in young Abe and encouraged him to study, and Abe, on his part, loved her as few children love even their natural parents. When an adult Abe said, "All that I am, or hope to be, I owe to my angel Mother," he was speaking of his stepmother.

Lincoln left Indiana when he was twenty-one and moved to Illinois with his family, but his tenure in Spencer County is honored in a series of memorials. The **Lincoln Boyhood National Memorial** is next door to Lincoln State Park on State Road 162, just south of Lincoln City. Abe's bio-logical mother, Nancy Hanks Lincoln, is buried at the former, and her grave and the reconstructed Lincoln cabin can be visited in this 200-acre park. A living-history farm that covers eighty acres of the Lincolns' orig-inal homestead is worked as Abe and his father once worked it and pro-vides a fascinating, accurate insight into a way of life that shaped one of the nation's greatest men.

At the handsome visitor center, you can view exhibits related to Lincoln's fourteen years in Indiana and see a twenty-seven-minute film about his life. You can also learn much about the human side of Lincoln, little-known facts that breathe life into the saintly image. Young Abe, for instance, loved to wrestle and was recognized as one of the area's best tusslers. His great physical strength earned him the nickname "young Hercules of Pigeon Creek," and he could hoist more weight and drive an ax deeper than any other man around. In 1828 his horizons widened greatly when he accompanied the son of the richest man in the community on a flatboat journey down the Ohio and Mississippi rivers to New Orleans. And one can only speculate how the course of history might have differed had Abe grown up in Kentucky, where slavery was tolerated. The national memorial is open 8:00 A.M. to 5:00 P.M. daily year-round, except major winter holidays; there's a nominal admission fee. Costumed interpreters work the farm from mid-April through late October. Contact Lincoln Boyhood National Memorial, National Park Service, P.O. Box 1816, Lincoln City 47552; (812) 937–4541.

The adjacent **Lincoln State Park,** which covers nearly 1,800 acres, includes the grave of Lincoln's sister, who died in childbirth; the site of the Little Pigeon River Primitive Baptist Church, where the Lincoln family worshiped; and the site of the first school attended by Abe, who was eleven years old at the time. At 8:00 P.M. each night except Monday, from mid-June to late August, the story of Lincoln's life in Indiana is depicted in *Young Abe Lincoln,* a musical outdoor drama that's staged in the park's completely covered amphitheater. Performances of award-winning Broadway musicals alternate with *Young Abe Lincoln.* For details and reservations contact Young Abe Lincoln, P.O. Box 7–21, Lincoln City 47552; (800) 264–4223 or (812) 937–4493 in-season and 464–0029 off-season. You'll also find many opportunities here for outdoor recreation, as well as campsites and housekeeping cabins. Open daily year-round, during daylight hours; nominal vehicle admission fee is charged from spring through fall. Write Lincoln State Park, Box 216, Lincoln City 47552; (812) 937–4710 or (800) 264–4ABE.

On the banks of the Ohio River just west of Troy, the **Lincoln Ferry Landing State Wayside Park** on State Road 66 preserves another historical segment of Abe's life. Here, as an employee of a local farmer, sixteen-year-old Abe operated a ferry across the mouth of Anderson Creek, a tributary of the Ohio now called Anderson River. To increase his income Abe built himself a scow to carry passengers to Ohio River steamboats in midstream. His first experience with the legal profession came when he was hauled into a Kentucky court for ferrying passengers on the Ohio without a license (the Ohio River was considered part of Kentucky). Lincoln pleaded his own case, stating that he didn't believe the law applied to a ferryman who went only halfway across the river. Agreeing with him, the judge dismissed the case. Abe's fascination with the law began with that encounter.

Following State Road 66 west along the banks of the Ohio, you come to Rockport, where the **Rockport Inn** offers one of the most unusual lodging experiences in southern Indiana. This tiny hostelry, originally built as a private residence around 1855, contains just six bedrooms. No two bedrooms are alike, but each has air-conditioning and a private bath. Thoroughly renovated with painstaking care in recent years, the building retains as much of the original aura and design as the owners could achieve. Early-twentieth-century furnishings throughout contribute to the overall effect. Open year-round, the moderately priced inn serves meals on a rotating basis in its full-service restaurant. A continental breakfast is included in the room rates. Lunch is offered Tuesday through Saturday and dinner Wednesday through Saturday. There's also a Saturday brunch, but no meals at all are served on Sunday or Monday. Contact the Rockport Inn, 130 South Third Street, Rockport 47635; (812) 649–2664.

Also in Rockport is **Lincoln Pioneer Village.** Although all the log cabins are reconstructions, they reflect the lifestyle of Lincoln's boyhood years, and you can learn more interesting facts about our sixteenth president here. Situated at 222 South Third Street, the village is open 9:00 A.M. to 5:00 P.M. Tuesday through Sunday. Contact the Rockport Area Chamber of Commerce, 302 Main Street, P.O. Box 85, Rockport 47635; (812) 649–4626.

Vanderburgh County

I f architecture is your cup of tea, you'll want to tour two aesthetic treats in Evansville. The P.O. Box 1816, *John Augustus Reitz Home* at 224 Southeast First Street was erected in 1872 when Evansville was the hardwood capital of the country and Reitz was the "pioneer lumber king." Encircled by a black wrought-iron fence, the French Imperial house boasts three stories, seventeen rooms, ten fireplaces, and a display of Victorian-era opulence in the parquet floors, gilded bronze chandeliers, stained-glass windows, pier mirrors, gold-leaf cornices, and rare carved woods. Some of the first-floor ceilings are canvas, hand-painted in oil to match the original rugs. All heating units were turned on their sides and placed under the floor so that the radiators wouldn't show. The fireplaces were apparently for ornamentation only—they were never used. In the basement is a huge clothes dryer where clothes were hung on movable racks and dried by a gas heater beneath them.

The Reitz home sits in a 17-block historic district amid other massive homes built by wealthy owners who spent a considerable part of their fortunes trying to outdo the next fellow, but the home of the pioneer lumber king is the showplace of them all. Now a museum, it's open to the public from 1:00 to 4:00 P.M. Wednesday through Sunday, April through October. Visitors are taken on a half-hour tour, with the last tour beginning at 3:30 P.M. There's a nominal admission fee. Special tours can be arranged by calling (812) 426–1871.

The **Old Courthouse** that dominates the Evansville cityscape, built between 1888 and 1891, is one of the grandest in the country. During its construction special excursion trains brought visitors from Louisville, St. Louis, and many other midwestern towns to admire what was then regarded as one of the most elegant buildings ever erected in the Midwest.

Its Indiana limestone face is encrusted with an unbelievable number of sculptures and stone carvings, some of heroic proportions, each intricately detailed—fourteen statues, national emblems, ornamental friezes, cherubs, innumerable garlands of flora indigenous to the area, and Indiana's state seal. Inside are marble floors and wainscots, oak woodwork, brass handrails, silver-plated hardware, domes, and an awesome rotunda.

Abandoned by the county government in 1969, the Old Courthouse now contains boutiques, art galleries, import shops, clothing stores, and a community repertory company. You'll find the magnificent old building at the corner of Fourth and Vine; it's open 8:00 A.M. to 5:00 P.M. Monday through Friday and 1:00 to 5:00 P.M. Saturday and Sunday. Guided tours are available by appointment. Contact the Old Courthouse Preservation Society, 201 Northwest Fourth Street, Room 114, Evansville 17708; (812) 423–3361.

At **Wesselman Park** you'll find 210 acres of primeval woodland. A virgin forest is extremely rare, but this one is particularly unusual because it lies entirely within the limits of a city and is of such high quality (most stands of woodland in or near cities have been adversely affected by pollution). A melting pot of northern and southern botanical species, **Wesselman Woods** is dominated by sweet gum trees. Spring here is bright with the blossoms of dogwood and redbud trees and with the wildflowers that are at their feet; autumn is a blaze of color. At the edge of the woods is a nature center where one-way glass provides a unique view of wildlife activity and a microphone brings sound and song indoors.

The woods, designated both a state nature preserve and a National Natural Landmark, make up approximately half of Wesselman Park; the remaining 200 acres offer typical recreational facilities, including a swimming pool. Along the park's northern boundary is a remnant stretch of the old **Wabash and Erie Canal,** the longest ever built in this country. Only two boats ever traveled its entire 468-mile length from Evansville to Toledo, Ohio.

The park lies on the east side of Evansville at 551 North Boeke Road. Admission is free. The grounds are open daily year-round, from early morning until sunset. The nature center is open 8:30 A.M. to 5:00 P.M. Tuesday through Saturday and noon to 5:00 P.M. Sunday during summer months. Hours vary the rest of the year. Call (812) 479–0771.

Moundbuilder Indians, too, found this part of the country to their liking. Sometime around A.D. 1300, they built a village on the banks of the Ohio River southeast of Evansville and stayed there for about 200 years before moving on. The eleven mounds they abandoned in this spot constitute the largest and best-preserved group in the state. One, the central mound, covers more than four acres in area and measures 44 feet in height, making it one of the largest such structures in the eastern United States.

After years of archaeological excavations here, the 430-acre site was opened to the public as **Angel Mounds State Historic Site.** Visitors can view a simulated excavation site and many artifacts from the digs in a modern interpretive center, then walk the trails that lead among the mounds and reconstructed buildings of the Indian village. The memorial is located at 8215 Pollack Avenue, 7 miles southeast of downtown Evansville. Admission is free. The site is open 9:00 A.M. to 5:00 P.M. Tuesday through Saturday and 1:00 to 5:00 P.M. Sunday, mid-March through December; (812) 853–3956.

Vermillion County

Journalist Ernie Pyle wrote about World War II as experienced by the common foot soldier. His newspaper columns were read by millions, and his writings were compiled in several books. When his life was ended by a Japanese sniper in 1945, he was mourned by millions and eulogized by the President of the United States. Today veterans of that war are among the more than 16,000 visitors who come to Indiana each year to pay homage to the beloved correspondent at the *Ernie Pyle State Historic Site* in Dana.

A focal point of the site is the house in which Ernie was born in 1900, moved here in 1975 from its original location about 2 miles away. It is adjoined by an interpretive center that occupies two World War II military Quonset huts. They are filled to overflowing with memorabilia from every part of Pyle's life, from the cradle he slept in as a baby to his high school report cards to the tattered wool jacket he wore when he had tea with Eleanor Roosevelt. Exhibits include re-created scenes from the war that Pyle wrote about so eloquently—Omaha Beach after D-Day, a Marine campsite in Okinawa that features a restored 1944 Willy's Jeep, and a soldier saying his last good-bye to his fallen captain, Henry T. Waskow. Pyle won a Pulitzer prize in 1944 for a column he wrote about Captain Waskow's death; a mannequin of the journalist sitting at his typewriter can be prompted by the touch of a button to read that famous column.

A 1945 movie, *The Story of G.I. Joe,* told Ernie Pyle's story. Pyle was played by Burgess Meredith, and Robert Mitchum, in the role that made him a star, played Captain Waskow. Years later, Pyle was also an inspiration for Charles Kuralt. Kuralt wrote that "Ernie Pyle was there first. He showed everybody else the way."

A sense of what Ernie Pyle meant to the soldiers of World War II can be gleaned from the fact that he is the only civilian who was allowed a burial plot in the National Memorial Cemetery of the Pacific in Honolulu, Hawaii. More than 33,000 veterans are buried there, but to this day more people request directions to Pyle's gravesite than to any other.

The homestead and interpretive center are located at 120 Briarwood Street in Dana; (765) 665–3633. Open 9:00 A.M. to 5:00 P.M. Tuesday through Saturday and 1:00 to 5:00 P.M. Sunday, mid-March to mid-December; closed Easter and Thanksgiving. Admission is free, but donations are appreciated.

Vigo County

The ocean came to the Hoosier State in 1993. That was when Morgan Lidster, with the help of his father, Richard, opened the doors to *Inland Aquatics* in Terre Haute. Begun as a part-time business in a 400-square-foot facility, it has grown into a full-time enterprise that now

Trivia

occupies a 13,000-square-foot state-of-the-art facility.

Inland Aquatics breeds fish and corals in a 40,000-gallon hatchery that is the world's largest. What makes their products unique is a patented scrubber system developed at the Smithsonian Institution's Marine Systems Laboratory that emulates what the ocean does—it cleans itself. The self-sustaining aquariums sold by Inland Aquatics allow customers to enjoy a little piece of the ocean in their homes without a need for water changes, artificial filters, or chemical treatments. Visitors to the retail showroom will see a 225-gallon tank with a miniature reef and corals and fish living in water that hasn't been changed in more than five years.

Inland Aquatics is a multifaceted business that includes a retail store filled with forty-gallon saltwater tanks, a gift shop, custom-designed aquariums, a classroom for educational programs, and the aquariums and production tanks of the hatchery.

Lidster describes a visit to his facility as being like "dry snorkeling." Visitors can view unusual marine animals and rare corals just as they would see them in the ocean—without ever getting wet. His business draws customers from around the globe; they include aquarium hobbyists and representatives from museums and zoos.

Inland Aquatics is located at 10 Ohio Street; hours are noon to 7:00 P.M. Tuesday through Saturday and noon to 6:00 P.M. Sunday. Guided tours are available; call (812) 232–9000 for additional information.

Bibliophiles and intellectuals will find the **Cunningham Memorial Library** on the campus of Indiana State University in Terre Haute of special interest. It houses what is said to be the world's largest collection of old and rare dictionaries—more than 12,000 volumes dating back to 1475 that represent the entire history of Western lexicography. Among them are more than 200 editions and issues of Samuel Johnson's *A Dictionary of the English Language*. Known as the **Cordell Collection,** it grew from an initial donation of 500 dictionaries by Warren Cordell, an ISU alumnus and executive with Nielsen's television-rating firm. The collection, located in the library's Rare Books and Special Collections section on the third floor, is open free of charge throughout the year. Hours vary; call (812) 237–2580 or 237–3773.

Warrick County

I n the early part of the twentieth century, it was not unusual for three or more generations of families to live together in the same house. People were born and died at home. The possibility of death was something confronted on an everyday basis, especially in rural America. Crops died, livestock died, people died.

When a family member died, he or she might lie in state at home for two or three days while a memorial wake and funeral took place. The tools of the local undertaker (originally a folklore term meaning "one who undertakes anything") were necessarily portable in those days, since he generally went to his customers rather than vice versa. All that

The Bottle Known 'Round the World

*U*ntil 1915 Coca-Cola was sold in flat-sided bottles. That was the year the Coca-Cola Company began bottling its product in the curvy bottle now recognized around the world.

It all started with the soft drink company's desire to market a product unique in taste in a container unique in shape. A nationwide campaign was launched for a design that would let customers know instantly what they were holding even in the dark.

The company that came up with the winning design was the Root Glass Company of Terre Haute, whose answer to Coke's quest was a bottle shaped like an encyclopedia drawing of a cocoa bean pod.

In 1950 a bottle of Coke became the first consumer product to be featured on the cover of Time magazine, elevating it to national icon status. In 1994 the state of Indiana placed a marker alongside U.S. Highway 41 in Terre Haute that officially recognizes the historic event. The marker reads in part: BIRTHPLACE OF THE COCA-COLA BOTTLE, THE WORLD-FAMOUS TRADEMARK CREATED IN 1915 ON THIS SITE AT ROOT GLASS COMPANY. . . .

In 1994 the Coca-Cola Company returned to Terre Haute to test market a new container for its soft drink—a twenty-ounce plastic bottle contoured like its original glass bottle. In 1997 the company once again came to Terre Haute to market another new container—a twelve-ounce can with curves. A spokesperson for the company said it chose Terre Haute because it was the place in which Coke's curves were born.

changed in 1939, however, when a state law was passed that declared funerals could no longer be held at home.

Although that era no longer exists, it can be revisited at the **Simpson Mortuary Museum** in Newburgh. The Simpson family, which owns a modern-day funeral home just across the street from the museum, established the museum to preserve our ancestors' views of death—and life.

Among the interesting artifacts, most of which came from a local turn-of-the-century funeral home, is a summer cooling board. Pans of ice were placed beneath the perforated board to cool the deceased throughout a wake. A rare Rockaway buggy was the typical mode of transportation for early-twentieth-century undertakers. When a person died away from his residence, he was discreetly transported home in a wicker body basket like the one at the museum.

The museum, housed in a small brick building approximately 200 years old, may be seen free of charge by appointment. Contact Simpson Funeral Home, 510 West Jennings Street, Newburgh 47630; (812) 853–8314. When phoning, call on weekdays before noon.

First settled in 1803, Newburgh perches picturesquely on the banks of the Ohio River. Footpaths lead along the riverbank, with views that include the Newburgh Locks and Dam. River traffic passing through these locks carries more tonnage than passes through the Panama Canal. The town contains some lovely restored homes, and a 4-square-block section in the downtown area is on the National Register of Historic Places. For additional information contact **Historic Newburgh, Inc.,** 100 State Street, P.O. Box 543, Newburgh 47629; (812) 853–2815 or (800) 636–9489. Historic Newburgh's office is open 10:00 A.M. to 4:00 P.M. Monday through Friday and noon to 4:00 P.M. Saturday.

PLACES TO STAY IN
SOUTHWEST INDIANA

BLOOMINGTON
Bauer House
4595 North Maple
Grove Road
(812) 336–4383

The Grant Street Inn
310 North Grant Street
(812) 334–2353
(800) 238–1350

Indiana Memorial
Union Hotel
Indiana University
900 East Seventh Street
(812) 856–6381
(800) 209–8145

Scholars Inn
801 North College Avenue
(812) 332–1892
(800) 765–3466

CLINTON
Pentreath House
424 Blackman Street
(317) 832–2762

DERBY
Ohio River Cabins
13445 State Road 66
(812) 836–2289

EVANSVILLE
Cool Breeze Estate B&B
1240 Southeast
Second Street
(812) 422–9635

FRENCH LICK
French Lick Springs Resort
8670 West State Road 56
(812) 936–9300
(800) 457–4042

Patoka Lake Village
Log Cabin Rentals
7900 West 1025 South
(812) 936–9854

GRANDVIEW
Grandview Guest House
and Gardens
611 Main Street
(812) 649–2817

GREENCASTLE
Seminary Place
210 East Seminary Street
(765) 653–3177

The Walden Inn
2 Seminary Square
Box 490
(765) 653–2761

JASPER
Powers Inn B&B
325 West Sixth Street
(812) 482–3018

LEAVENWORTH
Carefree Country Resort
RR 1, Box 408
(Mansfield Road)
(812) 739–4522

Leavenworth Inn
930 West State Road 62
(812) 739–2120
(888) 739–2120

LOOGOOTEE
Stone Ridge Manor
Bed and Breakfast
612 Kentucky Avenue
(812) 295–3382

MARSHALL
Turkey Run Inn
Turkey Run State Park
RR 1, Box 444
(765) 597–2211
(877) 500–6151

MITCHELL
Spring Mill Inn
Spring Mill State Park
State Road 60 East
P.O. Box 68
(812) 849–4081
(877) 977–7464

NASHVILLE
Abe Martin Lodge
Brown County State Park
State Road 46 East
P.O. Box 547
(812) 988–4418
(877) 265–6343

Allison House Inn
90 South Jefferson Street
P.O. Box 1625
(812) 988–0814

Always Inn Bed and
Breakfast
8072 State Road 46 East
(812) 988–2233

Artists Colony Inn
Franklin and
Van Buren Streets
P.O. Box 1099
(812) 988–0600
(800) 737–0255

Aspen Leaf Inn
2785 Clay Lick Road
(812) 988–0073

Day Star Inn
87 East Main Street
P.O. Box 361
(812) 988–0430

5th Generation Farm
4564 North Bear Wallow
Road
(812) 988–7553
(800) 437–8152

Lee's Retreats Log Cabins
1352 Oak Grove Road
(812) 988–4117

McGinley's Vacation Cabins
P.O. Box 386
(812) 988–7337
(877) 229–6637

Naumkeag
3240 State Road 135 North
(812) 988–8263
(800) 793–4586
Fax: (812) 988–0328

Olde Magnolia House
213 South Jefferson Street
(812) 988–2434

Orchard Hill Inn and Cabin
1958 North State Road 135
(812) 988–4455
(800) 968–7266

Russell's Roost Bed
and Breakfast
3736 North Greasy
Creek Road
(812) 988–1600

The Seasons Lodge
560 State Road 46 East
(812) 988–2284
(800) 365–7327

Story Inn
6404 South State Road 135
(812) 988–2273
(800) 881–1183

Tulip Tree Bed and
Breakfast
233 South Jefferson Street
(812) 988–6741

NEW HARMONY
Harmonie Bed and
Breakfast
344 West Church Street
(812) 682–3730

The New Harmony Inn
508 North Street
P.O. Box 581
(812) 682–4491

PAOLI
Big Locust Farm
3295 West County Road
25 South
(812) 723–4856

Patoka Chalets Resort
7355 South County Road
50 West
(812) 723–5544

Underwood Inn
405 North Gospel Street
(812) 723–4639
(888) 300–4683

ROCKPORT
Rockport Inn
130 South Third Street
(812) 649–2664

ROCKVILLE
Knoll Inn Distinctive
Suites B&B
317 West High Street
P.O. Box 56
(765) 569–6345
(888) 569–6345

Owl Nest Bed and Breakfast
303 Howard Avenue
(765) 569–1803

Suits Us Bed and Breakfast
514 North College Street
(765) 569–5660
(888) 4–SUITS US

SPENCER
Canyon Inn
McCormick's Creek
State Park
P.O. Box 71
(812) 829–4881
(877) 922–6966

TASWELL (PATOKA LAKE)
White Oak Cabins
and B&B
2140 North Morgan Road
(812) 338–3120

UNIONVILLE
Possum Trot Bed
and Breakfast
5067 Possum Trot Road
(812) 988–2694

VINCENNES
The Harrison Inn Bed
and Breakfast
902 Buntin Street
(812) 882–3243

WEST BADEN SPRINGS
E. B. Rhodes House
Bed and Breakfast
726 Rhodes Avenue
P.O. Box 7
(812) 936–7378
(800) 786–5176

**PLACES TO EAT IN
SOUTHWEST INDIANA**

BLOOMINGTON
The Bakehouse
125 North College Avenue
(812) 331–6029

Bear's Place
1316 East Third Street
(812) 339–3460

Encore Cafe
316 West Sixth Street
(812) 333–7312

The Irish Lion
212 West Kirkwood Avenue
(812) 336–9076

Ladyman's Cafe
122 East Kirkwood Avenue
(812) 336–5557

La Torre Restaurante
Mexicano
1155 South College
Mall Road
(812) 336–5339

Le Petit Cafe
308 West Sixth Street
(812) 334–9747

The Laughing Planet Cafe
322 East Kirkwood Avenue
(812) 323–2233

Lennie's Restaurant
1795 East Tenth Street
(812) 323–2112

Macri's Deli
1221 South College Mall
Road
(812) 333–0606

Malibu Grill
106 North Walnut Street
(812) 332–4334

Mother Bear's
1428 East Third Street
(812) 332–4495

Opie Taylor's
212 North Walnut Street
(812) 333–7287

The Peach Garden
Chinese Buffet
636 South College Avenue
(812) 332–3437

Peterson's
1811 East Tenth Street
(812) 336–5450

Puccini's
420 East Fourth Street
(812) 333–5522

The Runcible Spoon
412 East Sixth Street
(812) 334–3997

Snow Lion
113 South Grant Street
(812) 336–0835

The Trojan Horse
100 East Kirkwood Avenue
(812) 332–1101

The Uptown Cafe
102 East Kirkwood Avenue
(812) 339–0900

BOONVILLE
Lee's Garden
Chinese Restaurant
966 West Main Street
(812) 897–5420

Locust Street Cafe
118 West Locust Street
(812) 897–4724

BRAZIL
Blue Bonnet
903 West Jackson Street
(812) 442–1233

CAYUGA
Covered Bridge Restaurant
5787 North Main Street
(765) 492–7376

Logan 105
105 Logan Street
(765) 492–4477

CLINTON
Zamberlettis at the Castle
1600 South Seventh Street
(765) 832–3322

DALE
Colonial Cafeteria
U.S. Highway 231 South
(2 miles south of I–64)
P.O. Box 468
(812) 937–2330

Johnson's Pizza Plus
Barbecue
12 South Washington Street
P.O. Box 346
(812) 937–4431

Windell's Cafe
U.S. Highway 231 and
State Road 62
(812) 937–4253

ELLETTSVILLE
The Village Inn
309 East Temperance Street
(812) 876–2204

EVANSVILLE
Bernie Little's Sunset
Restaurant
20 Walnut Street
(812) 425–6500

Bockelman's Restaurant
4001 Big Cynthiana Road
(812) 963–9017

Canton Inn Restaurant
915 North Park Drive
(812) 428–6611

Dogtown Tavern
6201 Old Henderson Road
(812) 423–0808

F's Steak House
125 Southeast Fourth Street
(812) 422–6788

Greeley's
100 Northwest
Second Street
(812) 425–5553

Hilltop Inn
1100 Harmony Way
(812) 422–1757

Jacob's Pub and Restaurant
4428 North First Avenue
(812) 423–0050

Jojo's Family Restaurant
3901 U.S. Highway 41 North
(812) 425–1486

Jungle Restaurant
415 Main Street
(812) 425–5282

Shyler's Bar-B-Q
324 South Green River
Road
(812) 476–4599

TK Pepper's Restaurant
217 Main Street
(812) 422–2555

Wolf's Bar-B-Que
1414 East Columbia Street
(812) 423–3599

FERDINAND
The Covered Bridge
835 Main Street
(812) 367–1501

Ferdy Flyer
133 West Tenth Street
(812) 367–2222

Fleigs Cafe
905 Main Street
(812) 367–1310

Homestead Pizza
1510 Main Street
(812) 367–1808

GREENCASTLE
Almost Home Tea Room
17 West Franklin Street
(765) 653–5788

A Different Drummer
(The Walden Inn)
2 Seminary Square
(765) 653–2761

Hathaway's
18 South Jackson Street
(765) 635–1228

Jackson Family Restaurant
Double Decker Drive-In
11058 Indianapolis Road
(765) 653–4302

HAUBSTADT
The Haub House
Main and Haub Streets
(812) 768–6462
(800) 654–1158

Nisbet Inn
6701 Nisbet Road
(812) 963–9305

JASPER
Schnitzelbank Restaurant
393 Third Avenue
(812) 482–2640

LEAVENWORTH
The Overlook
State Road 62
P.O. Box 67
(812) 739–4264

LINTON
The Dutch Oven
90 Northeast A Street
(812) 847–4581

The Grill
60 Northeast A Street
(812) 847–9010

Stoll's Country Inn
State Road 54 West
(812) 847–2477

LOOGOOTEE
Stoll's Lakeview Restaurant
U.S. Highway 231 North
(812) 295–3299

MILLTOWN
Blue River Cafe
128 West Main Street
(812) 633–7510

MONTGOMERY
Der Deutsche Gasthof
North County Road
650 East
(812) 486–3977

MOUNT VERNON
Gundi's Restaurant
132 East Second Street
(812) 838–4661

NASHVILLE
Abe Martin Lodge
Brown County State Park
State Road 46 East
P.O. Box 547
(812) 988–4418
(877) 265–6343

Accent Dining Room
The Seasons Lodge
560 State Road 46 East
(812) 988–2284
(800) 365–7327

The Artists Colony
Restaurant
Franklin and Van Buren
Streets
P.O. Box 1099
(812) 988–0600
(800) 737–0255

Hobnob Corner
17 West Main Street
(812) 988–4114

The Nashville House
Main and Van Buren Streets
(812) 988–4554

The Ordinary
61 South Van Buren Street
(812) 988–6166

Remember When
Restaurant
51 South Parkview
(812) 988–2679

Story Inn
6404 South State Road 135
(812) 988–2273
(800) 881–1183

NEW HARMONY
The Bayou Grill Restaurant
504 North Street
(812) 682-4491

The Main Cafe
520 Main Street
(812) 682-3370

Red Geranium
508 North Street
P.O. Box 581
(812) 682-4431

NEWBURGH
Edgewater Grille
1 East Water Street
(812) 858-2443

The Old Homestead Inn
10233 State Road 662
(812) 853-3631

ROCKPORT
The Rockport Inn
130 South Third Street
(812) 649-2664

The Rockport Junction
Junction of U.S.
Highway 231,
State Road 45, and State
Road 66
(812) 649-2700

ROSEDALE
Harvest House
202 North Main Street
(765) 548-1102

SPENCER
Chambers Restaurant
120 South Main Street
(812) 829-9085

TERRE HAUTE
Cancun Mexican
Restaurant
3495 South Fourth Street
(812) 232-4347

Garfield's Restaurant
201 West Division Street
(812) 421-1171

Gran-Ma's Joys
3631 Wabash Avenue
(812) 232-6598

Louise's Restaurant
1849 South Third Street
(812) 232-4989

Runyon's Black Angus
502 South Third Street
(812) 235-5549

Western Rib-Eye
Restaurant
100 South Fruitridge
Avenue
(812) 232-5591

VINCENNES
Bill Bobe's Pizzeria
1651 North Sixth Street
(812) 882-2992

Charlie's Smorgasbord
630 Kimmell Road
(812) 882-5115

Market Street Station
Restaurant and Pub
106 St. Honore Place
(812) 886-5201

Marone's Formosa Gardens
101 North Second Street
(812) 882-0460

Oink's Gourmet BBQ
1003 Main Street
(812) 882-3311

WARRENTON
The Log Inn
Old State Road
(812) 867-3216

WASHINGTON
Black Buggy Restaurant
910 State Road 57 South
(812) 254-8966

The Washington Steamer
21 East Main Street
(812) 254-9973

WORTHINGTON
Front Porch Steak House
118 North Canal Street
(812) 875-2306

**SOURCES FOR ADDITIONAL
INFORMATION ABOUT
SOUTHWEST INDIANA**

Clinton/Vermillion County
Chamber of Commerce
292 North Ninth Street
Clinton 47842
(765) 832-3844
Fax: (765) 832-3871

Covered Bridge Capital
Convention and Visitors
Bureau (Parke County)
401 East Ohio Street
Box 165
Rockville 47872
(765) 569-5226
Fax: (765) 569-3900

Covered Bridge Country
Convention and Visitors
Bureau (Putnam County)
2 South Jackson Street
Greencastle 46135
(765) 653-8743
(800) 82-WINDY
Fax: (765) 653-6385

Crawford County Tourism
Board of Commissioners
6225 East Industrial Lane
P.O. Box 227
Leavenworth 47137
(812) 739-4747
(888) 846-5397

Daviess County Visitors
Bureau
1 Train Depot Street
P.O. Box 403
Washington 47501
(812) 254–5262
(800) 449–5262

Evansville/Vanderburgh
County Convention and
Visitors Bureau
401 Southeast Riverside
Drive
Evansville 47713
(812) 421–2200
(800) 433–3025
Fax: (812) 421–2207

French Lick/West Baden
Chamber of Commerce
P.O. Box 347
French Lick 47432
(812) 936–2405
(800) 748–7246
Fax: (812) 936–2904

Lawrence County Tourism
Commission
1116 Sixteenth Street
P.O. Box 1193
Bedford 47421
(812) 275–7637
(800) 798–0769
Fax: (812) 279–5998

Lincoln Hills/Patoka
Lake Recreation Region
Courthouse Annex
125 South Eighth Street
Cannelton 47520
(812) 547–7028

Linton-Stockton Chamber
of Commerce (Greene
County)
159 First Street Northwest
P.O. Box 208
Linton 47441
(812) 847–4846
Fax: (812) 847–0246

Martin County Chamber of
Commerce/Tourism
Commission
123 Cooper Plaza
P.O. Box 447
Loogootee 47553
(812) 295–4093

Monroe County Convention
and Visitors Bureau
2855 North Walnut Street
Bloomington 47404
(812) 334–8900
(800) 800–0037
Fax: (812) 334–2344
E-mail:
cvb@visitbloomington.com
www.visitbloomington.com

Mount Vernon/Posey
County Chamber of
Commerce
915 East Fourth Street
P.O. Box 633
Mount Vernon 47620-0633
(812) 838–3639
Fax: (812) 838–6358

Nashville-Brown County
Convention and
Visitors Bureau
P.O. Box 840
Nashville 47448
(812) 988–7303
(800) 753–3255
Fax: (812) 988–1070
www.browncounty.com

Paoli/Orange County
Chamber of Commerce
210 Southwest Court Street
P.O. Box 22
Paoli 47454
(812) 723–4769

Perry County Convention
and Visitors Bureau
645 Main Street, Suite 200
P.O. Box 721
Tell City 47586
(812) 547 7933
(888) 343–6262
Fax: (812) 547–8378

Spencer County Visitors
Bureau
P.O. Box 202
Santa Claus 47579
(812) 937–4455, ext. 209
(888) 444–9252

Spencer-Owen County
Chamber of Commerce
780 East Morgan Street
P.O. Box 87
Spencer 47460
(812) 829–3245

Terre Haute/Vigo County
Convention and
Visitors Bureau
643 Wabash Avenue
Terre Haute 47807
(812) 234–5555
(800) 366–3043
Fax: (812) 234–6750

Vincennes/Knox County
Convention and
Visitors Bureau
27 North Third Street
P.O. Box 602
Vincennes 47591
(812) 886–0400
(800) 886–6443
Fax: (812) 882–6441

Warrick County
Chamber of Commerce
224 West Main Street,
Suite 203
Boonville 47601
(812) 897–2340
(812) 897–2360

Index

INDEX

INDEX

INDEX

INDEX

Acknowledgments

If I were to personally thank each person who has contributed in some way to the writing of this book, the list would be longer than the contents of the book itself. I talked to many people during my travels throughout Indiana. They were, without exception, warm, gracious, and kind. We met as strangers and parted as friends. I am grateful to each and every one of them.